MW01595486

Memoirs In Toe Shoes

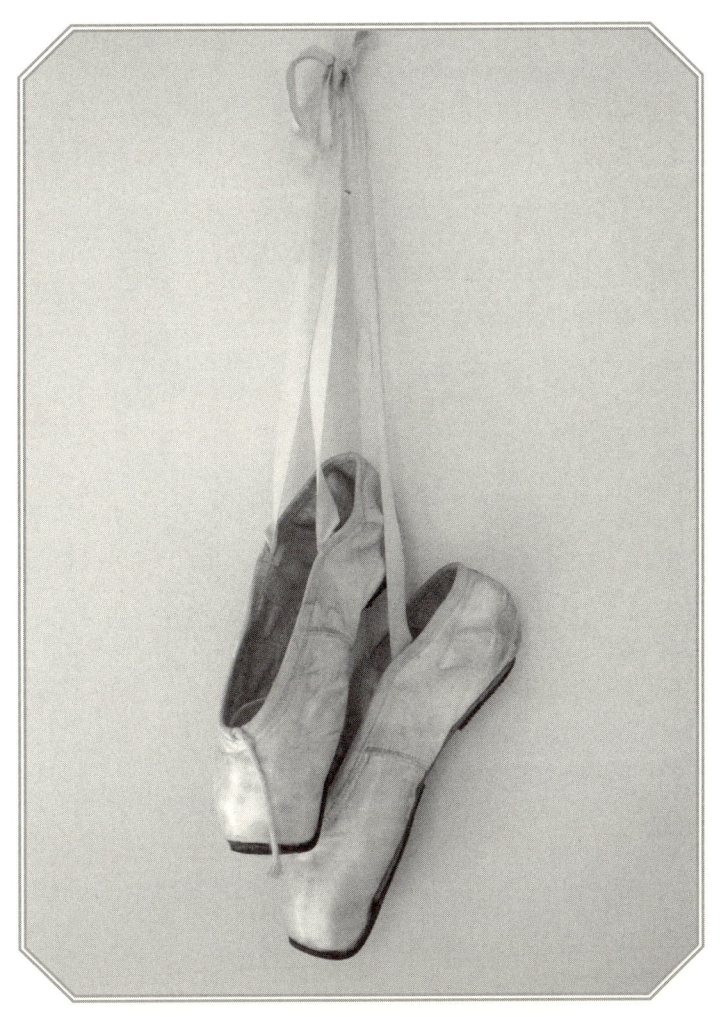

Also by

ERNA SEGAL
aka ERNA OLINGER

NOVELS

The Ademian Line

BioHazard Red

Transfers

SCREENPLAYS

The Medici

The Prague Affair

TRANSLATIONS

The House of a Thousand Floors (A Novel – From Czech)

Burning Sand (A Novel – From German)

POETRY

From Eden to Armageddon

Memoirs In Toe Shoes

The Unabashed Autobiography of
"CHIQUITA"
of the World-Famous Dance Team
"CHIQUITA & JOHNSON"

ERNA SEGAL

AKA "CHIQUITA"

FICTIONSPIN™
MALIBU, CALIFORNIA

FICTIONSPIN PUBLISHING

First Edition, September 2004

Memoirs In Toe Shoes
An Unabashed Autobiography

Copyright 1975 by Erna Segal
Copyright 2003 by Erna Segal

Published in the United States by FictionSpin Publishing Malibu, California.

To contact FictionSpin, please visit our website at: www.FictionSpin.com or email us at: FictionSpin@aol.com.

Library of Congress Control Number: 2004106554

ISBN 0–9724007–5–3

Printed in the United States of America

Some "Chiquita & Johnson" Reviews

At the Moulin Rouge, Hollywood, California

"It all began in Prague where a ballerina met an acrobat. The two promptly formed a dance team that's been making history ever since as Chiquita and Johnson. Dancing at Havana's fabulous *Tropicana,* they were spotted by TV host Ed Sullivan. He featured them on his *Toast of the Town,* and one hour later they were booked to open Frank Sennes' brand new *Moulin Rouge* nightclub in Hollywood. Awed by their sensational rise, the talented team attributes it to good luck. Spellbound audiences report luck has nothing to do with it – they're just plain GREAT!"

— EYE, People and Pictures, July 1954

At the Latin Quarter, New York

"…Outstanding were dance-acro team of Chiquita & Johnson. Splendidly produced as part of an Arabian Nights sequence, pair do tricks that are literally breath stopping. Overhead holds, splits, and sensational finishes are almost unbelievable."

— Bill Smith, Show Business, 1956

At the Cocoanut Grove, Los Angeles

"Opening dance act of Chiquita and Johnson was a fitting one for the splendor of the room because they're the best act of their kind on the circuit. Chiquita is refreshingly beautiful with a body that deserves display in the Museum of Art."

— Hollywood Reporter, April 26, 1957

At the Dunes Hotel, Las Vegas

"Stars of the show are the incomparable CHIQUITA and JOHNSON, two of the most accomplished artists of the dance it has ever been our pleasure to watch in action. Every number is meticulously carried out to perfection and contains graceful, but breathtaking lifts and spins to achieve a most exciting effect. This couple is undoubtedly high among the leaders of the world in the field of acro-ballet dancing."

— Fabulous Las Vegas Magazine, December 29, 1957

At the Dunes Hotel, Las Vegas

"PETITE PRANCER – One of America's inspired acro-ballet artists is bewitching Chiquita of the dance team of Chiquita & Johnson, stars of the current Minsky show at The Dunes…the petite Chiquita has moved show critics from coast-to-coast to a point where they are "dancing in the street" over her masterful dance styles… Chiquita's the most fetching little lass ever you did see, hazza style all her own."

— Las Vegas Review-Journal, 1958

At the Carillon Hotel, Miami, Florida

"Chiquita and Johnson have played the smartest rooms in this resort, and in this setting, come up with a big-mitt consistency as they walk out their acro-terps lined with fine ballet touch by the lithe, talented little Chiquita. They're show-stoppers, per always."

— Variety, 1961

Foreword

To write an autobiography is a curious thing. Is the writer exposing her life for public scrutiny as a form of self-analysis and using the reader as a sounding-board, a sort of collective of therapists, or is it simply an extension of the exhibitionistic tendencies dwelling in every person aspiring to fame and public recognition? Or is it merely for the money? Or a very private therapeutic cathartic process that eventually, or ultimately, demands to be shared? Can it be none of these, or all of these rolled into one?

None of these reasons seemed valid enough to give in to my friends' prodding and embark upon the task of so personal a vivisection. I always maintained that sort of thing is best left to the scruples, or lack of them, of the "soul pathologists" or the "digger-uppers-of-posthumous-dirt."

Why cater to the reader's morbid curiosity to learn all kinds of sordid details about the lives of people "in the limelight," I would say.

However, having done a lot of "soul-searching," that is, poking around in my psyche to find out why I spent two-thirds of my life on my toes and taking bows and the rest of it feeling weird about it and trying to convince myself I was really a very "private" person, I began to realize that exposing that kind of soul-searching might be of some intrinsic value – something I should share with my fellow creatures in an effort to, perhaps, shed the tiniest spark of light on some of their own drives and needs.

Thus the following narrative:

Part I – Becoming

Part II – The Career

CHAPTER ONE

Part I - Becoming

April 6, 1938

My mother used to say I came with the war which made me feel just dandy. But I came into this world by way of a natural childbirth, assisted only by a grumpy midwife summoned grudgingly by my father and that, only after my mother threatened to throw herself out of a ground floor window to demonstrate that she was indeed in labor.

I'm told I 'popped out like a bullet' (another of my mother's euphemisms) which, by some psychoanalytical standards today, should have assured me of growing up to be one of the few 'relatively well-adjusted neurotics' as neurotics go. This unlikely possibility, however, was promptly counteracted by my mother who, true to her conditioning, social training, or what have you, peculiar to that particular part of the world, Central Europe, the country of Czechoslovakia, the city of a hundred spires – Prague, to be specific – wrapped me tightly into a comforter which was secured by a wide pink sash wrapped around, neatly crossed and crossed again and then tied into a handsome bow. My spindly legs and arms straight as soldier's, I lay there – entombed – because of some moronic belief, handed down from one bloody generation to the next, that this insane practice would ensure the child's straight limbs.

Just imagine I – having 'popped out like a bullet,' undoubtedly due to the fact that I was anxious to leave the once comfortable and
spacious womb as it was becoming increasingly smaller, was confined in this dastardly fashion! Can anyone imagine the panic, the
sheer terror that overcame me? That must overcome every brand-new
human creature thrown into such a situation? When the undeveloped
brain hasn't been taught yet to rationalize its way into accepting all
the insanities, which are indeed bountiful in this mad world of ours, as
normal! (Ha! There it is – that universal euphemism which so cleverly
throws the blame off the blundering culprit! – The world? – What
indeed is the world?! What do we mean when we say "the world's
gone mad?" It's people, I tell you! People! You and me – and everybody else! We're all hopelessly mad! Anyway, I mustn't deviate from
this ghastly little tale.)

Instantly I began to wiggle and writhe and using something
which must have amounted to a superhuman effort, I pulled all my
newborn strength together and pushing and heaving and choking, I
managed to pull my feeble arms out of the suffocating confinement.
Thus relieved, I gave out a deep sigh of relief. Oh, give me freedom
or give me death! My legs were still imprisoned, but my arms, at least
my arms were free!

Thus the need for freedom came to me early. Or perhaps one
is born with it – even conceived with it, and spends all one's life
learning to have to do without it. We all exist within the limitations of
our own kind of prisons – prisons of our own making the way out of
which, most often, is only death, or, a totally new mental attitude. Too
harsh? Perhaps... But if you really care to take a look, you can see the
whole mess of restrictions starting from day one. Unfortunately, or
fortunately – perhaps – most people manage to bury most successfully
the earliest unpleasant childhood memories deep in their unconscious
and remember nothing. Why didn't I manage to bury them like every
other normal neurotic?

Anyway, no sooner were my arms freed when my mother, discovering the 'terrible' thing I'd done and fearful that my limbs were
already on the way to some grotesque curvatures, repaired the damage
and – to my nameless horror – I found myself in the same situation. I

really can't tell when the full recall of this particular episode occurred. But one of its manifestations soon became evident although at the time no one was aware of the reason behind it, least of all me. But in the nursery school I found that whenever anyone pinned my arms down I began to gasp for air and choke. Of course everyone assumed I was a supersensitive child prone to hysteria and eccentricity or whatever else they dream up when they don't have any idea why anything happens.

Today, even though I've finally made the connection and understand the whole thing, I still gasp and choke whenever I find myself restricted in any such fashion – (which clearly illustrates how fucked up I still am!) My idea of a chamber of horrors are those nasty little steam boxes people lock themselves into with only their heads exposed sweating in bliss.

As a child I used to have a recurring nightmare of waking up in a dark, narrow coffin – buried alive – screaming and choking with no one to hear and help. It was only later that I began to suspect that these early restrictions may have been the cause why I, as early as the age of three, was up on my toes flailing my arms and fluttering about like a lame bird in wild parodies of dancing. Of course, this drove my mother to distraction because all my shoes had holes in the toes in a matter of days. But for all the discouragement and punishment I received, I was firmly resolved, from then on, to become a dancer. To me, the prospect of dancing – free and effortlessly – across great open stages of theaters all over the world, was the epitome of heaven – regardless what I heard about that place from my grandmother whom I loved dearly in spite of her obvious naiveté and religious mania. And because I loved her, I used to listen to her with patient indulgence pretending to believe all those lovely and idealistic, but to me, so childish and unrealistic stories. Perhaps it was because my father, a devout atheist with strong socialistic tendencies (even though he was a practicing capitalist) sought to undermine her teachings at every opportunity.

It's amazing how quickly children absorb other people's convictions and after a while believe them to be their own. Today, I still wonder if anything I believe is truly mine. Or indeed if what I am – is the real me. Why can't they ever just let things be and allow the children to grow up along the lines of their own inclinations? But I suppose that's too much to expect of people eager to see perfect little images of themselves (or what they like to believe is themselves) running around – accomplishing, succeeding and conquering all they themselves were unable to? If you consider the number of varied and contradicting influences children grow up under, it's a wonder we can function at all, that is if we assume we are indeed functioning.

Anyway, (anyway happens to be my favorite word which I use often – maybe too often, but it's a handy means of getting back to my narrative.) So, anyway – I remember distinctly watching the behavior of the grownups around me with utter astonishment. The innocence, and the unerring instinct of logic, and justice which the child is born with is unfortunately stomped out by the grownups with much speed and determination. (There is nothing illogical people despise more than logic – ignorant people, intellect – the insane, sanity.) But while I still had it, I saw clearly how they continually contradicted not only each other, but also themselves.

My mother in particular was the real champion at it. She confused me so thoroughly and to such a point that I was mortally afraid to make any decisions of my own or act according to a previously established rule because I knew she was prone to change it according to her moods or whims.

Years later when I confronted her with her earliest crime, that is, made careful inquiries, she declared flatly that it's impossible I should be able to remember anything that happened to me before the age of three months. Because it was at that time, she claims to have discontinued wrapping me in that damn little straightjacket. Later however, she grudgingly admitted that she used to wonder why I was turning blue and how I managed to get my arms out since she made sure to tie it as tightly as possible to prevent me from doing just that.

Good God! I could weep for that helpless little thing – totally at her mercy – unable to tell her to fuck off with her goddamn sash! But the poor thing, she did only what she was taught to do. She was confused herself by my grandfather who used to beat the shit out of her for reasons known only to himself. So how could I really hate her? If it hadn't been for her, I might never have become a dancer, nor wandered all over the world in search of fame and recognition. Thus, the inevitable question: are we creative because of our neuroses, or in spite of them? I tend to believe the latter, but who knows?

In spite of her irrational behavior, my mother wasn't as stupid as my father would have liked me to believe. Although, for a long time, I did believe him. I suspect it was because he succeeded in convincing me he was 'generous' by never failing to add that I shouldn't hold it against her since "it wasn't her fault." "Your poor mother's a moron, but she can't help it – she was born that way." The soft, charitable tone he used when he said it made me love him for his kind and generous nature. Yes, my father liked to think of himself as a humanist, and for many years I looked up to him as the quintessence of wisdom and kindness. Of course, the fact that I hadn't seen him for many years must have helped.

But my career was a busy one, taking me all over the world (just as I'd envisioned at the age of three), except back to the tormented little country I sprang from. This may sound melodramatic and imply that I suffered being away from home but that wasn't really so. In fact I must admit I remember feeling little pain at the prospect of not seeing my parents, or if need be my homeland, for what I suspected from the start could turn out to be many years. But fortunately, at the age of twelve, I hadn't yet developed into a sentimentalist nor a fierce nationalist. Besides, by then the situation at home had deteriorated to such an extent there was little left to hold me there. It may sound callous not to miss one's parents or even country perhaps, but I sure cried bitter tears at having to do without dumplings and all that obscenely rich Czech food. You'd think such a diet would render people placid and compliant, but the world is constantly reminded that nothing could be further from the truth. The Czechs have always battled for their freedom against overwhelming odds even though they seldom come out victorious except in spirit – but that they always managed to hang on to – (how and why, in face of all the blows – God only knows). Perhaps it's the city itself that gives them the strength.

Prague is said to have been designed by alchemists who had built their houses right into its fortifications, the same way alchemy and spiritualism is built into the Czech character itself. Whatever these ancient occultists may or may not have contributed to the development of the city, Prague remains the last intact medieval city in Europe. Abounding with Gothic, Baroque and Rococo architecture, it is indeed a most beautiful city. Wherever you look you see countless turrets and spires reaching for the sky. The "Old Town," with its narrow, cobblestone streets, spreading across gently sloping hills is topped by the Hradcany Castle, once the residence of the ancient kings of Bohemia, which dominates the view of the city. In the midst of it all you can see the Moldau River – twisting its way past the ancient banks beneath the many handsome bridges where weathered statues stand solemnly gazing upon their trembling images reflected in the dark, deep waters. In the spring the city blossoms into a glowing picture of pink, white and fresh green of the spacious orchards and gardens lacing the splendid panorama.

I used to love to look down at all that from the big round windows way up in the top stories of the old National Theater where we had our rehearsal halls and dressing rooms. You could see the river just below like a dark ribbon sparkling with sunlight as it ambled lazily past the little islets lush with ancient, sprawling trees and gardens amidst which you could spot here and there the roofs of the marvelous old mansions that stood there for centuries. The fondness with which I recall it all seems to belie the notion that I never missed the old city and my country. Perhaps I never wanted to – couldn't face it – since there was no alternative for me and the dumplings only symbolized the whole thing. It's easier to say "how silly to miss something as stupid as dumplings" – it wouldn't be quite as easy to cope with the real thing.

CHAPTER TWO

Anyway, to get back to my career; as I recall, it wasn't only I who envisioned a 'glorious' future for myself. I had a kooky aunt who knew I'd have one. (Actually all my aunts were on the kooky side, but this one was extra special.) She was purportedly a medium. I dare say, I was the only child who, at the age of four, knew exactly what that word meant. How I came to know that takes some explaining. Since my mother was a hardworking woman, busy helping my father build up a business, I was packed off to my grandmother's as soon as I was through breast-feeding (yes – a breast fed baby. Another good beginning shot to hell.)

Up to that time I remember the constant sound of machines, dust and the smell of fresh wood. And, of course, of being left alone a lot. From that period, one particular incident stands out in my mind. I was ill. I didn't feel ill but they said I was. The general assumption was that I must have – again – eaten something rotten. But instead of digesting it without any adverse effects as usual, I was covered with big red blotches which didn't bother me in the least but which scared the shit out of my mother. Our family doctor stared at them in awe, and since he had no inkling what to make out of the blotches, he instructed my petrified mother to take me to the clinic at Charles University. At that glorious institution dating back to the 13th Century (everything in Prague dates back to who knows when) a lot of serious doctors looked me over shaking their heads in dismay. Finally it was decided I should be left there for observation. Even today, I can still see the indecision in my mother's face. I knew an instinct was tugging at her conscience trying to tell her not to leave me there, but 'authority' had spoken and her conditioning won out. I knew they were up to no good when a sassy looking nurse, to whom I took an instant dislike, took my clothes away.

Then I was carried off to a white, cold-looking room, with my mother trailing hesitantly behind, and put into a crib. My mother was there still wearing that hesitant, helpless expression. Somehow I knew she had no strength to resist them. The sassy nurse came back and told my mother she had better go. Of course, as soon as I saw her departing, I began to scream and yell on the top of my lungs. I could see her weakening. There were tears in her eyes and she rushed back to me. But under the hard, watchful eye of the nurse, she laughed nervously and began laying on me a lot of cheerful bullshit like I had no clothes so she couldn't take me and that she'd be back in a while and all kinds of things I knew to be lies. I kept screaming she should take me home naked but that brought only hard laughter from the nurse and fresh tears to my mother's eyes.

Another nurse came and they tried to distract me while my mother made it out of there. Oh, how I hated their guts. They were all around me, their hard, unfeeling faces forced into frigid smiles, telling me to stop being a little screamer. Had they shown a little real concern, real feeling, it might have helped. But they didn't.

Then they too left the room, and I was alone. Through the open doors I could see across the hallway into another room. A bigger boy in pajamas peered out and then wandered into my room. His own loneliness and fear wiped out by a sneer, he began to ape the nurses, calling me a screamer and dancing around the room repeating over and over in a hateful singsong voice I'd never get to go home again.

A smaller boy, stumbling over his pajamas that were too big for him, shuffled in and took up the chant. Did it ever occur to anyone that the railing of a baby's crib looks like prison bars? I rattled the railing in helpless fury and there was murder in my soul. I wanted to annihilate those little monsters.

But the crib was large and the bars tall. I knew I could never make it. Then I came upon a new idea. I became perfectly quiet and ignored them. This reaction seemed to startle them and after a while I could see the fear return to their faces and they stopped their nasty little game. Meanwhile I was busy plotting a revenge. There had to be something I could do to the nurses. Finally I came upon a brilliant idea. I had no diapers and the sheets were fresh and clean. I began to push and push to move my bowels.

A nurse walked by and peered at me suspiciously. I stopped my efforts. She went on, and I resumed my activity. It wasn't easy, I ate little that day. I was longing for a lot of loose shit. Oh, my kingdom for a pile of shit!!

Finally I managed to create a modest little mound. Dissatisfied with the amount as well as the consistency, I proceeded to smear it all over the sheets.

Nobody can tell me that a child doesn't know what it's doing. I know better! I remember!

My mother came back the next day bringing me a doll and grapes – my all-time favorite nourishment. But I didn't want any of it. I could sense her guilt. I knew these were tokens of atonement bribes. But I wouldn't let her buy me. I didn't even want her anymore. I played the injured game to the hilt. I saw her pain, and I knew I should stop, but I couldn't. And then it was too late. She had left – no communication had been reached. I never looked at another doll again. But I ate some of the grapes when no one was looking. The rest were devoured by the nurses. Much later I found out, my mother went all the distance to the clinic on foot, saving the tramway fare to buy me the grapes.

Anyway, back to my kooky aunt and my life at grandmother's.

If my aunt was a medium, she came to it quite naturally. Throughout most of her life, my grandmother would religiously pilgrimage three or four times a month to the most respected medium in the region. This much sought-after-lady happened to live, as far as I can remember, some four miles away which may not seem like much, but on foot it was plenty.

But my grandmother was a deeply religious person, as were most people in that part of Europe, and to her, life beyond the grave was not a mere belief – it was a certainty – and the reason for her weekly pilgrimage was to have a chat with the favorite of her children – my dear uncle Joseph who departed from this world long before I was born, but whom I knew as well as any of my living aunts or uncles because my grandmother would speak of him incessantly, of his goodness, generosity and beauty, of his devotion to the family, his sacrifices, etc.

Not like my uncle Stefan, who was lazy, ornery, drank, and to top it all, made it his business, much to my grandmother's exasperation, to teach me all the dirty words and limericks he could think of. Naturally, I was quick to repeat them as clearly and as loudly as I could, preferably in the most inconvenient places as possible. Like when we had company, when the butcher's shop was full of people, or when grandmother carried me through a busy street. It would be quite useless for her to try to get me to shut up. I knew perfectly well I was saying something I shouldn't but I persisted to embarrass my poor grandmother with perverse pleasure. Why I was such a little bastard, as so early an age, I can't seem to decide.

Anyway, my grandmother would take me along to these seances, and she would always be accompanied by at least one of my aunts and a number of friends, and everyone would take a turn in carrying me. The first time I was taken there, or I should say, the first time I remember being aware of where I was going and why, seemed like a very special thing – a sacred journey into some mysterious land. My grandmother spent a long time explaining it to me so that I had a vague understanding of what was going to happen.

Also, I was used to hearing gossip every week about what went on during the last seance. They would always speak in hushed tones, confiding whose departed soul visited whom.

"Oh yes, did you hear what Anna Chernik came to tell her husband? And Mrs. Mashek was finally visited..." (This practice was by no means restricted to superstitious old ladies.) But it was my grandmother who was looked upon as the owner of the most romantic spirit – my uncle Joseph. I only saw a poor, badly faded photograph of him but his face is etched into my mind still as clear and distinct as life itself. Young and handsome with a high, clear forehead and a mass of thick dark hair and eyes gentle and full of goodness – "he came so readily, coffin and all," my grandmother would say nodding her head sadly and relate the story of her first visit to the medium for the umpteenth time.

Uncle Joseph had appeared to the medium standing – in his coffin surrounded by bunches of violets – dressed neatly in his blue Sunday suit – his hair carefully combed – just the way my mother and grandmother laid him out. The good lady saw it all, to the last detail. The day I speak of, when we journeyed to the medium, I didn't know what to expect. I had never seen 'inside' before, and I was amazed to see the woman my grandmother spoke of as some kind of a saint – a wonder – was in reality a very ordinary looking person.

She sat in an ordinary armchair, in an ordinary room, wore an ordinary dress and an expression to go with her ordinary, totally non-descript, face. She hardly spoke as the pilgrims gathered around her – tiptoeing reverently to their respective places. My grandmother sat me on her lap and reminded me again – unnecessarily – I had to keep silent, no matter what. I had every intention of doing just that. I was too awed not to. Or so I thought.

Someone closed the shutters and the room became dark. Everybody settled down and the woman leaned her head back and closed her eyes. Soon, I heard her emit a sound – something between a sob and a deep sigh. Then she began to toss her head from side to side and shiver. The movement increased until she was trembling violently – erratically like a spastic. Everyone stared in tense expectation – scarcely breathing.

I, however, found the whole thing hysterically funny. She kept jerking and twitching, and I kept biting my lip until it hurt to keep from screaming with laughter. For a little kid, I think I stood it for a long time. Finally, I couldn't contain myself any longer and burst into uncontrollable laughter. I've never seen my poor grandmother in such a state. She was utterly mortified that her favorite grandchild should behave in such a disgraceful fashion. She was nowhere near as distraught when I shat into her hand in my first year. I could see the terrible disappointment and shame in her face and I was profoundly sorry for my 'criminal' behavior and wished fervently I could stop but the laughter kept gurgling forth just the same. Of course, she hustled me out of there as fast as she could, and that ended my adventure into the mysteries of the spiritual world.

Needless to say, I was terribly disappointed and furious with myself. It wasn't until I was five, when my life at grandmother's was over, that I saw my aunt Zia go into a trance and tell me what she saw in my future. I didn't laugh that time because she didn't go into the spastic bit at all. She was a small, pretty thing with clear, blue eyes that seemed to be smiling all the time but that could be sharp and cutting as broken glass when she was angry. But they shone with a strange light that day when she said in that precise voice of hers:

"There will be fame and fortune for you across the sea – and much traveling. Your path is bright with glory but studded with stones and thorns. People will admire you and want you, but they'll also take much from you..." (That should give some idea of the spiritual lingo.)

Of course, no one paid much attention to her prediction because she wasn't really a 'professional.' She gave it a go only rarely, and even then just for the 'benefit' of the immediate family. In the spiritual world, not to make use of the 'gift,' is considered a grave transgression. If I appear to be ridiculing the whole thing, I must insist I am not. I have to admit though that for a long time, due, undoubtedly, to my father's influence, I did consider such things pure nonsense. But lately, seeing the results of mankind's 'pragmatic and scientific' ways of thinking, I wonder. At that time, however, it was rather too soon for me to be initiated into the world of the occult and that might have had something to do with my subsequent recurring dreams of being buried alive. Of course, the tales I remember hearing around the evening fire about the plague and how gravediggers could tell who had been buried alive when they dug up the grave and found the skull upside down, might have had something to do with it. Not to make it sound as if my grandparents where altogether, well, strange, I must concede that the possibility exists these tales were prompted by my own questions which were tirelessly answered by my grandfather who, unlike most, never gave me stupid or evasive answers to my incessant questioning.

But all the nightmares, the gravediggers' tales and uncle Joseph's unearthly presence could have been just an extension or a manifestation of a deep fear of death which has plagued me ever since I remember remembering anything at all. Why this fear should have been with me so early in life, overshadowing all else, is another of those puzzling mysteries I had to learn to live with. Most people, when you mention this unmentionable of the many fears we have to grapple with, will argue they never even think of it or give you one of those condescendingly tolerant looks they reserve for children and morons.

Yet I believe we all have it and it is one of those inexplicable, unconscious forces motivating all our behavior. In my case, even though it has always been a conscious hang-up and as such should have kept me from doing all sorts of stupid things – it didn't. It seems that being conscious of something doesn't necessarily make it automatically disappear.

I have always been prone to do all the irrational things people who are totally ignorant of this fear are apt to do. I believe we all have to face the moment quite early in life when the reality of the transient nature of existence is brought home to us. The child is born ignorant of where this strange trip he has just embarked upon will lead and somewhere along the way – somehow – he will come to realize what's at the end of that trip and the manner in which he finds that out will unconsciously influence him for the rest of his life.

I wish I knew why the circumstances of my discovery of this fact should have remained as vivid in my mind and plague me all through my life. I still shudder when I think of it. I remember the feeling, the terror of it as if it were today.

It was at grandmother's. I remember feeling sorry to see the flowers fade and bloom away and I pondered why this should be so with a great deal of uneasiness and a kind of foreboding of something terrible. Then one day the drying, shriveled leaves of a dead rose made me think of my grandmother's hands. At the next feeding time I took a good look at the dry, brown skin thin as parchment covering thick, blue veins and bones – my grandmother's hands. When I pinched it the skin pulled up easy, it was so thin and loose.

I tried to pinch my own hand that way but couldn't. I must have looked puzzled because she smiled and said my own hands would some day be like hers as well. A terrible suspicion dawned on me then and I stared at her in awed terror. Could she have ever been a little girl as I was?

Later she dug up from somewhere an old photograph of a fat, little child that had been her. All I could think of was that some day my own hand would be just like hers, all brown and shriveled and faded like that rose. This filled me with a nameless dread and terror that is still with me. I realize I had to find out sooner or later – one way or another – acceptable or kinder way of learning of one's own mortality. It is a blow we try to compensate for as long as we live.

We try to beat the unalterable fate by attempting to achieve some sort of symbolic immortality. To have a child means leaving a piece of yourself behind, any kind of achievement or creative work represents 'leaving your mark' and is another form of immortality. Perhaps my ambition to become a great dancer was part of it as well.

My grandparents were poor, but at the time I lived with them, I wasn't aware of it. My home, which was actually the only stable home I knew, was their little stone house on the outskirts of the small coal town of Kladno some twenty miles outside of Prague. It was simple and old-fashioned, but it projected all the love and care my grandmother put into it. It was she who plucked the geese and filled the great, fat featherbeds with down, hooked the rugs, crocheted the drapes and spreads and doilies and did all the countless things that made the house a warm, cozy home.

She was a big, heavy woman with a broad, comfortable face settled into a myriad of good-natured wrinkles. There was an air of stoic resignation in her that held no tragedy – only wisdom and acceptance of whatever life held for her. Her big, capable hands were all weathered and work-worn, but they could be soft and tender in spite of their harsh appearance.

I remember her forever cooking, tidying up or sweeping the little stone-inlaid yard that separated the house from the garden. There was an old, weather-worn bench there that I liked to sit on and feel the sun warmed wood beneath my bare feet and watch grandmother peel potatoes or kneed dough for dumplings. Her thick, gray hair was always covered by a kerchief tied firmly beneath her chin. Oh, she was one ideal picture of a grandmother. I liked to sit close to her there and watch her every move. From there we could see the great, old lilac trees and smell their heavy, intoxicating scent.

That garden across the yard was another thing I loved. It was small but full of marvelous new things for a child to discover. There I made my first acquaintance with flowers, bugs, fruit trees and vegetables and all sorts of agricultural secrets all carefully tended and guarded by my grandfather. I remember his tall, gaunt figure forever bent over the flower beds or grafting, pruning and fussing about his apple trees, his small, bald head shining amongst the lush greenery.

To me, that garden was a paradise – a fragrant, wondrous world of strange, new things to get acquainted with, to examine, to taste. There, no one would ever tell me what I could or could not do. I could touch every flower, every bud, eat my fill of strawberries or the fat, tasty gooseberries that were my grandfather's pride. I could pick out rain worms after he had turned the soil and feed them to the chickens through a wire fence.

Across that wire fence was another world of thrills and delights. There were baby chicks and ducklings to pat and baby rabbits to hold. There was the chicken loft where I could rummage through the straw in search of freshly laid, warm eggs. And there was the cranky old goat named Byela who'd never let anyone milk her except grandmother and even then, aunt Emily had to straddle her to keep her from bucking up like a wild pony, but who could be induced by grandfather to give me a short, but very bumpy ride.

There was nothing my grandfather kept me from doing. From him, I never heard that sharp, grownup NO! I can't remember any place, in all my life, where I felt as happy, nor do I remember any person that filled me with the same sense of well-being and security as my grandfather. He was quiet and almost somber but to me he was a wonderful contrast to my aunts who were forever jabbering without saying much, or quarreling over some nonsense.

At the time I came to live there, grandfather was retired after having spent forty years of his life in the coal mines. Forty years of working deep underground, from dusk till dawn. Forty years of seeing daylight only once a week. I can imagine no greater punishment for any man. The soul-killing, spirit-numbing groveling in the darkness of the mines fills me with terror and endless pity for that kind, gentle man that my grandfather was to me. He's been dead for many years now but his image is as sharp and clear in my mind as if I had seen him only yesterday. I can almost see the small, birdlike face with eyes as blue as aunt Zia's except I never saw him get sharp with anger.

Although life hadn't treated him too kindly, grandfather didn't turn bitter or resentful. At least not that I could see. Some people believe each one of us is the master of his own destiny. It's understandable why they are in the great minority. If one would indeed have to accept the full responsibility for whatever happens to him, it would be a most crushing cross to bear. That's why it's so much easier to say "it's God's will" or any number of convenient sayings which are abundant in our daily repertoire of clichés.

What would we ever do without the crutch that religious or at least fatalistic thinking has to offer? To be sure, some of grandfather's misfortunes were not of his own making. He was born to the young daughter of a very wealthy landowner who gave herself, wisely, or unwisely (whichever way one chooses to look at it) to the man she loved just before he went off to a war somewhere. Unfortunately, the young man was killed in action and thus, grandfather was born illegitimate – the love child – a terrible stigma in those days. But my great-grandmother was a strong woman and she was determined to keep her child instead of stashing him away somewhere to be forgotten like a bad dream.

Nevertheless, she married but kept her first-born with her. The marriage was good but far from ideal. My great-grandmother was obviously a one-man woman and her child became her whole life.

Although she had another child, also a boy, my grandfather remained her favorite. Unfortunately, her untimely death left him penniless as it was claimed she had left no will, although she had told him otherwise, and since grandfather was illegitimate, whatever inheritance she had wished to bestow upon him was claimed by his younger brother. Characteristically, grandfather didn't defend his rights and as young as he was at the time, went to work in the mines.

CHAPTER THREE

The next most devastating thing that happened to grandfather, that I know of, was much later, after he was already married and most of his children had been born. Grandmother was a careful housekeeper and after years of saving every penny they could, they managed to acquire a house with several rentals to help feed the large family. Grandfather, a kind and trusting man, obviously, to help out his best friend, cosigned a note for a loan giving the house that they had worked so hard to acquire, as collateral. His friend took the money and vanished. Grandfather lost the house and had to start all over again. Whatever immediate effects this misfortune, that he had to realize was largely of his own making, may have had on him, by the time I came around he seemed at peace with himself and his lot. But mother says she can't remember him ever having reacted to it in any other way. His life's philosophy was simple and earthbound and must have helped him transcend all that.

And then, there was that little garden that must have also helped a great deal to keep him going, that allowed him to remain as he was. That garden and the woods. For when he wasn't puttering in the garden, he was off somewhere in the countryside gathering flowers and herbs out of which he concocted all sorts of oils and salves which were supposed to cure any number of ailments.

And once I had an opportunity to see it work. It was during winter. My sister, Kaya, was about two and a half at the time. When it got very cold grandmother burned coal in a small barrel stove which was a quick and most efficient way to heat the house. To fill it, she'd remove the red-hot top plate with a pair of iron prongs and set it down on the stone floor. It was precisely at that time that Kaya and I were playing and running around.

I was chasing her and she ran squealing toward grandmother when she tripped and fell and one of her chubby, little hands landed squarely on that red-hot plate sitting there on the floor. It didn't just touch it either. It stayed there for a few seconds before she pulled it away. It was all scorched and seemed to swell before my very eyes and the smell of burning flesh was everywhere.

She was screaming frightfully and grandmother held her arm very tightly but the little hand was twisting with all that pain just the same.

I felt terrible. Mother was there visiting at the time and she was dreadfully angry at me. Grandfather wasn't at home just then so mother took Kaya and raced to the hospital. When she came back Kaya was still screaming and the doctors had said her hand would remain badly scarred.

When grandfather came home he just listened to the story without saying one single word. Then he brought a jar full of yellow, oily liquid and took off all the bandages and removed whatever the doctors put there. It looked frightful. The charred skin was hanging in shreds and where it wasn't there were those terrible, huge blisters. Grandfather saturated a pad of gauze with the yellow liquid and covered Kaya's entire hand with it and bandaged it up again. She soon stopped crying – the pain seemed to have ceased. Skin formed back and within three to four weeks, her hand was healed new without the slightest scar visible.

Later, mother took her to the hospital "to show those doctors," but the doctors refused to believe it was the same child. If I thought

my grandfather was terrific, after that I thought he was the greatest.
Particularly since he didn't say one reproachful word to me, never as
much as looked at me cross for what I had done. What effect the
whole thing, especially my mother's anger and accusations may have
had on me, I cannot remember except it had to be significant since the
incident is so vivid in my mind and fills me with such a feeling of
guilt and pity for my sister who turned out none the worse for it.
Grandfather also made wine out of all sorts of berries and grew his
own tobacco which he took great pains in drying and cutting properly
and I, at four, was the neatest cigaret roller around.

Next to the main house he had rigged up a little lean-to which
was entirely his own domain. It was full of big vats of fermenting
fruit juices turning slowly into wine which required constant attention, row upon row of jars filled with strong aromatic mixtures of all
hues and consistencies, and boxes full of dried tobacco leaves and all
sorts of tools and gadgets.

As I think back of him it's hard for me to believe he could
have been the man my mother speaks of so rarely but always with
fear and apprehension, as being too strict and rigid, demanding, pun-
ishing, merciless. How cruelly he punished her for the slightest transgression, whether real or 'fabricated' by her sister Anna who was
supposedly his favorite child.

What is it that makes parents pick one child over the other?
Do they look at them like at a litter of puppies, searching for the right
blend of the best qualities of both? Or a likeness of one or the other –
or the lack ot it? Who can tell? (But try to tell any parent of his prefer-
ence – it will be denied with the greatest vigor and indignation.)
While my mother complained about my grandfather being too strict
with her, with me – he 'was too lenient – too permissive.' Perhaps he
was, but whatever damage it caused, he always made up for it, even if
it turned out to be an uncomfortable task.

Years later after I'd been taken from the sanctuary of their
home and came to stay only during school vacations, he would let me
read all the things my mother wouldn't. Since I took to reading like a
duck to water, my mother considered it harming. Particularly since I
quickly became bored with fairy tales and adventure stories 'suitable

for my age,' and poked around the library in search of some more 'interesting stuff.' She'd say things like: "I won't have you turn into a book worm." "Are you reading again?! In that light you'll wind up blind and hunchbacked from bending over so much!"

Thus, the only chance I'd get to read was before falling asleep, or in the early morning. Up to this day, I feel the vague, uneasy feeling of guilt when I sit down to read a book in the middle of the day. At grandmother's, however, grandfather would let me read not only all day long, if I so desired, but he even lent me his collection of cowboy mysteries and horror stories which I devoured with bated breath. "The Mystery of the Copper Mine," "The Headless Horseman," "The Pit and the Pendulum," "The Tell-Tale Heart," "The Frankenstein Monster," etc., etc.

Good or bad literature, I wasn't very particular, as long as it was good and scary. Of course, at night, should the need arise, and it often did, I was too petrified to go alone to the bathroom particularly since at grandmother's our 'bathroom' was an outhouse situated in the fenced area between the chicken loft and the stable, which housed the goat Byela who was my grandmother's most prized possession.

To get there I had to walk through the dark, cold hallway and open the heavy, squeaky front door. I never made it that far. I'd race to my grandparents' room and whisper fiercely into the keyhole: "Grandpa!" fearing that at any moment some monster would put his repulsive hand around my throat. Fortunately he was a light sleeper and in no time I could hear him shuffling toward the door. He never asked unnecessary questions. He knew. It seemed he never made any unnecessary gesture – every move was precise and carefully calculated.

He'd walk slowly across the front yard holding my hand, summer, winter, in snow or rain – leading me to my destination. Sometimes, as I sat there, I'd be afraid he had gone, it was so quiet. "Grandpa!" I'd call out to him in panic and he'd answer in that calm reassuring voice of his: "Don't worry child, I'm here. Take your time." And I'd sigh with relief and the demons would recede.

Sometimes I'd pretend my uncle Joseph's spirit was there standing guard. I felt a bit guilty taking him away from my mother who seemed to have a monopoly on him, but I'd figure she was asleep so she didn't need him just then. Grandmother had nine children – six surviving. Two died in childhood – uncle Joseph, at twenty-three. They say he walked to the coal mines, stopped, lifted his eyes to the lightening sky and, sighing deeply, keeled over dead. The company doctor examined him the day before but found him 'fit for work.' His chest pains were supposedly 'nothing.' He was to be married one week later.

No one took it harder than grandmother and my mother, who was fifteen at the time. That night, unable to sleep, she lay in bed staring into the darkness. It was then she claims to have seen a hazy, luminous shadow pass across the room. Her brother had come to say good-bye. Later, he told her through the medium, he'd always be beside her, watching over her as long as she lived – removing the heaviest stones from her path.

But in spite of her brother's reassurance, my mother was always prone to despair. As it was, there were always plenty of reasons for it but she should have had more faith in him and things may have been easier for her. The fact that I was at grandmother's all those years is a good indication how hard she worked to help father in the business.

They began with a tiny workshop manufacturing furniture. She was inexhaustible. A week after my birth she was racing downtown to buy hardware. She dragged the heavy carton into the tram and could barely stand up for the pain in her abdomen. She used to tell me for years she did all that only for her children. Of course, that was a carefully calculated strategy which worked most successfully. She managed to make me feel guilty about all sorts of things including my very existence.

My sister Kaya came around in my second year and, as far as I can remember, I loved her. She was all white and pink and blonde, a chubby, beautiful baby. I was dark and skinny and everyone thought I was sick with consumption or something. My mother would take me to the clinic for X-rays every six months but much to her disappointment, the doctors always gave me a clean bill of health.

My sister, who looked like such a sturdy, healthy baby, caught every disease a child is prone to catch. Although I remember loving her, I also did every nasty thing to her I could think of. My favorite mischief was to coax her into a big drawer and slam it shut. To drown out her screams I would sing at the top of my lungs. Obviously, since I inflicted upon her the torture I myself considered most horrendous, somehow I had a need to punish her.

Somewhere deep inside me there is a little tug of suspicion that I was probably jealous of her. That, perhaps, I may have even hated her. Which could have been another reason for my wanting to become a dancer – to attract the attention I craved – the attention I felt she usurped. That, of course, would blow my previous hypothesis all to hell. Or would it! It might have been a combination of all these things.

In any event, if I remember so vividly how lovely she was and how unlovely I felt next to her, it had to be a strong motivating factor. And if I felt unlovely, it's most likely that my parents must have made me feel that way. One minute I was the center of attention – the next moment there was this chubby cute thing that everyone swooned over. So... she had to be punished... What dark, cruel deeds a child is capable of in order to take revenge for the parents' injustices. Who suffers then is the small, innocent victim who cannot fight back. She was my mother's child. Was and is. Even today my mother and Kaya are as thick as thieves and I am, as always, the outsider. Oddly enough, my locking her in dark, confined places didn't produce in her my kind of phobia.

Another nasty thing I used to like to do was to ignore her. She would start talking to me, but I'd pretend not to hear. Soon she was pleading and crying and still I would behave as if she wasn't even there. I would carry on like that until she was really howling. Then, when I tried to make up, she would have no part of me. Today I know my mother's love was all she had. Father didn't want her and tried to induce mother to have an abortion. My mother would have gone along with it but at that time the marriage was already rotten and she refused just to get even with him.

She was in labor twenty-four hours and almost died. My father took one look at Kaya and declared that anything so ugly couldn't be his. I, on the other hand, grew up under the unshakable conviction that I was the apple of my father's eye. Whether I pretended it was so, or whether I really believed it, I don't quite know.

Yet my first vivid memory of my father is rather ambiguous in that respect. It must have been in my first year because I couldn't walk yet and my mother says I began walking at nine months. It was in the morning or evening because my father stood there in his pajamas, towering above me. He pulled me up and tried to get me to stand. I remember some words of encouragement and then, slowly, he was letting go of my hands. I tottered around uncertainly trying to keep my balance. Feeling I couldn't maintain it, I grabbed at my father to keep from falling. What I got hold of was soft and rubbery and my father yelled out sharply: "Erna!" It was the first harsh sound I heard from him, yet I knew it wasn't anger. It was pain, and I was amazed and immensely curious about the object I happened to discover so unexpectedly.

Children are incredibly curious and their imaginations are boundless. Before they know how to ask questions about the things they don't understand, they have to try to figure things out for themselves. We lived in the suburbs and the first time I remember my mother taking me to the city where I saw tall buildings, I was amazed to see people looking out of the high windows. Since I was familiar only with one storied houses, I was racking my brain to decide how they got up there and why.

The child can think only in terms of the objects it is familiar with. I knew of ladders and wood boards. So my first assumption was that they must have gotten up there using ladders. But then I saw some walk away from the window and they didn't go down – they receded. Thus I deduced they must have somehow used boards, like those my father worked with, and propped them horizontally below the windows. I didn't get the image of many boards placed side by side. I saw only a few boards and thought these people must have balanced precariously on top of them. Of course, I thought they were crazy. Since I couldn't ask, this mystery preoccupied my mind for a long time.

Anyway, back to my father. However much I thought he loved

me, my mother never failed to remind me what he did when I was one week old. It was the day she went to get the hardware and I was entrusted to his care. She was in pain, the carton was heavy, her breasts hurt and she knew I must have been hungry, so she ran as fast as the carton would permit, propelled by the old mothers' instinct. When she got there, my father was working at the machines and she didn't see me anywhere.

From here on, it always went something like this: "So I yelled at him: 'Where is the baby?' The machines were screaming and he didn't even hear me. 'Where is the baby?' I screamed louder.

"He looked at me dumbfounded then turned to one of our workers. Honza, did you see the baby? Where'd I put it? The man shrugged. Don't know? I think the last time you had it was outside. He hit his forehead. Must have left it somewhere in the lumber stacks. Well, I was ready to kill him. You know how forgetful he is, but to forget where he put his own child. I ran out to the yard where we kept the lumber. The sun shone brightly – it was high noon. I looked frantically through the stacks, but there was no sign of you. Your father (she'd always put a special emphasis on the way she said that, like saying: That's your father for you!) was looking around scratching his head. Well, look for her! I screamed at him. Don't you remember what you did with your own child? Just calm down, he said irritably. Nothing could happen to her! (Of course not! Tied up in that blanket the way I was, why, I couldn't even move! For god's sake, Mother! I shudder just to think of it! And it's not so much my father forgetting me somewhere.)

"The lumber yard was full of nooks and crannies and finally I found you in one of them – sleeping peacefully, your face all pink from the sun. Hell, I told him right then and there: I'll never forget this as long as I live – and she won't either, you can be sure of that! And you know what he did? (Here I'd look at my mother with dutiful curiosity.) He laughed! Yes, he just stood there and roared with laughter!"

I think it may have been my mother's constant attempts after their divorce to denigrate my father that made me turn a deaf ear to all she said and love him in spite of everything. It may have also been because he never disciplined me. I don't remember my father ever laying a hand on me, or even as much as saying a harsh word to me. But he would do things my mother deeply resented. On pay day, he'd sit at the dining table surrounded by the handful of employees he had then, counting money and drinking coffee. Everyone was having coffee. He'd sit me in the middle of the table and I could play with the coins and bills lying around. Then he would say: "Erna, stir the coffee."

And I would obligingly stir everyone's cup with my finger. He loved that. And I was happy I could please him.

My father was what is considered a self-made man. Born an illegitimate child to a young maid at my great-grandparents' house, he was marked for life with a social stigma he tried in vain to live down, or rise above, all through his life. My great-grandparents, being very wealthy and class conscious, turned the maid out and placed my father in an orphanage. To make up for his trespass, my grandfather was forced into a marriage with a girl that came from another wealthy, socially prominent family.

My father's description of his life at the orphanage sounds like Dickens's Oliver – only worse. He was forever hungry, and, as soon as he was able to, had to work all day. Six years later, his father, in spite of his aversion to his highborn wife, managed to sire a child, a girl they named Mimi. Thus, father had a half-sister.

For some reason, the 'orphan' was allowed to come to his father's house once or twice a month where he was grudgingly fed by the lady of the house whom he describes only as tightlipped, hard and very stingy.

Mimi grew up to be a holy terror that no one could cope with, least of all her mother. However, as spoiled as she seemed to have been, she was very fond of her 'big brother,' which didn't please her mother in the least, and whenever she could, slipped him something decent to eat. For that, and perhaps for having all that he himself could never hope to have, he adored and worshipped her. At that time she was probably the only human being that showed him any kind of affection. Why my grandmother made this cruel arrangement, I was never able to determine. But it can be safely assumed it was to ease my grandfather's guilty conscience. For the boy, however, it was the most inhuman punishment. To see – so rarely – the wealth and elegance of his father's house, the sharp contrast between him in his rags and his pampered sister, to receive a few begrudged crumbs from the rich table, and then have to return to the dismal poverty at the orphanage must have been a torment beyond belief.

Throughout all that – the only bright spot in his life – was that spoiled child that loved him for reasons he couldn't fathom. The only time he saw his father and mother together was during an illness at the age of seven which almost took his life. He had a high fever and was delirious. His recollection of that episode is rather sketchy but revealing. "I was in bed in the infirmary feeling hot one moment and freezing cold the next. Then suddenly I was running with the boys again up the hill to a cabbage field near the orphanage. I yanked out a head of cabbage and sank my teeth into it. It was cold and gritty with earth, but it stilled the gnawing hunger pains in my stomach. It was a wintry, early morning and I was freezing. I heard a boy yelling: Come on! Let's start back! Move your asses or they'll let us have it! Then I heard another voice – a soft, tearful voice coming as if from a great distance: Please, let me take him... I opened my eyes and found myself in bed again. My head felt burning hot and it was hard for me to bring anything into focus. Then I saw a woman's face above me moving in and out of focus. She was stroking my forehead and although I didn't recognize her, somehow I knew it was my mother. There was no joy or satisfaction in that realization. Then I thought I heard my father's voice drifting toward me. I tried to move my head but couldn't. It felt too heavy.

"What would you do with him?" my father was saying. "Besides, we agreed, remember?"

I saw she was crying – big, fat tears streaming down her face and I could feel them dropping on my hands.

"I don't care, I want to take him."

"You know that's impossible. Don't be such a goose."

She cried harder and called him coward, over and over."

At the age of fourteen my father escaped from the orphanage. Determined not to get caught, he kept moving until he reached Czechoslovakia. There he served as an apprentice to a carpenter. How he got together with my mother isn't very clear to me. Both are rather evasive on the subject as if trying to forget it ever happened. All my mother ever said, was that she ought to have had her head examined. She certainly had much better suitors than him!

But whatever she may claim, the fact remains she married him, in spite of her family's opposition to the 'penniless foreigner.' These little Balkan countries are really something. Everybody hates everybody else but when it comes to the Austrians or Germans, they put their hatreds together and turn them on the 'Krauts.' My father was a 'Kraut' and although he stayed there most of his life, he remained a 'foreigner.'

Today I realize why he was so determined to 'make it.' But oddly enough it was always my mother who worked the hardest and contributed the most. She, was doing it 'for her children,' and, of course, she never let us forget it.

In spite of father's determination, I am inclined to doubt he'd have made it without mother's perseverance. The first few years they were constantly in debt but mother scrounged and saved to make ends meet. She worked in the factory at those awesome, noisy machines that cut and planed and sanded the lumber that would be worked into beautiful pieces of furniture. She also cooked meals for the workers to save on wages. It must have been a very rough life and it is only today that I realize it.

Father, on the other hand, liked to frequent theaters, concerts and nightclubs, and where my mother saved, he spent. There were girl friends and scenes and long days of ominous silence. Days when even a kind glance at my father brought a look of resentment into my mother's eyes. Any move I'd make was bound to be the wrong one – one way or another and I'd be glad when the visit was over and grandmother took me back home again. Of their quarrels, one episode left a particularly deep impression on me. I must have been very little because there was no Kaya yet. Mother had a bowl of eggs sitting on the table intended to be marinated for the winter. They were carefully selected and my father liked to crack them and suck them out raw. My mother must have objected because suddenly, he said something sharp and began laughing and smashing egg after egg against the wall. I sat there staring at the yellow, slimy mess oozing down the wall and gather into a revolting puddle of broken shells and yolks. Mother must have been terribly upset because she refused to clean it up and the wall bore witness to their anger for a long time. Before each visit I'd wonder if it would still be there. It was, for as long as we lived there.

CHAPTER FOUR

By the time I was three, I made my first public appearance as a
dancer. It was at some civic affair and I knew I was terrible. I would
flutter around on tiptoes to some dreadful selection rendered by a
squeaky record player but everybody loved it. I knew I had much to
learn and was eager to begin. However, no one seemed terribly enthusiastic about it.

By the time I was five, my father had acquired a large piece of
land consisting of acres of walnut groves and all sorts of fruit trees.
On the vacant part, he had built a large factory and we began to pros-
per. The secret of his sudden success was a fat military contract with
the Germans calling for the manufacture of prefabricated barracks
which were transported wherever needed.

Father, although being a confirmed socialist and Marxist, had
no qualms about it. They were made as badly as possible and so he
felt he was 'doing his bit to sabotage the efforts of the Nazis.'
(Whether that was a rationalization or not – I can't say.) Of course, all
his communist friends found employment at the factory whether they
were carpenters or not. They, however, weren't allowed anywhere
near the furniture department. There, he had excellent craftsmen.

I liked best the woodcarving section. The foreman there was an old man whom I loved to watch. He'd sit me up on his work bench where I could sit for hours watching his rough, gnarled hands work the wood with such care and precision until it turned into flowers and delicate curlicues which would wind up gracing the fine smooth surfaces of the furniture worked on in the other sections. Due to the unprecedented affluence, our home became a house in the suburbs, and my mother no longer worked at the factory and I was brought 'home' to stay.

Oddly enough, I have a very dim recollection of that house except for the huge yard it had and the sprawling garden which had a kind of wild look to it. But what I liked best about it was an area way in the back of the garden where a cluster of huge granite boulders, haphazardly scattered about, nestled amidst tufts of grass and flowers and created marvelous little hiding places that no one knew of – away from everybody – away from my mother's irritated tone of voice, the constant reprimands and complaints. There were narrow, tunnel-like passages that only a child could crawl through which opened onto secluded, sunlit little areas carpeted with the softest grass and graced with lovely flowers and various edible weeds I could chew on. I'd lean against the smooth, sun-warmed stone and watch the drifting clouds for hours and hours. Somewhere in the distance, disturbing the infinite peace, I'd occasionally hear my mother's impatient calls – like echoes from another, hostile world – but I'd pay no attention because I knew whatever she wanted would be a drag. I knew it was because she was growing restless and insecure. She was like a workhorse, unable to relax and take it easy after the yoke's been taken off.

There is another recollection I have of that house that isn't at all pleasant. We had a pet duck we named Lida. She was just an ordinary duck but she was great. Kaya would always wrap her in her old baby blanket and quickly stuff her into her toy baby buggy and race around the yard before Lida had a chance to extricate herself from the confinement. She knew her name and came waddling the moment we called her. And she was better than a watchdog. As soon as someone approached the front gate, she'd start a fearful racket. Sounded like a whole flock of geese. But you could tell by the tone and volume whether it was a stranger or a friend visiting. Her home was a tool shed not far from the house which had a door balancing precariously on one hinge which no one seemed inclined to repair.

One early morning in my sleep, I thought I heard a slam. When we got up we found the door had collapsed and Lida was squashed beneath. Both Kaya and I cried for hours. Later we began to plan a fine funeral for her. But mother had other ideas. At lunch we found Lida roasted and quartered on a plate. I was horrified and Kaya wailed horrendously. Mother had to give us a few smart smacks accompanied by sharp words about it being a war and that it was a sin to waste food, etc., before we, reluctantly, and with constricted throats and fat tears rolling down our cheeks, forced a few bites down – I, feeling positively like a cannibal – eating my best friend.

I think it's grandparents who should be entrusted with rearing children. The parents are always much too preoccupied with building a life, money, position, mutual differences, frustrations and a number of things that only bewilder, disorient and confuse the children.

Grandparents, on the other hand, have already made all their mistakes, finished fighting their battles, are settled down, at peace with themselves, easy-going, with nothing but time on their hands and not even the faintest idea what the hell to do with themselves anyway no more than their children know what to do with them. Locking them up in rest homes only makes them older and crankier then they have a right to be while they could make themselves useful in this fashion.

Neither of my grandparents would have ever as much as dreamt of making us eat our pet duck. I may understand my mother's growing uneasiness and feelings of insecurity in view of all the developments, but I don't think I can forgive her for her lack of sensitivity and understanding. But that was my mother – bewildering, confusing, illogical and maddening, but at the same time sacrificing and devoted.

My father had a 'manager' whom mother was very suspicious of. But he refused to listen to her and there were many quarrels about it. I guess she began to feel expendable and I, being so adamant about wanting to take ballet lessons, made things only worse. But finally, the doctors found something wrong with me. I had weak bones and they recommended exercises. Well, I thought I had it made. But nei-ther of my parents were ready to concede and let me do what I wanted all along. That would have been too simple. Mother had a particular gymnastics organization in mind – one that she herself went to, and father, of course, had his own choice, which mother, naturally, was dead set against.

Anyway, it was then that father decided to take a trip to Vienna. The war was going badly for Germany and the end was near-ing rapidly. While we could obtain all the food we wanted on the black market in Prague, in Germany and Austria it was getting very scarce.

Father couldn't have picked a better time to come rushing to his father and sister's rescue. I am sure it must have been his plan all the time. As was to be expected, my mother was less than enthusiastic about the whole idea, particularly since father flatly refused to take her along. Only I was selected to accompany him. But in spite of her protestations and suspicions, she packed two huge suitcases full of food and even baked her best cake for me to take to my grandfather. But she'd bitch about it all through her packing and fussing.

"After the way they treated you, serves them right! Let them starve! But no, you must run and show off."

To make up for her hurt, she'd insist he couldn't even drag her there.

"I have my pride. I wouldn't crawl back where I was kicked out from."

This would go on until father stormed out of there – laughing furiously.

Of the trip itself, I remember very little except that it was long and full of stops and waiting once we crossed the border. But I have a vivid memory of the arrival. The railway station was partially bombed out. The city was a mess. Bombed-out houses, mountains of rubble in the streets, sad-looking people poking around in the ruins and all this, sweetly perfumed by the lush, green linden trees which grew amidst the devastation, unperturbed by all the human folly. What impression can all that have had on a five-year-old child? I don't remember feel-ing much – perhaps incredulity – I couldn't imagine, no matter what I was told, how all that could have happened – what caused it. But I was to find out soon enough.

And then I stood in front of the gray, four story house of my grandfather's, staring at its crumbling, but still imposing, facade full of baroque ornaments. A badly disfigured angel spreading his wings, graced the main entrance. Today, I can only guess how my father must have felt.

The next thing I knew, I was being hugged by 'my grand-mother.' I took in the wrinkled face, the thinning hair, the small, rheumy eyes that darted from me to my father and the suitcases – examining everything appraisingly. I glanced at the hands on my shoulders – huge, swollen knuckles, the fingers stiff and ugly like an old witch's. I began to withdraw. I looked up at my father and stared. His face was frozen into a forced smile and his eyes wore the strangest expression. I had never seen him look like that.

Mindful of what mother told me, I looked at her bravely: "Which grandmother are you? Not the real one..."

She began to laugh and fuss to hide her embarrassment. "Such a clever, pretty child you have there, Heinrich. Why, she's the spitting image of you. You used to have the same kind of look. Won't Papa be pleased to see you...and Mimi... ah...my God!"

Up to this day I believe I wouldn't have liked that old woman even if mother hadn't set me against her.

My grandfather turned out to be a big, jowly man that looked as if he had lost a great deal of weight. Everything hung on him. His skin, his clothes – even his eyes had a downtrodden, defeated look. How much my father could have enjoyed his triumph, I don't know. I doubt he found the satisfaction he sought. But I liked my aunt Mimi. She was a tall woman, a little taller than my father, with the same eyes as her mother but their expression was completely different. There was none of that calculating, appraising quality. She had a lovely, kind smile and beautiful, absolutely perfect teeth. There was some-thing very graceful, almost feline about her walk and I liked that. I really liked her very much and I knew she liked me too.

At one point, I remembered the cake (undoubtedly because I felt like having some) so I took the box and presented it proudly to my grandfather adding pointedly that I was hungry. The old lady quickly took my hand and marched me off to the kitchen where, much to my horror, she cut a slice of the darkest bread I had ever seen and, after slapping some jam on it, handed it to me. I must have looked terribly disappointed but she didn't appear to take notice. I will never forget my father's look when he saw that piece of bread. Somehow, I had a feeling it looked vaguely familiar to him. For a moment, I pondered if I should say anything but after taking a brave bite of it, I gave up. "I was hungry for my Mama's cake," I explained plaintively.

"Erna!"

I couldn't believe it was my father who had said that. I had never heard him speak so sharply to me. Before my father could say anymore, grandfather took the bread out of my hand and handed it back to her. His face was red and his eyes were very angry.

"None of your stinginess today," he said in a terribly quiet tone but which held a hidden threat. "Give her a piece of her mother's cake, and be quick about it!"

She looked astonished and flustered and rushed out of there.

My grandfather's house was in a section of town that was in a much better shape than most. It was situated near the Schoenbrun Palace and aunt Mimi took me there the next day. It was fantastic. There, the devastated city seemed far away. I don't remember whether my father went with us, but I don't think so. Later, she took me to some friends of hers that lived not too far from there. I had a feeling she wanted to show me off.

Everyone fussed about me and marveled at my German and, of course, I was well-pleased. They were very nice people, but it was their parrot that fascinated me the most. That clever bird could say all sorts of things and they said whenever they quarreled he would scream at them to shut up.

They lived on the ground floor of a big house, and I remember we were sitting drinking tea and having some excellent cookies when it happened. First, the air raid alarm began screaming its warning which was followed almost immediately by the sound of airplanes. Then I heard this strange, whistling noise and I ran to the window. Looking up I saw a whole cluster of bombs falling right on top of us.

At the same time someone was yelling that the door wouldn't open. Apparently the air pressure kept it shut. Then I was yanked from the window and dragged under a bed or something.

In the next instant all hell broke loose. The house shook, furniture was falling, from where I was I could see pictures and paintings smashing to the floor and above all, there was this fantastic noise all through which the parrot was screeching: Shut up! Shut Up! Shut Up!

I was laughing. I was laughing so hard I thought I'd never stop. Later, I remember my aunt carrying me out of the house. The row of houses opposite was leveled, and the street disappeared beneath a solid mass of debris.

I tried to look around but my aunt held my head to her chest. I could feel her trembling. She hesitated, then was stepping over something. I managed to peer out and saw a bleeding arm. The alarm had come too late. The street was littered with torn limbs and bleeding bodies. I don't remember reacting to it. I don't think I felt fear, or pity, or anything. Not anything! Yet there had to be some feeling – some tears.

Much later I was finally taken to see my real grandmother. I sensed my father went there only reluctantly, delaying the visit as long as possible. She was a tiny, delicate woman with small features and big, dark eyes. She reminded me of a bird, she was so light and quick in her movements yet very controlled as if keeping a check on the impulsive energy she projected.

She had married after father ran away. Out of the marriage, she had one son who had just been killed somewhere in Italy. Her husband was also dead. I remember her looking at me for a long time, searching my face. I saw her eyes were turning bright with tears and she turned away and began talking quickly saying father shouldn't have brought her anything and so forth. I felt terrible because he brought her just a fraction of what he took to his father.

She lived in a tiny, dark apartment which had that intangible something that tells you here lives old age and loneliness and it made me very sad. Everything was scrupulously neat and tidy – as if she were forever expecting someone to pay her an unexpected and long awaited visit. She pulled out some pictures telling me I had an uncle. I saw a photograph of a droopy-eyed young man that bore little resemblance to my father, or her. When I asked her where he was, she showed me an iron cross and a couple of other medals.

"He was a good soldier," she said in a thin voice. I could see my father could barely wait to get out of there. She held me close looking up at him asking to bring me back again. "She's all I have left now..." she said as if she knew she never really had him and never would.

But my father never took me back there, and I never saw her again. I tried not to let him see how sorry I was for her and that I really liked her because I was afraid he wouldn't have been pleased with me. Actually I didn't much enjoy my stay at grandfather's. I suppose I must have been impressed by the big, imposing house, but I didn't like it. It was a cold, aloof house – like the people living in it. They acted like strangers toward one another, very polite but cutting and sarcastic. There were always things left hanging in the air – unsaid – creating tensions until the elegant rooms bristled with it. There was the old lady (I never could call her grandmother as she asked me to) sitting behind the grand piano straining her swollen, rheumatic fingers to obey while she casually threw out biting words aimed at Mimi. But they would be directed either to grandfather, or my father, depending who happened to be handy.

She always made a point of keeping her eyes on the keyboard and Mimi pretended not to hear. But I could tell it affected her by the thin, little smile that tugged at the corners of her mouth. Yet she'd continue reading, or whatever she was doing, as if nothing had been said. When she wasn't around, grandfather didn't miss a chance to bitterly complain about her. About all the money he poured into her education and travels – to no avail.

It seemed she collected degrees, diplomas and beaus with the same unflagging persistency but never made 'proper use' of either. She had degrees in economics, business administration, both of which she despised – in Greek, Latin and who knows what else, and at the time of our visit, was working on a law degree. She also had years of vocal training and was good enough to have gotten an offer from the Viennese Opera House, which she rejected, studied piano to become a

concert pianist, which she had no intention of doing and – studied ballet for years with equal detachment. (I am sure her last accomplishment must have made a great impression on me and was most likely
an important contributing factor to my growing affection for her.) I
know my father would have given his life for but an iota of her education. Although he remained loyal to her, and defended her consistently, to a certain degree, he commiserated with his father.

As far as I was concerned, if it hadn't been for Mimi, I would
have regretted bitterly not having gone instead to my grandmother's
as usual.

CHAPTER FIVE

The most important thing that emerged out of that trip for me was my father's sudden change of attitude toward my ballet lessons. There were no more objections – I could do as I pleased. The abrupt change didn't fail to arouse my mother's suspicions. Even today, I still don't know whether my mother was a mistrusting, suspicious person, or a highly intuitive one. Sometimes it is hard to distinguish between the two. But most of my life I believed the former, and when compared to my father, she didn't come off so well.

On the other hand, my father had a few habits I wasn't exactly crazy about either. Where she was suspicious and secretive, he was overly extroverted. He would fall into intimate conversations with perfect strangers and pour out all of his problems in minutes. As much as I loved him, I found it highly embarrassing, and I used to pretend I didn't belong to him whenever he carried on like that. And his forgetfulness was unbelievable.

I remember distinctly a time he was taking me back to grandmother's. I must have been around two years old. I remember sitting next to him in an empty bus waiting for its departure. There must have been plenty of time left because he decided to go out and get something. He told me to be a good girl and stay put – that he'd be back in a little while.

Well, the bus began filling, the driver was getting all set behind the wheel, the motor coughed into action and I knew from previous experience that departure was imminent. I strained to look out of the window but there was no sight of my dear Papa. I don't suppose grownups ever consider the terror children experience under such circumstances. I knew my father surely didn't. Knowing I couldn't rely on anything, I managed to slide off the seat and waddled to the exit door.

Someone picked me up and yelled indignantly: "Whose kid is it? Can't you look after it?"

No one made an attempt to claim me, and I was too busy scanning the street for my elusive parent to try to set him straight. The bus was buzzing with indignation. Suddenly, I spotted my dear father, sporting freshly shaved cheeks, walking along the street in deep contemplation. I had already learned that was the way he looked when he strained his poor brain to remember what he was supposed to. Most often, it was lucky he remembered there was something he had to remember not to forget.

Seeing him wandering there aimlessly, racking his brain for a clue to remember what he was there for, I began yelling: "Papa! Papa!"

Regardless of what my mother may have believed, I had a good set of lungs.

He heard me. His face lit up with sudden illumination and he ran toward the already moving bus and jumped in just in the nick of time. I was so happy to have been thus saved from some unimaginable calamity, that I forgave him instantly and hugged him fiercely crying with joy.

As I look back on my childhood, I realize my parents split me up. I see clearly two distinctly different people. One was for Papa, the other for Mama. And it may still be that way. And the world is full of people who can be easily fit into these categories. Parents can be a real pain. They confuse, hurt; they mislead and terrorize. After a while the child's natural inclinations are buried under all the shit it has to put up with.

One of the things my mother was really big on was morality – modesty, propriety. She taught me very early there was something terrible between my legs that I had to hide at all times. Like make believe it didn't exist. We even have a cute little euphemism when referring to the poor nature's eliminating and procreating apparatus which clearly indicates the general attitude toward it: We call it shame. Translated, it sounds utterly ridiculous but that's exactly what it is. Shame. It's always been: "Put your shame away! A nice little girl doesn't lift her dress and show her shame. Erna! Your shame is showing!" Heaven forbid!

My father, on the other hand, didn't bother about that. He had other preoccupations. My ears stuck out a bit. It didn't matter that it was he who happened to pass them on to me. He wanted it corrected. Immediately. He dragged me from one plastic surgeon to the other but they all told him he had to wait till I was at least nine. It took me a very long time to face up to the fact, which was something I probably couldn't have done then, that he didn't like me the way I was. He didn't love me, sticking away ears or not, and it had to hurt.

My mother, to make up for the dismal fact that she bore an imperfect child, was quick to attempt to correct it. She used to put a tight-fitting cap on me which began pinching my ears in two minutes flat. Of course it didn't do a damn thing for my ears but it sure drove me up the wall. Then later when my second teeth came in crooked, father insisted I get fitted for braces. I would have liked to oblige him but I just couldn't bear the way they took the impressions of my teeth. The metal contraption filled with the revolting white goop that was to be jammed against my teeth, filled me with disgust and I began to gag at the mere sight of it.

To top it all, the dentist delicately dipped his finger into the goop and proceeded to smear it against the roof of my mouth. Well, that did it every time. We tried again and again, but I persisted in gagging and choking and during the last attempt, I became so infuriated with him, I yanked the damn thing out of my mouth and threw it at him. After that, father gave up. The net results – my ears didn't see the light of day until I was twenty-three. I kept them well hidden at all times. And, out of the thousands of pictures I accumulated during my career, there isn't one of me smiling.

On stage, my whole body, my whole face could project a smile, but my teeth – I showed as little as possible.

When I began taking ballet, my whole world changed. Five was a bit early to begin, but I was a mature five and I didn't just fool around – I really worked at it. I was so serious about it, it was ridiculous.

Soon after that aunt Mimi came to visit. And that was the beginning of the end. I think mother resented her from the first day she came. Of course, my father's attitude didn't help matters any. It was as if he became a different person. Where before he never used to be around in the evening, now he was always at home. Or, if he went out, aunt Mimi went with him.

My mother never wanted to join them wherever they may have decided to go. He also bought all sorts of presents for her which was bugging mother no end. Later I understood why he was doing that. To some degree he was trying to pay her back for the love and kindness she showed him in their childhood. But mother never saw it that way. As the visit was extending into a stay, her antagonism became more overt and quarrels grew more frequent. I was six at the time and going to school. Then one day something happened.

I remember coming home from school and seeing father's car parked in front of the house and the backseat full of suitcases. I'll always remember every detail of that day. I ran into the yard. Mother stood there, stone-faced, staring stoically at the front door. I couldn't see Kaya anywhere and I knew that someone must have taken her away.

Then I saw my father coming out of the house carrying his briefcase. I never saw it packed so full. He wore a hat and carried his overcoat over his arm. I knew something terrible was happening and there was nothing I could do to change it. My only concern at that time was me. What should I do? Where did I fit in? How to survive? He looked at me and I wanted to run to him.

I was about to say something when I caught my mother's look. It stopped me cold.

He gave me a funny look and walked on by me, never stopping, never trying to speak to me. And then I saw his back, walking away from me, slightly bent, and I knew. I knew he was walking away for good. He was leaving me. I would never see his back as he was leaving the house – only to return. It would never ever be that way again. I felt like running after him when I heard my mother's voice.

"Let him go!"

I didn't dare to move. Kaya was indeed gone, and I was alone with mother. All I remember after that is my mother's pain. The endless torrent of tears, self-reproaches, accusations, laments that went on day after day, night after night. When mother would hold me in her arms calling me her little girl one moment and pushing me away the next saying I was just like my father – unfeeling, selfish; I looked like him, talked like him, laughed like him.

I was terribly afraid. I could hear her weep every night and talk to herself and sometimes to other people but I knew there was no one but the two of us. Good God, the things people do to their children! They act as if they were unfeeling morons that cannot absorb all the madness around them.

But that wasn't the end of it. Some time later, mother sued for divorce. She didn't want to grant father visiting rights so it was to be a bitter, drawn out fight. He was an 'immoral degenerate' and I shouldn't want to see him ever again. I had no idea what these labels meant but the way mother said it, I knew it must have been something dreadful. This was brought home to me until I agreed I would testify in court. I didn't really want to do it but I knew she wanted me to. Somehow she made me feel l owed it to her. And I thought she might get to like me as much as she liked Kaya if I did it. Until today, I shudder whenever I think of it, which is as rarely as I can. But it's there, etched into my brain with bitter poison and burning acid.

I was afraid. Grandmother went along and I sat on her lap outside in the corridor waiting for my turn. I saw my father briefly, talking to his lawyer and I quickly turned away. I didn't dare to look into his eyes.

Then, against all my secret hopes, I found myself in the witness box. I did all I could to keep calm. I had to do what was expected of me. I had to spill out my whipped-up anger – for the sake of righteousness – and renounce my father.

I sat there, my hands balled into tight fists to keep from falling apart. The judge asked me one single, short question. "Do you want to see your father?"

"I want to stay with my mother." I whispered afraid my voice would crack at any moment.

The heavy-hooded eyes had a veiled look of sadness and compassion. "Of course you will stay with your mother. But do you want to visit your father sometimes?"

I tried not to think of the fact that my father was right behind me – looking at me. Taking a deep, shuddering breath, I blurted out: "He didn't even buy me a present for Christmas!"

I flashed the last, happy Christmas we all spent together and I had to keep swallowing in order not to cry. I had known then that things weren't going well, but for that Christmas they had made up, and we had a good time. It was in the new house and we had a fantastic tree decorated with all the beautiful, glittering ornaments my mother took such pain to collect over the year.

That Christmas will always mean to me a cozy, warm room filled with the fragrance of pine incense and mama's cookies, and open boxes, gaily colored paper and ribbons lying around – and in the midst of it all – two pair of tiny, but grownup-looking, leather boots trimmed with fur. They looked so warm and beautiful. Mama also got a pair and Kaya got a doll and I, a lot of books full of beautiful pictures.

Actually, it's the only Christmas that I do remember all of us together and it probably was. The Christmas that just came and went so uneventfully was lonely and no matter how hard mother tried, the fact that there was no sign of father or anything to tell us he thought of us at that time, made it very sad indeed.

I pushed the thought aside with great difficulty. I heard my father's attorney saying in that smooth, sarcastic tone of his: "You mean you like your father only when he buys you presents?"

I glared at that suave, hateful face. "He forgot me on the bus!"

I burst out never knowing why that suddenly crossed my mind or how it could be relevant to what was happening. "And he left us because of her! I don't ever want to see him again! I'm ashamed he's my father!"

Then I was crying and sobbing and through all that I could hear father laughing as I was carried out of the courtroom. Outside I was deposited into the safety of my grandmother's ample lap and burying my head in the softness of her sagging breasts, I cried and cried.

My poor, misguided mother. Misguided by her anger, her need to strike back. Although today I understand how she felt – having worked so hard for many years and not to have reaped the benefits of her labor – still I wish she'd have spared me that. It didn't accomplish anything, and later, it was I who was sent – by her – to collect the alimony which father so readily forgot to send.

If I sound like I am complaining – I am. I am complaining for all the children who have to go through the same shit and who grow up into torn-up human beings hurting deep inside – never knowing why. It's not that I'm against divorce. Not in the least. But I feel if a marriage is rotten, we should think twice before bringing children into it. They don't "cement it up." They just fall apart in the process of trying. If there are children already, we shouldn't "keep it together because of their sake." Just leave them out of the mess and end it as quickly and as painlessly as possible.

My father moved into a lovely eight room apartment in the finest section of Prague and furnished it with the best furniture his factory could supply. And we, after a little over a year of suburbia, after a breath of sudden affluence – had to give up our house and move into an apartment in the city. It wasn't as large, nor as elegant as my father's, but it was comfortable. At that time, however, I already felt pretty much out of it all. I didn't feel at home there. But it didn't matter. I had my dancing, and my main concern was how to obtain new toe shoes which were hard to get unless you could supply the cobbler with meat or some other goodies.

Food for shoes! Why not? After all, as mother never failed to remind us, there was a war. But aside from that, and the one experience we had in Vienna, war meant very little. To me it was the normal state of affairs. Even the fact that those stern, superior acting men in uniforms that were swarming all over the city evoked fear in the grownups was nothing unusual. It's always been that way.

A child is subject to constant authority and the occupation forces were just an extension of it. Whatever inconveniences there were, that too was quite 'normal.' The only unusual event was the revolution which gripped the city just a few days before the end of the war. By then it was all over everywhere except in my city. Prague was the last refuge of the disintegrating German forces. The allies were approaching from both sides and the remnants of the Eastern armies, fleeing from the Russians, were heading toward us.

With the news of the approaching German tank divisions, the people of the city took up arms. There were rumors of women and children being forced under the tanks of the Germans – of German nuns with machine guns firing into the people. The people moved into cellars and began setting up barricades in the streets.

To us children it was a great adventure. Everybody dragged down a mattress and a supply of food and the dark, musty cellar was transformed into a huge dormitory. We spent four days down there. Four days of not knowing whether it was day or night, of sleeping whenever it moved us, of getting acquainted with each other. There were children I never even met before. Down in that cellar the usual neighborly casualness turned into something much deeper and much more humane. We were all people thrown together by the same predicament and everyone was helping everybody else. I will never forget that – the beautiful feeling of solidarity and friendliness.

There was an old professor, our next door neighbor, who made it his task to keep the children under control. He was continually telling stories and anecdotes and devising all sorts of games to keep us occupied.

For the most part I remember having a marvelous time. For the first time in my life the passing hours didn't represent a regimentation of my existence. There were no regular meals, no set hours for sleep, no duties, nothing – not even dancing. We were all cramped together, cot next to cot, but it was all friendly and cozy.

Someone had a transistor radio going all the time. Our people had captured the radio station and we could hear the announcer's voice calling London for help. That went on for hours and hours. Prague calling London... please help... That's all I remember. Those were the first English words I learned.

Then somewhere along the way the voice faltered and was cut off in the middle of the sentence. The cellar turned dead quiet. Even the children became silent. A few minutes later a German accented voice began ordering the people to start removing the barricades and behave in an orderly, lawful manner. The mood in the cellar dropped drastically. The men fighting outside, coming in occasionally for a bit of rest and food, brought more news. Good news alternated with the bad. Pankratz Prison was captured and the prisoners released – then it was recaptured by the Germans who were going to blow it up.

The Americans had halted at Pilson and were proceeding no further. Everyone had a different theory as to why it should be so. The strange young man reputed to have been secretly harbored by Mrs. Ondrak, a widow living on the fifth floor whom no one had seen but everyone knew about and who had been the cause for much gossip and consternation, emerged as a member of the underground – a partisan – a freedom fighter – and became a hero instantly.

He was the only one who had a gun and every time he went out he brought in more weapons. Mrs. Ondrak was beaming with pride.

Our food supply was running low so mother and I ventured upstairs. There was no electricity so the elevator wasn't working and we had to climb the four flights of steps to our apartment. I could see a German airplane circling overhead. We took as much food as we could and raced down again.

Later mother volunteered to help with the barricades. Of course I insisted on tagging along. It felt strange being outside again. It was spring and the trees were getting green but the fresh smell of sap mingled with the sharp acrid smell of powder and the street was all torn up. A tram had been pulled across the street and the people were digging out the cobblestones and passing them from hand to hand until they were deposited inside the tram.

The sound of distant bullets frightened me, but I wanted to keep near mother. She had joined the line of people passing the cobblestones. The stones looked too heavy for her so I decided to help her. But I was more of a hindrance than help. Still, I wouldn't be put off and finally caused her to drop a stone. She was angry and as she stooped down to retrieve it, I heard the swishing sound of bullets right above her.

Everyone dropped to the ground. I found myself pressed into the hollow space left by the stones with mother right on top of me. For a while I was aware of nothing except the wild, erratic thud of her heart, and although she appeared perfectly calm, I knew she must have been terribly frightened.

Someone was still firing from the second floor of the house across the intersection. It was Mrs. Ondrak's young man who went up there and 'took care' of the sniper. I thought he was the bravest and the most wonderful human being in the whole world. He returned later to the cellar carrying two suitcases. Just as I was falling asleep I saw him slipping a gold watch on Mrs. Ondrak's wrist. She laughed, showing him the bracelet was too large for her. Then late at night I heard the professor's maid whispering to mother she saw him drag more suitcases upstairs to Mrs. Ondrak's apartment.

My admiration for the young revolutionary suffered an irreparable blow. In my childish fantasy, the hero was a noble-hearted creature, never stooping to bagging the spoils. It took me a long time to fall asleep that night. I was wondering what father was doing, but was afraid to ask. I knew mother wouldn't have liked it. But, as I later found out, he survived well those four crucial days.

Everything has a way of passing and people learn to adjust to new conditions. Only my mother never did. Her anger and resentment never subsided. She was bitter he hadn't suffered – what with him and aunt Mimi being Austrian and all. But where before he was 'the Communist' (fortunately she never expressed this except in private) now he was 'the Nazi' – the collaborator and so forth.

As it was, father had some minor problems in those first few days of the German defeat, largely due to my aunt's incapacity to speak Czech without a thick German accent, but my father's socialist friends came quickly to their rescue. Thus, postwar life brought little change for my father and aunt Mimi – much to my mother's disappointment. But there was one satisfaction mother had during the first year of their separation. Her suspicions about father's 'manager' turned out to be justified. That man, whom father trusted implicitly, together with his personal secretary, succeeded in defrauding the firm of over a million crowns in less than a year. But, at the time, father was doing so well it would have taken a lot more to break him.

Not even the end of the war could do that. He swung right back into action and carried on until the new communist regime came around to nationalizing whatever he owned. Because it didn't happen immediately, he believed he was safe. A rich man within the socialist system, he felt he had every right to be. He was after all a self-made man. He didn't inherit anything so he had a right to keep what he had. Those were the Marxist rules. When at last it happened anyway, it was quite a blow to him because he had such faith in Marxism. Even when I was quite little, I remember him telling me all about the 'system,' and as soon as I was able to, he had me read "Das Kapital" and we'd discuss it at every opportunity.

I doubt if I understood it fully, but he was proud I could carry on a halfway intelligent debate about it. I soon learned that if I sounded off about it among his friends, it made him very happy and since I was eager to please him, I never failed to lay it on thick. It is only today that I realize how much I craved his love and how much I was willing to do for it. It is only today that I am consciously aware that I – as I was – was never enough.

He wanted me perfect. In looks – and mind. I tried very hard, but I just couldn't make it. There were my teeth, my ears, and even my nose began to develop a tiny bump like his. And my attitude about the 'system' must have been disappointing as well. I found the ideology, on the whole, admirable and thought Mr. Marx a kind, humane man but in practice I couldn't see it working very successfully. Whatever the advantages, I thought it sounded too restrictive and individuality stifling. But that was before I found out that happens under any regime and that one has to fight hard to maintain it or accept the alternative. I was always very big on individuality. No matter what, I wanted to be the master of my own destiny. To do as I pleased – go wherever it moved me. To be free. And freedom to me was dancing. Dancing would take me wherever I wished to go.

CHAPTER SIX

My first 'break' came when I was eight. I was a soloist in a children's corps de ballet in an opera-like treatment of a fairy tale. Of course, I had danced before but that was just individual performances here and there, sponsored by the school. This, however, was to be a steady engagement.

I was terribly excited about the whole thing. To me it was the beginning of a 'dream come true.'

I still have a picture somewhere taken during the first performance. There I was, in a pale lime tutu, looking every inch the ballerina I always wanted to be. But having been rather thin, and the single spotlight having cast deep shadows which blended into the background, my arms and legs looked like veritable skeletons.

Much to my surprise, the whole family came to the opening – including my father, although he arrived late. But it turned out to be like a wake. Everyone cried, with the exception of my father who got out of there as soon as the performance was over and I never even saw him.

My grandmother insisted that my ankles were too thin and predicted they would break if I kept it up. Everyone agreed I was much too skinny, most likely due to the strain and all the hours of daily dancing and performing, and that mother should make me cut it out. My mother, never too happy to have me all that involved in a career at such an early age, a career which was gradually removing me from her influence, was quick to follow their advice.

Terrible scenes ensued, the details of which I don't, nor do I care, to remember, but the outcome was – I won. I kept on dancing. But it was a struggle. Anytime it appeared that I was neglecting school and homework because of dancing, she'd hide my toe shoes and threaten to make me stop. It drove me to distraction.

The war was long over but things weren't back to normal yet. Of course, I had no idea what 'back to normal' meant since I never experienced such a thing. All I knew was that toe shoes were still hard to get and cost a lot of money. And my 'salary' wasn't even enough to keep me in toe shoes. And my mother, although I believe she rather enjoyed my 'success' (at times, anyway), when she was sore for one reason or another, sent me off to get the money I needed from my father.

"I've spent enough money on you at the expense of your sister. And who's ever going to pay me back for it, I want to know? See if your father will do for you even half as much as I have."

The absurdity of these constant challenges never failed to infuriate and frustrate me and I swore to myself countless times I'd get away as soon as possible. She thought this would make me hate my father, but it only strengthened my resolve to show her I could get from him what I wanted. But I didn't mind that in the least. Besides, I liked to visit with him.

The factory no longer meant just the good old smell of wood and pretty curls of wood shavings to play with and the comfort of the old woodcarver's affection. Now it was status. My father was rich and I could cajole him into lending me his chauffeur and have him drive me around. I learned quickly I could connive him into giving me whatever money I needed. All he had to do to get rid of me was to give me what I wanted.

I also liked to go to his apartment. Mother insisted aunt Mimi lived there too and it had certain sinister overtones which I grasped only vaguely but never believed. But mother was wrong. Aunt Mimi occupied the top floor of a small apartment house my father had acquired which was located quite a distance away in another section of the city. Although she was often at father's, there was no evidence that she lived there except for the grand piano father bought her. But that was there because in her apartment there was no room for it. She had agreed to make use of her degree in business administration and help father run the business since he, after the dismal fiasco with the 'manager,' was reluctant to try with someone else. Or so it appeared. But I suspected he did it to keep aunt Mimi occupied so that she could stay away from her parents.

I loved that apartment. Every room was exquisite. One had huge clothes closets of polished walnut and a wall full of mirrors. I liked that one the best. When no one was home I could fool around in front of those mirrors and wander from room to room. There were lovely sofas upholstered in burnt orange velvet and real Persian rugs on polished oak floors. There was also a maid who would cook a meal for me, should I so desire, and serve it wherever I pleased. Often aunt Mimi played the piano and the full, rich tones would fill the airy music room which opened upon a balcony curving along the length of two walls of French doors.

Father, who fancied himself having a terrific voice and that opera suffered an inestimable loss because he couldn't study earlier, liked to belt out the closing aria out of Aida. But his belief was a complete delusion. I cringed because he sang hopelessly off-key, but aunt Mimi never said anything. She was either too kind or had long given up trying to correct the 'slight' imperfection. When she sang with him, it was better.

She had a beautiful, velvety soprano, that clearly showed the years of fine training and it was indeed a shame she didn't put it to better use. When it came to my father's singing, I wasn't as kind as aunt Mimi – particularly when I had reason to be angry with him. I'd wait for him to hit a real stinker, then put my fingers into my ears and squeal in terror.

Or on the contrary, when I wanted something I'd tell him he was getting a 'little better.' That never failed to get him. Or, I'd clown around and try to dance as badly as he sang. That would break up aunt Mimi and in either case, the singing was over. Of course, that was just one of my methods. At times, there were things that worked better. It depended on the situation and what I wanted. In certain cases, particularly when everything else failed, complaints about mother accomplished the objective and even produced better results than expected. But I stooped to that only rarely. I considered it too common a practice. Every child learns to do that in no time.

But finally, the inevitable happened. It began with the frustration at not being able to communicate with my mother in a logical, realistic fashion. There I was, nine-years-old, well into my career, convinced that I knew exactly what I wanted out of life and mother completely failed to take into account that I was indeed a maturing, logically thinking individual and to deal with me accordingly. She never listened to reason, she would never try to discuss things calmly and try to see my side of it. There was just one side to everything that had to do with my life – and that was her side.

I was a very serious, dedicated person and to me, dancing was all I wanted to do. At school I managed to get good grades with the exception of mathematics. Mother hit the ceiling when she had to hire a tutor to help me with the subject. I hated it. To me, mathematics and anything remotely related to it was an unbearable bore. That I almost failed in physical education didn't bother her in the least. That was because phys. ed. classes were held separately, in the afternoon, and since I had my ballet then, I never showed up. I did exceptionally well in art classes and mother wanted me to take more drawing and painting because the teacher told her I could really be good at it. She must have seen me as a famous painter already. She never seemed to understand that, although I liked drawing and art work, dancing was my chosen profession to which I had already dedicated almost half of my life and I wasn't about to give up.

Today I don't even know which particular incident caused it and why, all I remember is one day I decided to pack my things and go live with my father. Kaya, who depended on me in everything, was inconsolable. What would she do? Together we held a steady front against mother's occasional tantrums and irrational behavior. We sustained each other in times of stress – pulled together in any emergency and – never once snitched on each other. On her part it took some doing, particularly when I used to lock her up in those drawers. Whenever I think of that day, for some reason, the one and only air raid we sustained just before the end of the war, pops immediately into mind. Perhaps it is because it was the only other crisis we faced together – just Kaya and I.

Mother was at the dentist and we were alone. Quite suddenly the air alarm sounded which in itself was rare enough, but no one believed anything would happen since it never did because the allies took into consideration that we were a country occupied and subjugated by the Germans.

Whether I remembered my earlier experience in Vienna, I don't know. At any rate, we were still too little to be really alarmed. Then we heard distant explosions which apparently came from the part of town where I knew my mother's dentist to be. I imagined her sitting in the chair squirming under the drill. Anyway, it was then that I became frightened and apparently, so did everyone else.

A commotion set in outside and Kaya began screaming. I looked out of the apartment. Everyone was rushing down the stairs, heading toward the air raid shelter. Kaya followed me out and stood there on the cold stone floor barefooted screaming in terror. "Shut up!" I kept telling her. "You know you get a nose bleed when you yell like that."

But no words of endearment could get her to stop. I looked out the windows and down the stairwell, but there was no sign of mother. As I predicted, Kaya's nose began to drip blood and other things. I was staring at her in dismay unable to decide what I should do when our neighbor's maid came out and looked at us aghast.

"What did you do to her?!"

Isn't that just like people? What the hell could I have done to her? I was scared shitless myself and it took a lot of doing not to join her in screaming.

"Well, we have to do something about her," the woman declared stoutly and began wiping her nose. "Where in the world is your mother? To leave two little children all alone at a time like this, tsk, tsk..." she was muttering to herself and I hadn't the slightest desire to remind her that my mother couldn't have foreseen that this would happen since, after all, she wasn't a clairvoyant – although at times I wasn't so sure.

Furthermore, I thought it was none of her damn business anyway. If she wanted to extend a helping hand, that was one thing. But she had no right to degrade a woman in front of her children, the dumb bitch.

"Where are your bags?"

"I'll get them," I offered obligingly, having no idea how I'd budge even the lightest of the few bags we had prepared – as advised – for an emergency that no one believed would arise.

Then I heard my mother's voice shrill with panic coming from below. "For God's sake! Let me through! I've got two little children up there!" she kept yelling over and over as she fought her way up against the downpour of people. I can still see her slim, shapely figure dressed in a tight fitting black coat trimmed with fur tearing up the steps in spite of the high heeled shoes she always wore.

She was a fine, handsome woman, the years of hard work notwithstanding, and in many ways, I was very proud of her. In times of need, she was a champ, in an emergency, such as this, she was a panic. But I was so happy to see her I could have cried, but fortunately, managed not to.

As it turned out, the damage to the city was minor, only one American bomber, having strayed off course, unloaded a few remaining bombs out of necessity as it was rumored. But it just happened to be over the center of the city and my mother had a close call.

Anyway, back to my imminent departure some years later. Kaya looked terrified when she realized I was indeed resolved to move out. "You mean you'll leave me here all alone?" she asked plaintively. When I think back on it, it was a strange thing for her to say because, after all, there was mother. I knew she'd start bawling any minute and I was racking my brain how to reassure her.

"I've got to go, Kaya, don't you see? I've got to go. But I'll come back for you... I really will."

I don't know whether I actually meant it. I certainly had no idea if and when I could do that.

She looked at me uncertainly. "You promise?"

I nodded. But she wasn't convinced.

"Cross your heart and hope to die?"

I nodded again and added quickly: "Mind you, I don't know when... but I will come."

She studied me for a while longer. Mother raised us to be insecure, suspicious kids and often we were afraid to even trust each other. But apparently Kaya decided I meant it. "All right. Just remember I'll be waiting."

That's the last thing I remember her saying. Then she calmed down and helped me pack. I took just a few things I liked best, there wasn't much time, we were afraid mother might come any minute. Then I carried the bag downstairs and hid it in an alcove on the ground floor while Kaya was keeping watch. At that point, my greatest worry was my toe shoes. I wanted to pack them but they always hung in the hallway in a loosely woven straw bag and if they hadn't been there mother would have immediately suspected something was wrong.

Up to this day I don't know why I didn't leave. I might have been afraid of running into her right then and there on the street carrying my bag and I suppose I must have been afraid of her. Afraid she'd stop me and I'd never have the guts to try again. Whatever the reason, I waited for her to come back. Today, it makes no sense to me whatever, but then, I suppose I wasn't as bright a kid as my father would have liked to believe.

When mother came home, I could tell she sensed something was up immediately. At one point I grabbed my coat saying I had to go out. In the hallway I took the bag with my toe shoes and headed out the door. But she was quick to intercept me.

"What do you need your toe shoes for?" she demanded while her eyes sharpened with suspicion.

All I could think of saying was that I wanted to show them to a school friend who lived nearby. It didn't sound like me at all and I knew she wouldn't go for it but that's the best I could come up with on the spur of the moment. "I've just got to get out." I repeated stubbornly. But she was holding the straw bag and wouldn't let go. I knew it was useless. I think I really hated her then. Her constant suspicions mixed with fear and insecurity and a dash of true insight.

I let the bag go and tore out of the door and down the stairs with her calling after me: "Come back here! Come back, I said!" I was surprised to hear the tone of authority mixed with fear. I never heard that before, at least not while she was talking to me.

She knew... But I was past caring as I ran on muttering curses and crying all the way down.

I realize I should have discussed the plan with father before actually going ahead. I guess I took it for granted he'd go along with whatever I wanted. But he looked startled when I arrived at his apartment declaring I had left mother and wanted to move in with him. The first thing he did, was to ask why. I thought it was a strange question coming from him.

"You know how mother is. I feel the way you did. I couldn't take it any longer. So, here I am. – Oh, Papa, it'll be just you and me. We'll have such a good time," I promised enthusiastically, but the colors of that picture didn't seem to look as bright to him as they did to me. He looked at me soberly.

"Erna, you can't stay here."

I couldn't believe he had said that.

"Why not? You've got so much room."

He seemed impatient and ill at ease. "It's not that. There's no one to look after you."

"But there is Tanya – besides, I don't need looking after anymore. I'm not a child!"

"Look, you'd be better off with your mother."

I can't imagine why it's been only recently that I became consciously aware that he didn't want me. It took me all these years to realize and to admit to myself that he actually didn't want me then. At the time I am sure I never allowed myself to see it that way – not consciously anyway. I fought him. I yelled and pleaded and insisted I couldn't and wouldn't ever go back to mother and that he couldn't make me. But that time, I didn't win. He didn't press me into going back to her, but he didn't let me stay with him either.

He moved me in with aunt Mimi. I didn't like it as much as I'd have liked staying with him, but it was better than going back to mother.

CHAPTER SEVEN

The top floor apartment which aunt Mimi occupied was rather small and, stuffed as it was, it looked even smaller. Wherever you looked there were shelves jammed with books and neat stacks of note books and magazines, all carefully sorted out. Aunt Mimi was a collector and every available place was filled with something. She managed to find a little room for the few things I brought along, and there were two convertible couches so I had a place to sleep. As I think back on it, it must have seemed like an unstable, impermanent existence, but if it made me feel insecure, I don't remember it. And then, every situation has some advantage to it.

With aunt Mimi I had freedom. She never told me what to do, what to eat, when to go to bed. We simply roomed together. And I got to know her pretty well. First thing I learned about her was that she couldn't cook at all. Since I couldn't either, we either ate out, or lived on sandwiches. Most often father would take us out for dinner or she'd take me to her favorite vegetarian restaurant. She was really big on that.

She was into a lot of strange things. Actually, she was a strange person altogether. She adored taking long walks, particularly in the evening. Unfortunately, father's apartment house was situated near a cemetery which spread into a huge square covering many blocks so that there was no way of walking around it or evading it. Because of past experiences with the world 'beyond,' I wasn't exactly keen on walking by there.

I had three performances a week at the theater and most often my classes ran late as well and so by the time I got back, it was getting dark. Whenever I could, I'd try to get a ride in my father's car and when I couldn't, she'd wait for me at the tramway stop and we'd walk back together. We must have made a strange pair. She, tall and lanky, walking in that sleek, graceful way of hers and I, a tiny, skinny thing hopping along or dancing to the accompaniment of her lovely voice.

She just loved to take a stroll in the evening along the deserted streets and sing her heart out. When I saw someone approaching, I'd stop hopping around, but she'd go right on singing, at the top of her lungs, totally oblivious to her surroundings. People would stop and stare at us in amazement. Looking at my stay with her today, I realize I must have been in the way, and I probably felt it in a vague, unconscious way but there was nothing I could do about it. I am grateful to her for making the best out of a bad situation. She tried hard to make me feel at home by including me in as many of her activities as she could. Mainly, she treated me like a grownup human being, like an equal – trusting me to look after myself, letting me decide how to structure my day and involving me in all kinds of things. Like testing her for the exams for her law degree, for instance. That involved my having to read all sorts of confusing things that made little sense to me, but I was pleased I could be of some help. But leaning somewhat toward the practical side of life, in some instances anyway, I'd ask the inevitable question:

"What will you do when you get your law degree? Open an office here?"

She looked at me astonished. "Certainly not."

"Then in Vienna?"

She shook her head. "Nowhere!"

"But if you want to have clients..."

"Bah!" she interrupted disdainfully, "I could never stand the client's petty grievances and caprices a lawyer has to cope with."

"Then why do you bother with all this?"

I thought she looked at me rather oddly and I was sorry I asked. There was surprise and disappointment there, and I felt I had said something that reminded her of what she constantly heard at home. I felt afraid suddenly. What if she stopped liking me... But she laughed then and the whole thing seemed forgotten.

And she did like me. I am sure she did. I always wore my hair long and my mother had never ceased tormenting me with setting it in curlers and combing it into a whole bunch of long, thin curls that bounced like crazy when I ran. But aunt Mimi liked it as straight as it's always been and she liked to pull it back saying I had such a good face all that hair only took away from the good lines.

Of course, that made me feel terrific since I always thought next to Kaya I looked like nothing and here were two people, Mimi and my father, who actually preferred me. I was infinitely grateful she took such an interest in me. She even insisted on giving me singing lessons. I remember till today all that she taught me although I never made any use of it. She knew more about the techniques of singing than anyone else I ever met. She used to say, if I could sing the way I whistled, I'd have it down pat. I was always a great whistler. Which isn't too hot for a girl.

Another thing I learned about aunt Mimi was that she inherited her mother's stinginess. But she was aware of it and since she despised her mother and anything even remotely related to her, she worked very hard on herself to suppress this not too attractive trait. It became my function to remind and reproach her whenever she displayed the slightest sign of it. Naturally, I was quick to take advantage of it. I'd take whatever I wanted and if she objected I reminded her she ought not to give in to the 'worst part of her nature.' It always worked. Thus I expropriated most of her watches (I used to have a passion for watches) and other goodies.

Sometimes aunt Mimi would come along to watch the ballet class but most often she fell asleep, much to the teacher's consternation. Of course, a ballet class isn't the most exciting thing to watch.

It's mainly a lot of hard, repetitive work. And it takes a great deal of self-discipline and dedication. But when it came to dancing I was practically a fanatic. My main worry was to do my homework as quickly and efficiently as I could so it wouldn't interfere with my 'profession.'

It's not that I hated to go to school, dancing was simply more important. To me there was nothing more satisfying than to spend the whole afternoon taking one class after another. Today I can't imagine how I did it. How well I remember the steamy, sweaty rehearsal halls, the black-clad bodies reflected in the mirrors and the familiar smells of perspiration, leather, resin and traces of various L'eu d' Colognes and perfumes fighting a losing battle.

To me, there was something tremendously satisfying about it all – the effort, the pain, even the blistered, bleeding toes one is bound to come up with now and then.

I will never forget my first ballet teacher. She was a small, fat lady with a big mouth and a stick to match and she wielded both with an equal lack of discrimination and restraint. In my beginning classes, which consisted exclusively of little people like myself, I escaped both. But I progressed rapidly and in less than two years was promoted to the 'professional' classes – and was the only child amongst grownups. It was then that I made my acquaintance with the lady's sharp language and the sting of her stick.

I soon learned that to react to either was an unforgivable trespass. Actually, I felt the smack of the stick only once. From then on I was determined not to give her any cause for displeasure, and I didn't. I can still see the wild, unruly mess of blonde hair framing a fat, baby-ass of a face with a wide, crimson slash of a mouth spewing obscenities that even a sailor could be proud of and shrewd, appraising eyes that never missed even the slightest mistake. Today, I remember the coarse, raspy voice with great nostalgia.

"Straighten that leg, asshole!" The voice would explode frequently drowning out the sound of soft-soled feet on hardwood and the clean, pure tones of the piano caressed by long, slender fingers of the accompanist, a slim, graceful and totally ladylike creature that never bat an eyelash no matter what emerged out of that crimson, vulgar mouth of our venerable maitresse de ballet.

Miss Lola, as everyone called her, would sit there poised and aristocratic looking, oblivious to all except the music and the dancer's feet while that raspy voice would shout and abuse, mock and ridicule with inexhaustible fervor.

"Hey, dummy, is that supposed to be a plie or are you taking a shit? Tuck in your ass, dammit!"

The unfortunate culprit, caught with his butt in the wrong position would hasten to correct his error before the stick helped him along the way.

She had all kinds of such endearing things to say. If anyone ever dared to snicker, she would turn and give him or her a haughty, annihilating glare. I found that once one became accustomed to the vulgarities, they barely registered. Most often I had but the vaguest idea of what "Madame" was talking about. But it was obvious to me she was very ass-oriented. She'd say things like: "Hey, take that cork out of your ass and start working before I smash the balls you don't need."

Of course, I was well aware that most of the male dancers were more feminine than the female and that they weren't like 'real' men, but I was fond of them, and I felt sorry when she attacked any of them in such an obvious manner. But she had no preferences. She could just as well tear into anyone.

"Look at our Carla! Walks like she still has it in her. Tighten those ass muscles for God's sake!"

You never had to look whether she was approaching to scrutinize you with those sharp, critical eyes. The clatter of her shoes would tell you. I don't think she owned any other kind of footwear except the wedgies that she had made up specially for her. Her feet must have been size 4-E. Round and chubby like her face. Designed to give her at least five extra inches, they were made of thick cork and pink suede.

Pink was her favorite color. Shocking pink yet. When she'd get all dressed up it was quite a sight. Pink hat, coat, even the fox trim was dyed pink, and those incredible wedgies. It may not sound all that terrible today, but at that time, in Eastern Europe particularly, people never wore bright, clear colors. In a world of sober, muted colors, her attire never failed to attract much attention and astounded stares. It would be as if today someone walked around in a coat made of flashing Christmas lights.

She'd come on like a hurricane, her coattails flaring, behind her a pair of yapping Pekingese dogs and an entourage consisting of her spinster sister, grandmother and her child, an awkward little fatso whom she tried desperately to transform into a graceful ballerina. Her chances at success were about as good as she'd have had with the little Pekingese horrors.

Furthermore, the child had no intention of following in her mother's clopping footsteps. Her one and only interest in life was to lock herself in the bathroom with a couple of enormous slices of thickly buttered or larded bread and stuff herself in all peace and quiet – and relative safety. Whenever there was a lot of yelling and pounding on the bathroom door, everyone knew "Madame" was trying to flush her daughter out of the toilet to stop her from gorging herself.

"Come out this instant you little bastard before I break down the door!"

And out would come a choking, muffled whine: "I can't mama, I've got cramps..."

"Don't give me any of that shit and get out of there or I'll break every bone in your goddamn body!!"

Her daughter was several years older than I, but she looked like an oversized toddler. For some strange reason, she liked me and I felt sorry for her. The torment she had to go through, the endless starving diets, sabotaged by the grandmother that, of course, never did any good. But the most amazing thing about "Madame" was her husband. He was an incredibly handsome, refined Englishman who never raised his voice or got angry no matter what happened. He looked very tall and slim quite a bit like Robert Taylor except much more handsome so that next to him, she looked like a pudgy midget, her wedgies notwithstanding. It was a bloody shame the little fatso didn't inherit even one iota of him.

Sometimes, toward the end of a class, he would come in and help. All he'd do was stretch us. Push the leg up as far as it would go while she stood on your other foot with those damn clodhoppers yelling: "Keep the knees straight!" right into your ear.

The procedure would be repeated to the side and back. It looked like torture, but it sure helped with the extensions. Now when you see a ballerina extending her leg high or holding a beautiful arabesque, you know how it's done. But he was very gentle and knew just how far to go and refused to press beyond that no matter how much she hollered. It seemed all the vulgarities went right by him. No matter what she said, he remained unperturbed and polite.

The one thing she hated more than anything was anyone chewing during class. One guy refused to give up his wad of chewing gum and when all else failed, she kicked him in the ass then pried his mouth open and poking her chubby fingers in there, pulled it out.

To me, she never said an abusive word. Perhaps it was to make up for subjecting my young ears to her unsavory repertoire. But that would be giving her undue credit. Most likely, she used me to spur on the older students. She'd never miss an opportunity to rile them. Whenever anyone seemed tired after a particularly exhausting exercise, she'd sneer contemptuously:

"What's the matter with you? Look at that little kid! She'll out dance you anytime!"

At first I used to blush with pride and pleasure. Soon however, it made me feel uncomfortable and guilty. I sensed that I became just another stick – another form of punishment. But that was her way of prodding people on. Although, in my opinion, it's a poor system which tends to get the opposite results, I have to admit she was very effective. In spite of the language which usually breeds disrespect and familiarity and a breakdown in discipline, she succeeded in producing the exact opposite.

I have never met a teacher who was more admired and respected and got better results. I don't know of anyone else who could talk that way to homosexuals without repelling them. At first I used to resent it, but seeing their acceptance of it, I learned to ignore it the way they did. Having grown up in that environment, to me words like faggots, queers, queens were never derisive or taboo. And I always preferred the gay dancers to the so-called 'straight' ones.

Actually I only knew one that I could be sure of. But that was later when I was studying at the National Theater on a scholarship. I was eleven then.

For a while a visiting Russian choreographer was conducting some of our classes and training the corps de ballet. Before his departure he staged a gala performance at the theater and I was among the dancers selected for a solo performance. Of course I was thrilled no end even though it meant a lot of extra work and long hours of rehearsing. We would work after classes and he worked me to exhaustion. His, as well as mine.

Anyway, that kept me at the theater long after everyone had gone. Now, the assistant of our regular 'maestro,' or teacher, if you will, was a dancer by the name of Mirek to whom I took an instant dislike. I really don't know why. Perhaps it was because he always tried to act smart and wore an obnoxious, condescending smirk on his face. But it was more than that. It was a feeling I had about him. Particularly during the pas-de-deux class which has always been my favorite.

For those who don't know much about ballet, that's when the dancer joins the ballerina for a duet – usually the highlight of the ballet. Well, the Russians, particularly, go for a very elaborate style. By that I mean lots of exciting choreography and lifts. The ballerina gets lifted, tossed and carried about. And, of course, with the Russian choreographer, we had lots of that. I loved it. No matter how complicated and difficult a lift anyone wanted to try, I was ready and willing to oblige. Of course, weighing some eighty pounds, I was the darling of the gay set. There is nothing more disconcerting than having to lift a one hundred and forty pound ballerina. By golly, they almost fought to get me. It was sheer bliss.

The only thing upsetting me was Mirek. Being the maestro's assistant, he always managed to work with me more than all the other dancers. It was there that I got that strange feeling – a dislike, perhaps even apprehension. He didn't behave like the others. There was something about him that bothered me. Something in that smirk that I was wary of. I never really knew what it was. But there was none of the usual camaraderie between us. Perhaps it was because I suspected he wasn't a fag. But then there were a few others who weren't either, but they never affected me the way Mirek did.

Anyway, one evening after particularly long and tiring work on my solo routine which he often watched for who knows what reason, and which I resented because it made me uncomfortable, I was in the girls' dressing room getting ready to leave. I liked that huge room on the top floor of the theater. It was so relaxing to sit there for a while and look down to the Moldau River. I liked it best when no one was there. I liked the quiet, the smell of greasepaint and costumes, the slightly moldy, musky smell so peculiar to theaters, that permeates every corner.

I had washed up and was finishing dressing when I heard a knock on the door. "Yes?" I called out.

The door opened and Mirek stood there, his face twisted into the usual condescending smirk.

"What do you want?" It sounded strangely hollow in that quiet room and it felt as if we were the only people in that ancient building.

For a long while he said nothing, just stood there grinning. Then he began strolling toward me, slowly, casually, picking up something here and there off the dressing tables cluttered with cream jars, paint sticks and the usual paraphernalia.

I was by no means a timid child nor a fearful one, but it wasn't easy for me to shake off that strange, numbing feeling I had.

"Well? What is it?" I managed to come up with as authoritatively as I could.

"Nothing... really... Say, that's gonna be a swell little number."

The way he said it, I didn't consider it much of a compliment but that didn't bother me in any way because his opinion hardly mattered. I didn't think he was a particularly gifted dancer.

"Thanks," I said drily. "I'm in a hurry now, do you mind?"

That he seemed to ignore. "Say, I noticed you don't sweat much."

He always began a sentence like that, and I thought it was rather stupid and affected. But he was right. I never perspired no matter how hard I worked. I didn't think of it as being particularly remarkable except that it was rather convenient in team work. It keeps you from slipping and sliding all over the place – mostly out of your partner's arms.

"That's right. I don't. So what?"

He laughed. "Nothing. It's great. Maybe it's because you're so skinny."

I gave him a dirty look. That was my sore spot mainly because mother kept trying to fatten me up and lamenting about her lack of success.

"But you got great legs. Good muscles," he said in a conciliatory tone. "And a terrific ass... How old are you?"

I stared at him suspiciously. "Eleven."

He sat down on one of the chairs and leaning against the dressing table, stared at me appraisingly.

"Hmm... your face sure looks older."

He was right again. I was one of those strange kids with ageless faces. At eleven, take my scrawny, skinny little body away, I could have passed for sixteen. At twenty, I could have passed for eleven.

"I'm aging rapidly," I agreed quickly. "It's all the damn work." I didn't like the way his eyes kept examining me. I remember wearing a pair of woolen, itchy tights knitted by my grandmother out of the softest wool she could find (but they still itched me) and a short, pleated skirt and sweater. In this get-up, plus the school case which I had with me because I hadn't been home yet, I was painfully aware of looking like the little schoolgirl I was rather than the ballerina I hoped someday to become.

"Why'd you get dressed so quickly?" he asked suddenly and leaned over slapping my thigh. His face was quite close and I thought he seemed excited. "Say, why don't you take off your pants for me, huh?" he said it very quickly and sort of breathlessly and had a leer on his face I didn't like. "What do you say?"

I stared at him incredulously.

"I'll show you something too..." he added in a tone that seemed to promise something extra special. "Well? Come on!" he snapped impatiently, and as I still stood there staring at him stupidly unable to decide what the hell to do, he got hold of me and began pulling at my tights.

I don't remember exactly what I did. I don't even know whether I was frightened or what. I don't remember thinking or wondering about what he was after. At eleven I must have had a pretty good idea although I am sure I didn't think in terms of specifics. I knew damn well though he wanted to show me his dick, but I sure wasn't curious to see it.

One afternoon when walking home with a group of girls we saw a dirty old man pulling at his penis and rubbing it against the wall. He seemed well-pleased with himself seeing us peering at him.

Having satisfied our curiosity we fled, shrieking dutifully in a fine demonstration of terror. But in reality, I didn't find it too exciting nor horrifying. Therefore, I wasn't at all enthusiastic about Mirek's proposition.

We struggled for a while, but somehow I managed to push him away. I may have hit him with my briefcase, but I'm not sure of it. At any rate, I was free and I ran out of there as fast as I could. It took me a long time to decide what to do. Should I go back to class the next day as if nothing had happened? I had no idea how I could face him again, but I certainly wasn't about to give up the theater – my whole future – just to evade him. But I needn't have worried. He never bothered me again, never as much as looked at me, not even in the pas-de-deux class.

CHAPTER EIGHT

As I think back, I realize that it was then that I was approaching the most crucial time of my life. I realize I was very lucky to be at the theater at all. The exams had been very rough. There were some thirty applicants for the scholarships and I was very doubtful that I'd make it.

Most of the girls were older and taller than I. We were called in one by one and that in itself was pretty intimidating. When my turn came, I slipped reluctantly into the rehearsal hall I had never seen before and found myself facing four somber people sitting behind a long table busy scribbling into the pads before them and a dainty, wrinkled man in sloppy pants and soft shoes with a long, black stick who was obviously the maitre de ballet.

Each gave me an indifferent, cursory glance, and I was wishing I had listened to "Madame" and waited another year.

Suddenly the maestro gave the floor a smart tap with the stick and rattled off a series of steps, naming them all by their proper names, which I was supposed to instantly execute. Of course, I was well acquainted with the French terminology for each step but I couldn't make out what he was saying. I was used to Madame's bastardized version that bore little resemblance to the original French words. Pas de chat became 'patcha,' rounde de jamb, 'rondcham' and so forth.

Instead of concentrating on the combination of the steps and their proper transition, I was racking my brain to relate his version of the word to the one I was familiar with. I had but one chance. He wasn't about to repeat it.

He stood there staring at me expectantly. I had no choice but to do whatever I thought it was – rightly or wrongly. They let me do it once, nodded, and sent me out. I was sure I had failed and crept out of there humiliated beyond imagination. I would have liked to just disappear and pretend it never happened.

I got dressed as quickly as I could without looking at anyone, eager to flee from there. I was sneaking past that dreadful door when the maestro poked his head out and called out two names. One was mine. I almost fainted. I couldn't believe it. It was just too fantastic. Finally, I'd have a chance to get to the real thing. If I just kept it up – and grew quickly, I'd make it and from then on, anything could happen.

And then there was the gala performance. I was very pleased about that. But much too quickly it had come and gone. After weeks of work, in one night, it was all over. But it was worth it. It was like doing a real grownup performance. There were no kids there. None. And I didn't look like one either. I guess I've always wanted to be grownup so that I could dance in all the ballets I wanted and to be able to do as I pleased. But I had so much to learn.

After every pas-de-deux class a few of us always stuck around to try out all sorts of new ideas. It was great fun. Some of the guys went often to nightclubs where they saw acrobats and commercial dancing teams and then we'd try some of the stunts they did. Sometimes they brought some of these people to the theater and we would all work out together.

There was one young man by the name of Ivan with whom I liked to work. He wasn't a dancer, but it didn't matter. He knew some extraordinary lifts which I wanted to learn. There is something incredibly marvelous about being lifted and tossed up into the air. It's like a continuation of dancing except it moves up – you float, graceful, easy, like a cloud – free as a bird. I found out Ivan was part of a quartet, but he wanted to quit. I had no idea what he wanted to do and I didn't care. All I wanted was to learn all the lifts I could. Occasionally he would leave, but a few weeks or months later he'd be back and we would start working again.

One day he brought an older man who must have been at least as old as my father. But he was in great shape physically, and he knew more fantastic stunts than anyone I ever met. For some reason or other he looked vaguely familiar, but I didn't give it a lot of thought. I had a feeling Ivan brought him to look me over. He had narrow, heavy-hooded eyes that had a sharp, penetrating look which I didn't find quite pleasant. But he was incredibly good. No matter what he decided to do, I had absolute confidence that I'd never get hurt. And that's something. It's not at all impossible to land on your ass or even on your head when doing some of the more elaborate lifts.

We rehearsed for a long time and before he left he smiled casually and said he knew my father.

"You do?" I asked casually wondering where or how my father would have come across someone like him.

He shrugged. "I've known him for a long time. He comes often... to see me..." he hesitated as if to find the right word.

Of course, I remembered mother's complaints about father's nocturnal escapades. Somehow nightclubs always had an unsavory feeling to them. And it wasn't just because of what mother said. As a legitimate dancer I looked at nightclub performers as being rather amateurish and the connotation of commercialism took further away from the legitimacy and merit of that kind of occupation.

"I am sure Papa will be glad we met."

"We met once before," he said. "But you wouldn't remember. You were just a baby then."

Apparently there are many things in my childhood I don't remember. I certainly didn't remember having met him before.

Later Ivan said he was a noted nightclub artist and an aristocrat. As far as I was concerned, there was no such thing as a 'noted' nightclub artist, and I didn't see anything aristocratic about him either.

But, of course, I didn't say anything.

After that we practiced as often as possible and I was becoming more and more enthusiastic about what he called 'adagio.' In ballet, adagio is something entirely different, but I didn't want to argue the point. Later, he went on a tour with his troupe which worked under the name of "Jonny Johnson and Co."

I thought it was pretentious as hell considering his real name was Johann von Kralik. But at that time, all the traveling they did seemed very attractive to me. It must have been because I was probably anxious to get out of the situation I found myself in. It wasn't that I didn't like living with aunt Mimi. But there was something very transitory and unstable about it all. Also, I must have felt instinctively that I was in the way. It was almost as if I had no home. There was no going back to mother although we agreed on a truce between us and after that I went to visit her occasionally. But everything was rather strained and awkward and even the old camaraderie between me and Kaya was all but gone. It was almost as if Kaya was afraid to be too friendly so as not to upset mother. But she was always near tears when I was leaving.

Now suddenly mother was ready to give me my toe shoes, but I didn't want them anymore. She tried several times to make me take them, but I wouldn't. I could have used them but for some reason, I was resolved not to take them no matter what.

By that time the factory was nationalized and the apartment house as well, although they let us use the apartment and father still had the big, lovely apartment near his offices which weren't his anymore either. I knew the whole thing was a terrible blow to him because he hardly left his apartment for over three months after every effort to forestall the inevitable failed. They bastardized their own rules as governments are apt to do, and took it all away. The one thing he lived for and strove toward all his life was suddenly gone and with it his faith in a system that he believed to be more humane than any other.

To add insult to injury, they offered him a job – to manage his own company for them. At the time, for some obscure reason, I wasn't really touched by it all. There was my father, suddenly silent, almost morose, on the verge of catatonia, and I didn't much care. Perhaps it was because he failed to come through for me when I really needed him. And even now, as depressed as he was, there weren't too many thoughts for me. I still felt like an outsider trying to get in, to be accepted and loved. I didn't know it then, but at that particular time, I was about to arrive at the crossroads in my career and indeed my life.

CHAPTER NINE

As a result of the Russian choreographer's visit, a few dancers at the theater were offered scholarships to the Bolshoi Ballet. I was one of them. Before I had a chance to recover from the shock and began to realize what that meant, I was asked to join Jonny Johnson and Co. and Ivan told me he had left the quartet and wanted to work with me.

How can I possibly explain what that meant? There was an opportunity to get away from everything and everyone. Today I don't know whether I really wanted to do that or just to punish them all for neglecting me, for not loving me, by removing myself from everyone. But who did I really punish? I hadn't consulted anyone about it. I figured I had to work it out by myself which wasn't an easy task by any means.

Old von Kralik, whom I learned to call Jonny the way everyone else did, confided that he planned on leaving Czechoslovakia and going west – his final objective being – the USA. Ivan had a similar plan but much less experience and to top it all, projected a great deal of insecurity and doubt about having done the right thing in leaving the well-established act he had been with for the past few years.

The Bolshoi Ballet was a real challenge but – it was in

Moscow. How can I explain how I felt? When I was a little kid, the American bombers we spotted occasionally, way up high so that they looked like toys, crossing our city on their way to some obscure destination where they would drop their fearful cargo, might have just as well been from Mars. They seemed just as remote, mysterious and intangible. Everything American was secretly deified, and everything Russian, openly feared and hated. The latter was accomplished most efficiently by the Nazi propaganda machine which bombarded the people's consciousness with a relentless intensity and such a simple but effective campaign that even Madison Avenue could learn from them (and probably did).

I grew up with an ogre's red, taloned hand, branded with hammer and sickle, with claws dripping blood hovering above the city of Prague ready to grasp it and tear it apart. The first words I laboriously learned to read were: IF IT GETS YOU – YOU'LL PERISH!

I can still see the wretched placard pasted all over the city, staring at you everywhere, even riding with you in the tram – like an ominous warning of some impending doom – the result of a terrible hate propaganda – the never to be forgotten Nazi heritage.

America, on the other hand, represented an image of hereto unknown total freedom, vast, open spaces, easily attainable fortunes, fame – I imagined huge, glittering, glamorous cities ready to be conquered – by me. I would like to believe that was why I joined the Jonny Johnson Co. but there is an unpleasant suspicion gnawing at the heart of my conscience that I chose the easy road. That I didn't have the balls to hack it alone – on my own – one little dancer trying to excel above all the others – in a country – a hard, gray country where nothing else mattered but hard work and the ultimate ability; that I preferred to fall into a ready-made position, rising on someone else's merit – someone else's 'supposedly' already established niche in the hall of fame.

Perhaps it's all too easy to say – how could I have done otherwise? A kid with crooked teeth and nose and fucked-up ears? But why blame them and their insecurities? It was I who bought it all. I could have had the guts and courage to try it anyway. But I didn't. Instead I listened to a lot of fairy tales and dreamt of far away places and how everyone at home would be staggered once I made it out to the prom-ised land.

"See, Papa! My awful ears and teeth and all!"

Also, I suspect, I was testing my father. Would he let me go? Perhaps he wouldn't. And if he didn't then – perhaps – he loved me after all.

But he signed the guardianship over to the man he met at some nightclub and knew only superficially – signed me away with-out hardly a moment's hesitation, and readily made arrangements for me to get my Austrian passport – even bribed someone to speed things up before mother got wind of the whole thing and could stop it – as we all knew she would. Not out of love for me, I was sure, but just to spite father.

Oh God, is it any wonder I was dying to get away?

CHAPTER TEN

Part II - The Career

"Chiquita. We'll change your name to Chiquita."

"Why?" I asked worriedly.

He looked at me with the kind of paternal indulgence one reserves for the mentally retarded.

"Everybody's got to have a stage name."

"Not everybody," I insisted. "Why can't I keep my own?"

"Because Erna just doesn't have the right ring to it. Besides, in America we'll need a catchy, exotic sounding name."

Exotic? I thought it sounded phony and pretentious.

"What kind of a name is it anyway?"

"Spanish."

"Well, I don't like it," I declared as resolutely as I dared.

How could I cast my Slavic and Teutonic heritage to the winds and assume a Spanish name?

His eyes turned a shade closer to steel. "I will choose the name I consider best for you. Besides," he added in a softer tone, "the name of Chiquita and Johnson is well established all over the world."

(That, as I discovered later, was a gross overstatement.)

"I've had two other partners I've worked with under that name."

"How about Tamara?" I suggested hopefully.

"Blodsinn!" (There is no English word which adequately captures the feel of that word. It's something like idiocy or stupidity, but neither comes even close to it. In any event, that was one of his favorite expressions and he used it with the kind of emphasis and gusto intended to imply you have just suggested the most idiotic thing imaginable.) "A Russian name for America?"

I sighed deeply knowing I was licked. I had already learned there was just no arguing with him once he had made up his mind. Then the otherwise kind and compliant man was transformed into an opinionated and adamant tyrant.

So – I was to become Chiquita number three. But I never got to like the name and later when I learned Spanish and realized it wasn't really a name at all, I really got to hate it. But once outside the country – like with my guardian – I was stuck with it and – for better or worse – had to make the best of it.

We arrived in Nuremberg with a contract to work for the USO. A Belgian impresario Jonny knew arranged the engagement. Jonny Johnson and Co. had disintegrated in Czechoslovakia because most members were Czechs and couldn't get out. Jonny had a German passport, I an Austrian one, and so we had relatively few problems getting out. There was just one drawback to it; we couldn't come back. In view of this minor detail, I knew I had better keep it from mother because she'd do anything to keep me from going – so – she never knew I had left until I wrote to her several months later.

In Germany, where we moved in the circle of artists, everyone seemed to know him and he quickly assembled a new group of people and once again he had his 'troupe' which now centered around Chiquita and Johnson. Now it was "The Chiquita & Johnson Show." It consisted of a juggling act, a magician, a ballroom team, and a contortion act.

The first act we put together was a disaster. (As far as I was concerned, at least.) When I began learning all the lifts, I had the idea that combining all that with legit ballet would make for an unusual and exciting routine. But that was before I found out he really disliked ballet and had no intention of using it in the act at all. Even the music he chose was some schmaltzy, unballetic number he neither knew how, nor was inclined to follow. All of these things I didn't know before I committed myself to the whole thing.

We had departed in such a furious hurry, these very important things were somehow left to be resolved on the spot. Whenever the subject came up of setting a routine, he was always quick to claim that since we had all the lifts down pat, he could put an act together in a day. Now I found out that he didn't really want me to dance and not only that, I had to ignore the music and let it be just window dressing – an unimportant background. But you can't unlearn what you've been learning most of your life.

The whole concept of ballet rests on music. Every step is carefully choreographed, using every note, every nuance of tempo, to interpret the music according to its rhythm and dynamics. Ballet is the physical expression of music. As the actor uses language to express a feeling, the dancer uses his body to express – and interpret – music. Jonny, however, couldn't follow two bars without losing his place. He had no ear for music whatsoever. His idea of a top act was one acrobatic stunt after another accented by a drum roll, and the drummer would have to use his own judgment when to lay it on thick, and the music was purely incidental.

God, did I hate it! However, I did have a ballet solo which I choreographed myself that he was willing to let me do. But I sure hated the act. I knew I just had to change it somehow. Since there was no way I could reason it out, I had to use subterfuge. There are all sorts of devious little means of persuasion people call psychology that can be used to get what one wants. And of course, I was a past pro at that. But that was just the kind of thing I was trying to get away from. I was tired of people who wouldn't let me be myself. Who liked me only if I conformed to some obscure image they had of me which I constantly had to try to define and follow or lose their love and interest.

It took me a while but finally I found the right approach. I dreamt up a lift that couldn't be done except in toe shoes. The classic arabesque in the palm of his hand. Of course, he was quick to assure me he had a faint recollection of 'someone' having done it before. I guess he didn't want me to think I came up with something original. Still, he was willing to try it. I also found various new ways (very balletic, of course) of getting in and out of the various lifts and even invented a few more lifts. Whether this impressed him or not, I couldn't really tell – however, he did begin to give me more free rein. In those days we practiced every single day and the routine went through continuous change.

Next in the line of my attack was the music. It consisted of little, strategic jabs which I planned as meticulously as a general with a whole army at his command. Except my army consisted of words and innuendoes and every attack had to be flexible, open to improvisation as I went along. It was psychological warfare. There was one thing I've always had – determination and, I suppose, cunning. I kept hinting that the 'proper' kind of music would automatically enhance each lift without having to resort to the 'worn-out old drum roll' – kept hinting at the advantages of being original – innovative.

After weeks of careful nudging, cultivating of the soil, so to speak, he finally agreed to let me select new music – subject to his approval, to be sure. To some extent I understood his feelings. He had been in the business since he was fourteen, which at the time was twenty-eight years, and there was I, going on thirteen, trying to tell him where he'd gone wrong. Yet in his line of work, he was better than anyone I'd ever come across – in all the years of my career – except he lacked taste, finesse, or what is commonly termed 'class.' And I felt that if I could change a few basic things such as choreography, music and costumes, we'd really have something.

Ever since I was a kid I had a compulsion to change things, to individualize whatever I could – no matter what it was – to my taste, to my way of doing things. I must admit, however, that my way of doing things often tended to be rather odd – to say the least. Still, it's a style, a way of looking at things, an individual approach to whatever I came in touch with. I find that anything original, if it is allowed to remain static, if it doesn't undergo changes and reformulations, in the end becomes boring. To look at it objectively, I would say, I am not an original thinker, or innovator. I think my originality rests in my constant search for contrasting, or even seemingly opposing genres and unifying them into a new style which then in itself becomes original. Perhaps it's an unconscious attempt to merge the two different people I had to be for my parents into one whole harmonious personality – which, of course, is next to impossible. The ideal would be to discard both and be yourself.

In my childhood, this trend made itself apparent in the oddest, and certainly most impractical, ways. In winter I wanted to wear sandals and in summer, sweaters and boots, and suddenly wool didn't itch me even if I didn't wear it over a blouse. I also thought one should wear white for funerals and black for weddings. Of course, it could have been simply a need to attract attention which later channeled itself into more useful areas. This began during my ballet training when I would always astound my teachers with the strangest combinations.

Now, in my 'new profession,' I had very definite ideas as to how the act should be changed to achieve the maximum effect and success, and I never, not even for one single moment, considered the possibility I could have been wrong.

The music we finally selected was "Bagatelle" by Ricksner, a not-too-well-known German composer, and I could choreograph it myself. Well, I soon discovered the safest thing to do about my 'partner' was to have him move about naturally without setting any specific steps or poses – and it worked. The contrast between the two different styles created the effect I had hoped it would. The complexity and purity of ballet combined with the simplicity and strength of those lifts made for a most effective and startling blend.

Although Jonny never admitted I had done anything to improve the act, his silence was eloquent enough. But there was one thing I couldn't budge him on until much later – his 'costume.' He insisted on wearing, and was convinced it was a gas, a glorified version of Spanish type flared pants, made, preferably, out of lace and satin, and a net shirt. It looked the way it sounds. The only thing that kept him from looking like a screaming faggot was his unmistakably male personality that contained a certain feel of brute strength and a look that defied anyone to disagree or cross him for whatever reason. But at the same time you knew that if you didn't press your luck too far, he would be the kindest, gentlest and most generous person you'd ever want to meet. I am sure to me he represented the father figure, and I to him the child he never had a chance to look after. (At that time he had two illegitimate children he had never seen.)

Another thing I absolutely had to get him to stop doing was yelling. If something didn't work out right during the performance, no matter who was at fault, and of course it was never him, he'd yell and holler until he was hoarse.

At first it scared me shitless but when I realized he was just letting off steam, I stopped reacting to it. But I had to be careful not to seem indifferent because that tended to infuriate him even more.

Out of the members of the troupe, I had one friend, the girl who did the contortion act. Her name was Hedda. She was already thirteen and stacked. I used to look with great envy at those bulging boobs of hers that looked as if they'd pop right out of her costume. She was very limber and Jonny had put together the contortion act for her. Later he actually asked me to teach her a few steps and set up a little routine. I didn't make the mistake of trying to teach her anything she couldn't handle. And – it went with the music. It was all easy, simple, but graceful. It was great to see her gradually turn into a pol-ished performer. Naturally, she too was given a 'stage name.' Hedda became Clarissa and up on that stage, with her big boobs and high heels, she looked more like eighteen than a kid of thirteen. If I didn't look quite like that – at least I tried to act like it. I guess there is a time in everyone's life when the most desirable thing is to be older and do all the grownup things that seem to represent freedom. Kids get into their parents' clothes, try to smoke, drink and act sophisticat-ed whenever there's no one around to cut them down to their size. Well, we could act older and sophisticated and there was no one to tell us we couldn't. But it was just a facade.

In some respects, Jonny was worse than my mother and father put together. In fact, the way he behaved, people automatically assumed he was our father and he never said anything to correct their mistake. He also had a guardianship over Hedda whose father was a hopeless drunkard and cared little what his children did as long as he had some money for booze.

Hedda was a pretty, blonde girl, a little taller than I and although she looked great on stage, in reality she was a little peasant, coarse, uneducated and already had a weight problem. But she was a warmhearted, loyal friend and if it hadn't been for her, I'd have been even lonelier than I was. She kept telling me I was crazy to fill my spare time with reading and studying for my correspondence courses which she felt were a total waste of time. As far as she was concerned, what she needed, she already knew.

CHAPTER ELEVEN

Working the American G.I. clubs in Germany was a strange, unsettling experience for me. The contrast between theater and nightclubs was so staggering I couldn't get over it and, in a sense, never did. All the noise and rowdiness, that whole environment totally devoid of such things as respect, understanding and appreciation of art or culture which are vital to the performing artist made me feel I had degraded myself and my work beyond redemption. And there was no turning back. But the tour in Germany was over quickly, and I had little time to torment myself over it. Of the country itself, I remember little. There was never any time for sight-seeing, even had it been worth it, what with the constant rehearsals, studying, packing and unpacking and all sorts of tedious little tasks filling the day of a traveling artist.

Out of all the places we'd been to, I have a faint recollection only of Baden-Baden and Heidelberg – probably because these were two of the very few places where we couldn't see the terrible scars left by the war.

In 1950, most of the German cities were still in a terrible mess and so it was better not to have the time to look around and depress myself by contemplating the useless devastation of wars. My life was centered around my work, the only people I came in contact with were those connected with it.

It was here that I learned Jonny's past 'reputation in the business' didn't quite measure up to his claims. His colleagues and 'friends' were quick to inform me that although he always had a flashy act, it had lacked finesse and never played in first-class houses. They called it a circus act and looked down on it as I had once looked down upon them and to a degree still did.

Strange how people always have to put down something, or someone, in order to make themselves feel more important. Anyway, I received this 'revelation' with ambiguous feelings. In a way I felt they weren't exactly what I'd call friends, and Jonny should have known it, and yet it was nice to be told I had added the necessary ingredient to elevate the act into the top category. It convinced me that I had succeeded – that I indeed was important and needed. But I had succeeded in more ways than I had then realized. In a way, I had achieved the impossible. I had made myself indispensable, acquired a substitute father figure, had everybody believing I was sixteen and lived the life of a grownup.

I worked diligently to change that unbending man into the kind of person I wanted my father to be. Yet I knew he could never measure up to the fantastic image I had built of my father – an image that would remain bright and shiny and irreproachable until years later I tore it down and destroyed it myself. In a way, Jonny fitted formidably into my scheme of things. If I sought to merge opposing styles – he was the embodiment of two distinctly different personalities that alternated according to circumstances. All you had to do was push the right button – be nice and he was a lamb – pressure him, and out would come that unreasonable, adamant person demanding utter obedience and blind loyalty.

He was right, even when he was wrong and you had to admit it and accept it. Slightly schizophrenic? Perhaps. But aren't most of us to some degree? All we have to do is scratch a little beneath the surface and the most astonishing things begin to emerge...

Baron Johann von Kralik, the circus artist – or bullshit artist as sometimes I called him, only in my thoughts to be sure when I was angry and longed to be really grownup and independent so that I could 'do as I please,' (oh, the never ending struggle for that illusive, intangible something we call 'freedom'...) was indeed a formidable subject to tackle.

The von Kraliks can be traced back to the Middle Ages when they were traveling knights moving from one principality to another as traveling minstrels, the robbing knights or whatever. Later, the family had split up. Some moved to Germany, some to Austria, some remained in Bohemia. Those who remained in Bohemia turned to stained glass artistry and their names can still be found on many fine stained glass windows of the Central European churches. Those in Austria were prominent patrons of the arts. Today in Vienna, there is still a Richard von Kralikplatz named after Jonny's granduncle, and the Kralik Palace – where cultural gala soirees were held, attended even by Emperor Franz Joseph – still houses descendants of the Kralik family.

Jonny's father, who was a chemist, was born in Germany where he worked for the Bayer pharmaceutical firm. It is reputed it was he who had discovered aspirin for the firm but was never given credit for its discovery by his Jewish employers which subsequently turned him into a virulent anti-Semite and later into a Nazi sympathizer. Embittered as he was at the time, he quit his job and moved to Hungary taking all of his notes and research papers with him, vowing he would never reveal how he came upon the formula. This may or may not be true, but as it is, there are a couple of trunks full of his records and notes somewhere which he carefully preserved and guarded throughout his life. What might lend added credence to this fantastic story is that even to this day, no one really knows the full story about aspirin. Perhaps the key to it all is in those trunks sitting somewhere in the eastern part of Germany now, guarding some very interesting secrets.

Jonny's mother, a Hungarian, came from a family of fierce revolutionaries who were considered traitors – or martyrs, depending on who's in power – and right now many a street in Budapest bears their name. One of his uncles, with whom he lived in his childhood and who practically raised him, was the notorious Bela Kun who, in 1919, succeeded in overthrowing the Racosi government and seized power in Hungary instituting a communist regime. But his reign lasted only a few short months. He was deposed in a countercoup and was forced to flee to Russia where he became Stalin's right hand man. Jonny was eleven at the time and after his uncle fled, his aunt, who stayed behind, was taken prisoner and Jonny was taken in by another relative. He remembered his aunt as a kind, gentle woman with long, dark hair which he used to hang on to when she took him swimming in the Danube. In prison he saw her tortured as they attempted to obtain whatever secrets and information they thought she knew. He saw her hanging from hooks in the ceiling by that long hair of hers, screaming over and over that she knew nothing. Later, Stalin released a number of political prisoners in exchange for her release and safe conduct to Russia.

Jonny was born in Budapest (as Janos or Jani as his friends called him) the second of three sons and by the time he was three, his father had decided to move back to Germany. He had sold their house and the money it yielded was supposed to help them get a fresh start. But the family waited in vain at the railway station where he told them they would meet. His father kept all the money and took off with another woman. His mother, heartbroken and penniless, had to turn to her family for help. The boys were taken in by various relatives while the mother went to work, struggling to provide for her children.

While Jonny remained with his uncle Bela until the disaster of 1919, his two brothers were sent to a fine military school. Later, he was taken in by another uncle who was a well-to-do tailor and Jonny earned his keep by being the delivery boy. Since at times he was also collecting money, this gave him an opportunity to filch a few crowns and afford himself a few luxuries here and there. The result of the instability and uncertainty of his childhood was restlessness and a need to 'get away.' He yearned to join the circus and ran away several times. Once, shortly after his uncle fled to Russia, he succeeded in setting their schoolroom on fire by igniting a mixture of phosphorus and magnesium which created a spectacular explosion and impressed his schoolmates. Failing to put out the fire by ingeniously reaching for the most immediate type of extinguisher handy – namely pissing on it, an example followed readily by his school friends – and terrified by the prospect of having to face the consequences of his misdeed, he ran away as far as Italy where he was finally picked up and delivered to the Hungarian consulate from where he was dispatched back to Budapest.

Two years later, he made better plans. He ran away again and this time joined a gypsy caravan. Somehow they accepted him and he accepted their way of life which included, among other things, stealing whatever they could to keep eating. He stayed with them until they'd traveled far enough for him, and after finding a suitable circus, that is, one that would hire him, he left the pleasant, carefree gypsy way of life.

At the circus his jobs were many and varied. He had to work his way through every facet of the circus life. At one time or another he worked every type of act one is likely to see at the circus – from the clown on, leading ultimately to the flying trapeze – and worked his way up to such name places as the Circus Medrano in Paris and the Circus Bush in Berlin. Meanwhile, in Budapest, his brothers were growing up as fine military cadets while his mother still slaved to keep them there and used every penny Jonny ever sent her on the two boys.

Then, the older brother got himself involved in a duel with a fellow cadet over a girl. Since the other cadet was a better swordsman, Jonny's brother was killed. The younger brother, true to the code of honor, also challenged the cadet to a duel, even though he knew he didn't stand much of a chance, and was killed as well. For their mother, the shock was too great, and she fell seriously ill.

Jonny, who was in Paris at the time, receiving the news of the tragedy and his mother's critical condition, dropped everything and took the first train back to Budapest. Quite characteristically, he ignored whatever codes of military honor there may have been established and went after the guy in his own way.

Jonny must have had quite a reputation among his contemporaries (I think he had been good at boxing or something similar), because the guy apparently decided he had better keep himself scarce or seek safety in crowds. Still, Jonny finally traced him to a dance held in the main ballroom of the Grand Hotel. When he got there, the oval marble floor was packed with cadets and ladies in evening gowns. Seeing him, the cadet ran up to the balcony which encircled the huge lower floor. There, Jonny managed to corner him and picking him up, threw him down to the shiny marble floor below.

Jonny departed never stopping to check the result of his action. He grabbed a train out of Hungary again, this time never to return, stopping only long enough to see his dying mother. On her death bed, the old woman, blaming all her misfortunes on the treachery of her husband, made him promise never to help his father in any way, invoking a curse if ever he should do so.

Interestingly enough, during the war in Germany, Jonny did allow himself to be moved to help his father, but no sooner did he finish furnishing an apartment for him to live in, it was bombed out. This happened three times in succession.

Jonny's entire life story sounds something like a Hollywood B-movie, jammed with the most fantastic adventures, but it just happens to all be true. Over the years I've pieced it all together mainly from things I've heard from his friends and foes and from the few things he would say about himself. Oddly enough, about his private life he never liked to divulge much – in word and even less in writing. He always seemed to be suspicious and afraid to leave himself exposed and therefore vulnerable.

Back in Paris, he threw himself into his work again and put together an act which was very dangerous and therefore extremely well paid. High wire balancing act – without a net. That's when a guy walks on a tightrope – way up high – carrying a long, balancing pole and a few people on top of him. But in spite of the money, they couldn't keep it up for long because it was too nerve-racking. So he turned to something easier. High trapeze. That's when someone hangs by his knees way up high and holds a short trapeze in his teeth on which a couple of people are performing slow acrobatic things. How this is done is really simple. The trapeze is attached to a mouthpiece and one has to have a set of good teeth to chomp down on it like a vise and very strong jaw and neck muscles. That's supposed to be so safe you don't even need a net. But of course, there are 'unforeseen' circumstances.

Jonny was bitten by a stray dog and had to undergo a series of anti-rabies shots. The doctor assured him there should be no adverse reaction so Jonny did the performance that evening as usual. However, the doctor couldn't have been quite clear on what kind of work Jonny was doing because while hanging down by his knees and holding his two partners in his teeth, he lost consciousness. Once the bite slackened, the weight tore out the mouthpiece breaking his front teeth and the two went crashing to the floor below. The woman died on the spot and the man suffered from extensive internal hemorrhaging and multiple fractures but survived. If Jonny's wrists hadn't been secured by the straps, he'd have crashed down as well. Instead, he hung there limply until he regained consciousness and came down by himself. As it was, his wrists were shot and he needed a few caps on his teeth, but that was all.

What it did to him psychologically, was another matter. To overcome the shock, he decided to go up again as soon as possible. But when he climbed up to the top platform, he knew he'd never go up there again. It took a lot out of him just to come down again. And that ended his glamorous career as a trapeze artist forever. I am sure that to Jonny, coming down to earth from these lofty heights was as much a come down as it was to me leaving the noble concept of traditional ballet and the theater. To him, being on the floor – reduced to the role of 'dancer' (the ultimate in self-delusion, to say the least) was the final degradation. To him, ballet, or what he assumed to be ballet, was a line of girls, dancing their little numbers between the acts, whom he regarded as worthless tramps and strictly forbade me to associate with them in any way.

Often even an exchange of greetings would provoke a tedious paternal tirade. It took a long time before I could induce him to come and see the Bolshoi and then he only judged it by what lifts they did, which he considered far inferior to what we were doing, but as far as my dancing was concerned, he boasted from then on that I was at least as good a dancer as anyone of them.

And later, when the Bolshoi began using an increasing amount of lifts, he insisted they must have seen us. But he still didn't like to go to see a ballet and in all the years we worked together, I managed to drag him to only three performances. And his opinion of the 'line' in the nightclubs remained the same.

In a way, we had a constant running battle about which direction the act should take and whenever we'd set a new routine it was warfare. I'd try, in my own 'diplomatic-strategic-psychological method,' for a more balletic treatment, while he fought in his own inimitable way, for more acrobatic lifts. But I was unbeatable. Any lifts I didn't like, or considered unsuitable to the 'image' I wanted to maintain, I simply 'couldn't' learn.

Suddenly I'd turn into the weakest, most incapable thing apologizing profusely to 'daddy' for my ineptitude. Still, I loved the lifts – but only certain kinds. What I loved was a combination of steps – pure ballet – which would end up in some kind of a jete, like a grand-jete, for instance, (that's when the dancer takes a long leap in a split) and land with just the toe in his hand and from there soar up high where he'd hold me in a pose that would twist into all sorts of strange, graceful things and end with him tossing me up and I'd come down in a swan dive and he'd catch me but a few inches from the floor. That, of course, was very effective and the audience almost jumped from their seats. The beauty of it was that with the type of dancing I did, no one ever expected these things.

But the greatest thing about it was Jonny never once missed. And lucky too, since if he had, I could have easily knocked my teeth out, cracked my skull or, at best, broken a few bones. But oddly enough, I never thought of such a possibility even though I'm certainly not fearless. If anything, I consider myself pretty much of a coward. Under no circumstance would I even dream of venturing up to such heights as the flying trapeze. I used to take a dive from eighteen feet high, perfectly confident Jonny would always catch me, but nothing could ever get me up on a trapeze. Even in this, I'm a strange contradiction of qualities – the fearless and daring, against the meek and cowardly.

Anyway, back to my brief, quick recount of the incredibly adventuresome and turbulent life of my venerable partner-parent-warden all rolled into one.

After having thus messed-up his wrists, which are as important to a trapeze artist as toes are to the ballet dancer, he had to turn temporarily to some other profession, one which would make no demands on his wrists. So he became a gigolo. It's amazing that as much money as performers make, for some reason or other, most wind up spending it as fast as they make it. To this, Jonny was no exception.

After his 'accident,' he was broke. This represented a serious problem since one of the most important assets of an aspiring gigolo, I'm told, is an ample and elegant wardrobe – aside of good looks and physique, which Jonny claimed to have had in his early twenties. For me it was hard to believe since I always thought his features were such they couldn't have been called attractive at any age. There are some faces that just never make it – but then – tastes are as varied as slaps in the face.

Around that time he was dating a girl, the daughter of the owner of a very famous variety theater in Paris – the result of this association was his first illegitimate daughter – and through her he met Josephine Baker (the star attraction at the theater at the time) who bought him, for some 'unimaginable' reason, the wardrobe he needed thus launching him on his brand-new 'career.'

From his sporadic accounts of this venture about which he spoke as little as possible (actually I got most of the choice details from his 'friends' – to get anything out of him on that score was like getting fleas out of a long-haired dog), I learned his best clients were Mrs. Grundig and Mrs. Krupp. They were middle-aged ladies who loved to dance and their husbands didn't, so Jonny obligingly filled a great void and provided peace of mind for the husbands who were grateful enough to befriend him and invite him to all their parties. Mr. Grundig even made him a gift of a radio. What Mr. Krupp did, I don't know. He could have hardly given him a hunk of steel.

This career, however, didn't last too long which was fortunate for Jonny since everyone knows what happens to old gigolos.

As soon as his wrists were mended, he began working on a new act. His partner was a lovely, limber girl and they worked up an acrobatic-contortion act and before long, Jonny was back at the circus again. This act didn't last too long either because there were other complications. The girl's mother had some strange ideas with regard to maternal functions which seemed to include nudging her daughter into an affair with Jonny and providing them with all sorts of contraceptives as well as acquainting them, rather graphically, with their proper application. (Sounds like a dirty, old lady bent on voyeurism.) Either she was a rotten teacher, or they inept pupils, because the result was Jonny's spawning his second illegitimate daughter. The unfortunate thing was that the enthusiasm with which the mother threw herself into this new role extended beyond Jonny. While he was off working with another act which he joined because of the girl's pregnancy, the mother couldn't refrain from prompting her into other affairs which resulted in her eventually passing to Jonny some unmentionable disease (I think it was the clap). This ended their relationship rather drastically as well as their plans to continue the act after the baby was born, and left the girl alone, pregnant and – unmarried.

CHAPTER TWELVE

Jonny's first departure from a strictly acrobatic style was a trio he formed with another man and a girl. It consisted of the two men tossing the girl around like a baseball to some wild Spanish music no doubt to match the wretched name of Chiquita – (not that I have anything against bananas, but what's good enough for a banana isn't good enough for me).

She was a tiny, light thing with wild black hair and eyes and a disposition to match. She was also Jewish which, at the beginning of the Nazi era, was one hell of a combination. But such 'minor' problems never fazed Jonny. He arranged top notch false papers for her and they performed blithely throughout Hitler's mad purge of the 'master race' and through most of the war. Believing the best hiding place is smack in the center of the lion's den, and that the best defense is an offense, Jonny booked the act to work for the K.D.F. Kraft durch Freude – the German equivalent of the USO, and during the war they toured the Russian, French and Italian fronts entertaining 'the boys' hellbent on conquering the world for their 'fuhrer.'

Soon Jonny was promoted to a top position among the K.D.F. functionaries, which meant it was his task to select acts and performers and put shows together and send them to the various fronts. He always claimed that that was the time he made the most money and lived the most exciting and satisfying life. I could never understand it because I'd have gone stark raving mad in such a situation. So there he was, in the midst of the Nazi elite – not only with a Jewish partner, but frequently with a whole Jewish show. This sounds impossible and extremely risky but, as he claimed, it really wasn't. In his position, he wielded quite a bit of power because nothing was ever good enough for 'the boys on the front' and under that policy all sorts or red tape could be eliminated and all sorts of shenanigans could go unnoticed. This enabled Jonny to help many Jews to safety. He would arrange papers for entire families and put them to work. Whenever possible he'd somehow work them into various acts as assistants or put them in some position where they'd attract as little attention as possible and place them in shows heading to a place from where it would be possible – where he had connections – to smuggle them to safety. Then, as soon as the show reached such a place and the necessary arrangements were made to get them across the border to a neutral country such as Switzerland or Sweden, they would vanish from the show without anyone being the wiser and their place was quickly filled by others.

Of course, these people knew they owed their lives to Jonny and they showed their appreciation accordingly. Jonny was loaded with jewelry and various valuables which he took when they were offered but also helped those who had nothing to give except their gratitude. I was never able to determine whether Jonny did all that out of sheer humanistic consideration, pity or simply materialistic drive because his attitudes were so conflicting.

From the fate of his uncle Bela, he seemed to have learned one lesson – never get involved in anything political. As far as he was concerned, this applied doubly to the artist-performer. So how he could rationalize his way into this activity was a puzzle. Materialism? That didn't seem plausible either. His money was spent almost before he had made it, mostly on his friends, generous gifts – and gadgets. (He loved gadgets and dogs.) His friends could get anything from him.

Later, I used to accuse him of being so insecure that he had to buy his friends to which he replied there was no such thing as a 'friend.' Yet he continued doing it anyway. It seemed he had the need to have people around who'd look up to him as the pinnacle of strength and generosity. He could conquer anything, buy anyone. Already in his youth, when he pocketed some of the money belonging to his uncle the tailor, he used it mainly to treat his friends to whatever they wanted. Perhaps it was also an unconscious rebellion against his father who was such an anti-Semite.

Still, for whatever reasons he did it, the fact remains he put his life on the line to help save these people. Since he continued to carry on with these activities without a hitch, Jonny grew bolder and more confident. And as their show, which was headed by his act, frequently performed for the highest officials in the Nazi government, to Jonny, he found nothing more thrilling than to see his Jewish partner admired, fussed over and courted by all these Nazis who'd have dropped dead had they known she belonged to the race they so hated and were busy exterminating.

It's interesting that it's always been the artist who has occupied a privileged position close to the heads of governments. Perhaps the artist's presence added an aura of culture and refinement and elevated their self-esteem. Perhaps it's because the very concept of art implies something ennobling, something outside and above political intrigues and maneuvers. Perhaps the best reason is – as expressed by Lorenzo de Medici in defense of his spending so much money on supporting the arts: "Posterity will not judge me by the wars I've won or lost, but rather by the works of art I've inspired that are left behind."

Jonny's greatest triumph took place in Nuremberg. The Nazi elite at the time used to stay at the Grand Hotel (the same hotel which would later house the judges who had to determine the fate of these men), and so did Jonny, Magda, his Jewish partner, and Helmut another partner, together with two dogs and three puppies which Jonny dragged with him wherever he went.

They moved in with all the pomp and style on the floor below the one exclusively occupied by Hermann Goering, his staff, and various other personages of the Third Reich and their entourages. After settling into the elegant three room suite, imposingly elegant with deep burgundy rug and heavy velvet drapes gracing the slim, tall windows and fine furniture representing the ultimate in style and decor, Jonny set up his wireless and proceeded to listen to London.

He had just got it going well when he heard a soft, discreet voice close behind him; "Herr Johnson, when listening to London, I would suggest you keep the volume a little lower."

Jonny stared at the frail, little man in stunned silence – too petrified to utter a sound. But the man, having voiced his warning, just smiled and left again. People were shot on the spot for a lot less. Later, Jonny saw the little man again in close proximity to the venerable Field Marshall and realized he was one of the many secret police surrounding him at all times. When he saw Jonny, he approached him casually and asked with a disarming smile. "What's new at the front these days, Herr Johnson?" Then without waiting for a reply, he moved on, chuckling to himself.

Whichever way the war was going at the time, those in top positions lived like kings. After the show that evening, Jonny and Magda were Goering's guests at a sumptuous party abounding with the finest French champagne, Russian caviar and other delicacies. Magda sat next to Goering listening with a whimsical smile to his compliments. The smile turned to one of triumph when upon their departure the rotund, bemedaled man gallantly kissed her hand – the hand of a Jewess. I can well understand the feeling of triumph they must have felt at that moment. It's like pulling off the gag of all times. But, unfortunately, Magda wasn't exactly what you might call diplomatic. That's why she was constantly having arguments about everything imaginable not only with Jonny but also with Helmut, a dull, stubborn German, simple and unattractive, but strong as an ox whom she called, "the horse head."

"My name is Helmut!" he would hiss through clenched teeth. "You better get her to stop calling me that or I will no longer be able to control myself!"

Besides being a troublemaker, Magda was also a blabber-mouth. Intoxicated with the staggering success of their deception, she liked to confide and stagger her 'bosom-friends' (she had quite a few) with the revelation of her ancestry and even hint at what Jonny was up to. One of these 'friends' was a better German than a 'bosom-friend' and betrayed Magda's confidence by telling her husband about it who then confronted Jonny demanding to know how he could do such a thing as harbor and protect a non-Aryan?! In spite of the man's 'generous' pledge not to betray his best friend, Jonny was afraid to trust him and stopped all of his activities on behalf of the Jews for a while.

Whether it was this particular couple or someone else – their secret was finally revealed. Someone informed the Gestapo and Magda was arrested and sent to Therezienstadt, one of the infamous concentration camps everyone claimed to have known nothing about. Before they could get around to arresting Jonny, he managed to remove himself from the immediate vicinity by assigning himself a tour heading to the place he considered the safest at the time: The Eastern front. In those days the communications were in disarray because of the war and by the time the communiqués dictating his arrest caught up with him, he was gone again.

This method of keeping himself at large seemed risky but in reality worked rather well, and for a long time. Also, the elaborate underground with its network of spies, would inform him when he was in danger. He had a few close calls, but also here, his method of defense, although amazingly simple, was most effective. He always carried a handful of pepper in his pocket. A couple of times when he had, unwisely delayed his departure a little too long – the Gestapo did manage to catch up with him. Because of his important position, a couple of plainclothes Gestapo men were sent out to arrest him. Jonny would consent to accompany them without much ado. As soon as they reached a convenient spot, he'd reach into his pocket and throw the pepper in their faces and race to the nearest railway station and head out of the city to the next 'relatively' safe place.

The final place – the place of his downfall – was Czechoslovakia. Prague, to be specific.

It was in April, 1944 – just about a year before the end of the war. Again, he received word that the order for his arrest came through and the Gestapo was about to arrest him. He was on his way to the railway station when he was approached by two Gestapo men. In Prague, the headquarters of the Gestapo was at the Petschek Palace which is right across the street from the railway station. They caught up with him in the lobby of his hotel which was on Wenceslas Square, less than two blocks from Petschek Palace.

Jonny went with them readily, confident he'd get away again. At a suitable corner, he reached into his pocket for his usual weapon, but much to his horror, the pepper was gone – run out through a hole in his pocket.

The shock was so sudden and overwhelming that he couldn't pull himself together in time to come up with an alternate plan of escape until it was too late. Thus, Jonny landed in Prague's Pankratz Prison.

Having examined all past records, the Gestapo managed to determine the number of all the Jews he had helped to escape and refusing to believe him when he said no one else was involved – they interrogated him again and again, trying to beat out of him the names of the people involved in the 'plot.'

His interrogating officer, a sadistic bastard, whom Jonny swore he would kill with his bare hands if he ever came across him, would put on thick leather gloves and use a heavy steel chain and beat him until he was bloody and unconscious.

Finally, Jonny was sentenced to death by guillotine – a quaint little touch the Nazis dreamt up to bring the feel of antiquity to the 'modern' days – and that was the means of execution at Pankratz. But in their customary efficient way, the Nazis found a way of improving even that. The victim was placed on the block in such a way – head up – that the blade would cut diagonally from the ear down to the lower neck. That way there was less bleeding – less cleaning up.

Once Jonny was among the 'guillotine candidates,' as those in that part of the prison called themselves, his life centered around the news received from the outside which was communicated throughout the prison by tapping in Morse code on the exposed water pipes. It was a race against time.

Jonny was to be executed on April 28, 1945. Every bit of news of the advancing allied armies meant a step closer to freedom –

and each day meant a step closer to death. Each morning they would sit in dead silence, counting the number of executions. Situated as they were, the dull, heavy thud of the guillotine descending upon its victim reverberated against the walls like a distant, ominous thunder. As soon as the echo of the last thud died away, they were marched into the grizzly chamber carrying mops and pails. It was their job to wipe up the blood flowing bright and fresh in the gully leading from that horrendous contraption that many didn't even dare to look up at. The pails contained strong, pungent disinfectants but nothing could remove the terrible stench of blood and death.

Then one night in mid-April, the guillotine candidates were awakened by noises coming from the nearby execution chamber. The next morning they listened in vain for the ominous thud of the guillotine. There were no executions that day. Rumors began circulating that the guillotine had been dismantled that night and sunk in the Moldau river.

The allies were approaching rapidly from both sides. The circle was tightening and its center was Prague. The wardens were becoming less cruel and hostile – some even tried to be friendly and helpful. The wind now blew from another direction and they began to fear for their skins. When the top-brass secretly departed one night leaving the prison in the hands of the underlings, everyone was breathless with excitement. The end was approaching rapidly – and it wasn't theirs.

News of the revolution raging outside reached them and everyone longed to join in the fighting. Then at last the Czech revolutionaries captured Pankratz and all the prisoners poured out into the streets.

How could I have possibly known that, not too far from the cellar where I played with other children and absorbed the realities and the dismal results of human conflicts, the man who would several years later affect such a profound change in my life, escaped so narrowly a gruesome death?

CHAPTER THIRTEEN

If Jonny's final goal was to go to America, he certainly went about it in a roundabout way. After Germany, we headed in the opposite direction – the Middle East. I really didn't mind because, at that time, traveling was still new and exciting – full of magic, fantastic promises. The orient, to me, seemed a different planet – a different world.

It began with many firsts: my first plane trip – Frankfurt to Milan; my first trip to Italy – which in itself was full of excitements. In those days all countries rang with exotic languages I yearned to learn. I didn't know then that once you do, half of the magic is gone.

In Genoa we took a boat to Beirut via the island of Cypress. I was thrilled with everything. The seas were rough and everyone was seasick, but I was forever hungry. I would get into my leotards and practice on the deck every single day for at least three to four hours and watched the huge waves with delight.

The people puking across the railings into the Mediterranean never bothered me, nor the dirty looks they were apt to throw in my direction. It got so bad that even the cooks stopped cooking and the very few of us that were able to eat were served cold meals. I spent every moment I could on deck, watching that raging body of water.

Of my first trip to Cypress, all I remember is a hot, hot land dusty and dry, and my terribly sore feet. I wore a pair of new Italian sandals and got huge blisters and was panicked out because I would not be able to put on my toe shoes for at least a day. Oh, the blessed naiveté of youth! In those days I was sure I'd fall behind by at least a year, if I were to skip one day's rehearsal. Strange, how some things stick in my memory with a clarity and persistency that defies years while others, often far more important events, blend into the monotony of constant excitement and change.

Of Beirut, I remember most vividly the purchase of my first gold coins and smuggling them home. I guess to impress my mother was very important, because I didn't send anything to my father. Granted, they were little coins, gold sterling pound pieces, I think, but I can feel the gratification of doing it to this day.

I bought a package of dates, carefully opened the cellophane, removed two center dates of the rows of three and six across. Then I dug out a bit of the center and placed the coins in the hollow spot. Replacing the two top dates was easy. Then I had to fold and glue back the cellophane in such a way that it never showed that it had been opened. Immensely satisfied with my work, I added the package of dates to other goodies I knew were scarce at home and mailed it. I was sure to write a letter cautioning them to "eat the dates with care because they were extra-special good."

The other thing I remember with great fondness was the hotel we stayed at – the St. James. It was built close to the sea around a picturesque little cove, crystal clear and blue where I swam every free moment I could spare. I hadn't even had a glimpse of the sea until that sea voyage, but it was love at first sight. I don't suppose anyone growing up near the sea can understand the awe, the sheer wonder of seeing it for the first time. No matter how much you hear or read about it, no matter how many photographs you see, nothing can in any way duplicate or approximate the real thing, the surprise at tasting the salinity for the first time, the feel of the salty water on your skin, the texture when it's dried by the sun.

To me the Middle East is the strangely disturbing, persistent sound of Arabic music drifting endlessly through the streets and the smell of mutton emanating from countless little shops mixed with the strong, intoxicating scent of jasmine which grew profusely, particularly up in the mountain regions. By the time I was through with the Middle East, I couldn't stand lamb (they even fried eggs in lamb fat unless you ask for butter) and for a long time, I couldn't bear to hear that kind of music. But up to this day whenever I smell jasmine, all I have to do is close my eyes and I am back in Beirut and the picture of that friendly little cove materializes instantly in my mind.

Then we were off to Egypt. Jonny had met King Farouk on his first visit to Egypt many years earlier and I was terribly anxious to meet a 'real king.' I was thrilled with Cairo – the magnificent mosques, the minarets, the pyramids, the camel rides, and particularly with the white-robed Arabs in their neat fezzes sitting cross-legged on the floor of the bazaars munching on lettuce, their cocks hanging beneath the hems of their long shirts. I used to walk around slightly bent, peering absolutely spellbound by their long, dark peckers. I thought it much more fascinating than all the gold so lavishly displayed in the gold bazaar, or even my first glimpse of the King.

It's a pity that illusions are created only to be shattered. The fat man in a white shirt with sleeves rolled up to expose fat, hairy forearms looked more like a butcher than a king. But he was quick to jump up and remove a chair a careless stagehand left in my way, showing deep understanding, consideration and respect for the performer. Also, he spoke a good German which was the only language I could get by in those days, except for my Czech, of course. But I was quickly learning French and some English.

King Farouk was the first of a long row of important personages I danced for and met. There was King Paul and Queen Frederica in Athens, Prince Phillip of England who was visiting. Ditto, the President of Turkey, etc., etc., and they all faded into faceless figures – faint ghosts dwelling in the far recesses of my memory. Strange how the most breathlessly anticipated events recede and become unimportant when tempered by years while other, seemingly unimportant and insignificant events loom as large as life in that great, unpredictable computer we call the mind.

I am apt to remember more clearly and with great fondness

particularly those places where the swimming was good and the water warm and sparkling clean.

In Cairo we stayed at the Mena House because it was close to the pyramids and Auberge des Pyramides the place we appeared – a large, beautiful club frequented with regularity by the king. It also had a pool that I could jump into right after the rehearsal.

The Mena House had an even larger, lovely pool but there was hardly anyone ever in it except me. In the cool shade of terraces, however, long-robed Arabs would sit cross-legged taking an occasional long pull at their water pipes. They sat like statues, always silent, always distant and solemn, curiously relaxed, one might say, at peace. They'd sit there seemingly gazing out toward the desert, but their eyes were most often closed. I used to walk by them as silently and quickly as I could. There was something about them that filled me with a vague, inexplicable uneasiness.

Then one day, after I got out of the pool, I noticed an Egyptian sitting on the coping nearby, his feet dangling in the water. He was slim, almost skinny but the muscles beneath his smooth, brown skin were firm and strong. The skin on his face was taut and shone like silk. I guess I must have been staring because he looked up at me and smiled showing perfectly shaped white teeth. His hair was a mess of long, dark curls and he had the beautiful, dark, luminous eyes one finds only in Arabs, Jews and Africans.

Knowing it was taboo for me to get into conversations with strangers, Jonny's rule, I trotted dutifully toward my "warden" lying nearby on a lounge. But the man walked over, sat down and began chatting with us. I noticed he was toying with a dark-brown object which looked rather like rabbit shit. Seeing me eyeing it, he held it up between his two fingers like some rare gem and let me examine it.

"Do you know what it is?"

I shook my head.

"It's magic," he said in a reverently enthusiastic tone of voice.

I must have looked skeptical because he said it once again and with greater emphasis.

"You take this and anything you want to be, you will be! You want to be a king? – You will be a king! You want to jump across a

mountain – you can! You can do or be anything you want...
Anything!"

I figured the guy must be stark raving mad. His big luminous
eyes shone with the mad gleam of a fanatic. But it was obvious he
really believed what he was saying. He was not putting us on.

Jonny, whose French didn't exceed the barest essentials kept
saying: "Was sagt der Kerl? Was?!"

"How can a little piece of that... (I thought better than to call it
turd) do all you say?" I demanded derisively. "What do you do with it
anyway? Hang it around your neck or something?"

He laughed like a maniac. "Mais non! You eat it, or smoke it
like they do," he said, still laughing and pointing toward the terraces.

I looked at him startled. Could it be those men there were
really smoking this thing?

"What is it?" I asked.

"Hashish!" He whispered the word with such awe and rever-
ence as if he was letting me in on the world's best guarded secret.

"Oh, hashish," I retorted with disappointment. "I heard it
makes you crazy."

I instantly regretted I had said that. His eyes flashed angrily.

"Only fools believe that. Only fools see things upside down.
This makes you see!..."

"See what?! Those guys have their eyes closed!"

"Ahh, but they see! They see it's the world that makes people
crazy. Hashish opens their eyes to what really is. Would you like to
try it? – Here, I will give it to you!" He offered as if he was just making the supreme sacrifice and offering us the world.

I looked at the thing with distaste. What if it was really a turd
and the whole thing was a gigantic put-on? No, whatever it was, I
wasn't about to smoke it (even if I knew how) much less eat it. Of
course, Jonny declined as well. Jonny didn't even drink alcohol! –
Debilitates the muscles! What else?! But I never forgot the young
man's enraptured face when he talked about the little ball of resin.

Another thing I remember – most vividly – is my first mental
breakdown, or perhaps, one might tend to call it a childish tantrum,
and all that led up to it.

It was in Asmara, a small, beautiful city in Eritrea. We appeared at a new, modern theater with a whole show which we assembled and choreographed. That part of it, of course, was up to me. It wouldn't have been so nerve-racking had I had the cooperation I needed instead of the constant interference.

I set up two production numbers, one ballet solo and a new routine for us. I designed the costumes and spent exasperating hours trying to get seamstresses, inexperienced in theatrical costuming, to understand what I wanted. I chose a sixteen-year-old Greek girl out of the chorus line who had fair ballet training and set for her a lyrical ballet solo. I was very pleased with her work and the routine came out well. However, Malvina had a boyfriend, a hideous, greedy individual, who ever so often failed to appear for rehearsals. Subsequently, she had trouble remembering the routine and was generally a nuisance. Jonny, instead of helping, kept complaining about the same old shit: the new act was turning out 'too balletic.'

During dress rehearsal the dancers couldn't lift their arms, the sleeves were too restrictive. The costumes had to be altered, and I had to spend more time with the seamstresses explaining all over again what had to be done. Up to the last day, I had to dance every step along with Malvina, she just couldn't remember the sequence. But opening night everything went great. She was beautiful, and I was glad I fought for keeping the routine as it was – pure ballet which Jonny kept insisting it should be jazzed-up somehow. She was a hit.

I was immensely pleased to see it went over so well. I think one of the hardest things is to choreograph a show and take part in it as well. You tend to forget your own thing and concentrate on everyone else's. However, the entire show was a success and I, exhausted and worn out, nevertheless felt a tremendous satisfaction.

The next day, I guess it was because the whole strain and tension was over and I could finally relax, I was more vulnerable. Jonny again complained about some parts of the act: Malvina's boyfriend sent a note saying he represented her and demanded an increase in salary, since she was now a soloist, or else she would not show up that night.

I sort of stood there, in the dressing room, letting all this wash over me. I remember being amazed how utterly calm I was but in the next instant I heard someone screaming horribly. There was a sort of lapse in time, I suddenly had no idea where or what I was, or where all that screaming was coming from. I touched my face and it was then that I realized that it was me who was SCREAMING. My face was taut and wet and I was on the floor and there were people around me putting something cold on my forehead. I felt like I had been drowning in terribly cold, icy water and I had just come up for breath. It seemed as if I had barely managed to escape some unimaginable calamity.

Jonny was surprisingly kind and apologetic, but the whole thing embarrassed me terribly. I felt everyone must be thinking I was too young to assume such a responsibility and that really upset me. I knew I was perfectly capable of coping with the whole thing and that no one really understood that it was all these extenuating circumstances that caused me to flip out like that. I guess my insecurity stemmed largely from the fact that I was pretending to be something I was not – a grownup. I was still a child, only playing at grownup and very discontented that it was only make believe. I'd like to know what makes us always so dissatisfied with what we are? I doubt everyone feels that way, but I am sure many do indeed.

CHAPTER FOURTEEN

We were to continue with the show all through South Africa and the Middle East, but Malvina and her boyfriend continued to be a problem, and somehow, the people were hard to keep together. Everyone spoke a different language and there was little closeness among the various members. I had just come upon a system which allowed me to learn a language sufficiently to converse within two to three months.

By the time we got to Sudan I spoke French (in Sudan I was learning English) and in Eritrea I picked up Italian which was considerably easier because of the French I'd just learned. It's really terribly simple and anyone can do it. The first month just listen to the rhythm and melody of the language and pick up vocabulary. Every language has its own melody. Once you pick it up, you can start. The next step is to learn the tenses of verbs of the most frequently used words, and before you know it, you are speaking fluently enough to have everyone think you really speak it well. Well, that's the way I figured it out and made it work.

In our little international group (and international it was! We had Frenchmen, Greeks, Armenians, Arabs, Hungarians...you name it) the unifying language was French. Still, some spoke it poorly and so there was a great gap from the word go. Also, we were getting engagement offers just for the act alone because no one knew about the show yet and rather than spending the time and effort publicizing it and hacking it with the whole group, Jonny decided we would go on by ourselves.

Some, I was sorry to leave behind. There was a French singer in her late twenties, which to me, being thirteen at the time, seemed ancient. She was a marvelous person, charming, warm and friendly. She was the only one who never made me feel as if I were a kid reaching beyond my ability. Instead, she treated me like a real grownup – an equal – with respect and understanding. We kept in touch for many years and even now, although our letters became progressively scarcer, we still write to each other from time to time.

But Africa was much more than these disturbing events. To me Africa had such a unique feeling that if I were set down anywhere in East Africa today, not knowing what part of the world it was, I believe I would know immediately where I was. There is something very special about that continent. Perhaps it's the feeling of vast, windswept spaces, the feeling of freedom and exuberance of spirit. Yes, I believe every place has its own specific spirit, or soul. If that be so, Africa has a fantastic, fiercely free spirit. Whatever goes on there – that's the one thing I'd like to believe will always shine through.

I remember vividly the drives in bumpy jeeps across the flat parched desert, the tall, rippling grasses, the slanting Musanga trees with their flat, umbrella-like crowns throwing rare patches of shade upon the hot ground. I still have a picture in my mind of a bunch of bush men dancing solemnly in the shade of one of those trees to the sharp, rhythmic sounds of drums and other primitive instruments. I was fascinated by the simplicity and grace of those movements, the mesmerizing rhythm, the cool, precise concentration that excluded the presence of any casual intruder – leaving them unaffected – alone with the purpose and meaning of that dance. There was something very concrete and important about it that made supreme sense. They appeared completely self-confident and free, their torn dusty clothes, proper and dignified. They "belonged" – we were the intruders whom they graciously tolerated in their unconcerned silence.

I saw the same feel, the same attitude, in all the Africans, whether it was in Sudan, Egypt, Eritrea, Ethiopia or Uganda. Even the Sudanese servant, busy pressing my dresses and moistening them by filling his mouth with water and expelling it in an impressive shower of mist, did so with utmost detachment and dignity. But I was most impressed by the Ethiopian and Eritrean Africans. Undoubtedly the aristocrats among the Africans, they were extremely slim, tall and fine-boned with beautiful sculptured faces and enormous naturals which they cut into various shapes. They walked tall and straight and regal as if nothing could ever faze them.

Africa was many things to me – it was a land of contrasts and surprises. Dry, flat desert lands where trees were rare and the air shivered with heat alternated with mountainous regions and lush vegetation and heavy humid atmosphere. The vast flatness of the desert reminded me of the ocean. As far as the eye could see, there was nothing but that barren, flat land where one could drive a car the way he would a speedboat. Instead of the bumpy waves, there were the deep furrows in the cracking, parched soil. The similarity struck me the day we went out, a party of nine, in two jeeps, to shoot birds. They called them sand grass and they tasted somewhat like squab.

We left Khartoum early in the morning heading toward Omdurman but bypassed it and continued further into the desert which is where the birds can be found. There, for miles and miles, you could see nothing but that incredibly flat surface – the horizon, even as the ocean, shivering in the hot air. We drove around erratically like a couple of hounds hot on a scent. Both cars went their own way and soon I could see the other jeep far off in the distance racing about like a busy ant, in chase of the elusive birds.

At one point the motor of our jeep went out and no amount of coaxing and fussing could get it started again. We honked and hollered then began to shoot furiously, but the other jeep was too far for them to hear us. We figured that eventually they would have to notice us sitting there in one spot, so we tried a visual tactic.

Someone tied his shirt to the end of a rifle and began waving it around. Nothing. Another hour passed and they still appeared too absorbed in their own pursuit and paid no attention to us. We sat there for a few more hours in furious exasperation, watching the other jeep, ignorant of our dilemma, driving about in carefree abandon. Unfortunately, as we were soon to discover, most of our drinking supply, which had consisted of a lot of beer, ginger-ale and plain soda water, was in the other car. Everyone was getting terribly thirsty while the sun was getting hotter and hotter. And the shade within the jeep offered little relief. I thought it might as well be a sailboat stranded on a calm, dead ocean, its sails useless in the absence of even a breath of wind.

Finally, one of the men, a big, powerful Greek who was reputed to have the rare talent of being able to polish off a dozen sand grass at one sitting, decided to hike to a nearby village to get some water and a chain or rope which we were bound to need eventually. I had never seen a primitive village so I wanted to go along. Of course, so did Jonny. The Greek gave me a dubious look but then decided I should be able to make it.

I found out quickly that there's more to walking in the desert than just physical exertion. Driving in a car, you get a lot of breeze even though it's so hot it takes your breath away. Walking, you soon become conscious of the incredibly hot ground burning right through the soles of your shoes, and the heat gets you tired in no time at all. It's just like a sauna. There is something terribly desolate about the great, lonely span of even land so dry and full of deep, sharp cracks it feels like being on another planet altogether – a dead, dried-out planet devoid of life. It's also a bit scary – even with other people around.

I don't know how far we walked but it must have been several miles, (at least it felt like it) when at last we came upon the village the Greek knew about. That village was probably the most astounding thing I had seen in Africa. The first, most startling thing was the seeming absence of color, or I should say, the presence of one color – sandy brown. It was as if that color absorbed every other and remained unchallenged, permeating every single thing in sight; on the ground, the houses, the people, their clothing and even their skin and hair. I saw none of the great variety of shiny mahogany shades, all was dulled by the uniformness of that sandy brown color. The houses, built mainly out of camel shit which stinks terribly when fresh but dries into sturdy, solid substance, appeared to have grown right out of the ground. They seemed to melt into it – one with the other.

There were naked, dusky children playing around and a few grownups, occupied with various chores. Our arrival caused the minimum of excitement. Perhaps the children showed the greatest reaction of all. They peered at us curiously and examined us with the same delight I examined them. An ancient crow, with only a rag tied around her hips, holding a big wooden bowl against her sagging belly in which she kept stirring some brown doughy mess, came walking toward us. Her head was a mass of dusty braids – like dozens of thin, decaying snakes twisting around her skinny shoulders. Her brown, dull eyes, almost buried in a myriad of dusty wrinkles examined us with open, indifferent curiosity. I stared fascinated at the loose folds of her breasts hanging down, almost touching the bowl, swaying as she walked.

The Greek asked her something and she nodded then croaked something at a young man who then ran off. Soon we had the water we needed and an old, rusty, but perfectly serviceable, chain. They offered us some food which we graciously declined. Fortunately, we didn't have to walk back because in the meanwhile the people in the other jeep, having exhausted their lust for killing, discovered our stranded car and came to our rescue.

Yes, Africa was indeed a land of many changes and contrasts. Khartoum, the capital of Sudan and the main seat of the British colony, was in many respects still very primitive in the early fifties. The greater part of the city had primitive housing, only slightly better than the little village we visited. Things like flushing toilets were to be found only in the sections which housed the British colonists and the government and in places like the Grand Hotel which is where we stayed.

The rest was provided with toilets which had big metal containers, or cans, beneath the toilet bench and in the early morning hours the "Khartoum Express," as the camel-driven wagon was called, drove through the city picking up its "load." If one happened to wake up in the middle of the night and go to the bathroom, he might sit there and hear a sudden, loud scraping noise beneath him breaking the silence of the night and the can would be pulled away in the middle of his activity. The collectors of these cans were not about to wait.

I heard a story about an Englishman driving home late at night from the club, drunk. He must have been really soused because there is no mistaking the aroma of the 'express' once it hits you. Of course, it depended on which way the wind was blowing. Anyway, the old chap, driving in his small convertible – fast – smashed head on into the side of the wagon leisurely crossing an intersection. Several of the cans turned over and – you guessed it – he was covered with shit. Actually, he was perfectly all right, not a scratch on him, but he died anyway. People speculated it was out of sheer disgust. Whether it's true of not, who can tell? You get to hear many a story late at night when a gust of wind brings a whiff of the familiar ole stench and with it all sorts of things to mind.

Asmara, on the other hand, was very modern. The Italians, unlike the British who did very little for their colonies outside of exploiting them, tried to act more civilized about the whole thing. Mussolini is reputed to have spent several billions of lire each year on Eritrea. That's why there was such a vast difference between those two countries, and it wasn't just the climate and logistics.

Asmara, the capital of Eritrea, which, at the time I was there, was an English territory, was an exquisite little town high in the Hamasen Mountains, and could have just as well been anywhere in Europe. It had a mild Mediterranean climate and when the winter rains were plentiful the cactus pears were big and juicy as nowhere else. Children, their hands roughened by the tiny, irksome stickers, would sell them along the road smiling their happy, self-assured smiles defying anyone to feel sorry for them. Whatever they may have been suffering from, it wasn't emotional poverty. I think that's the one surprising facet of the African personality which I found so puzzling and moving.

To my fondest memories belongs the Red Sea some forty miles away from the city. The roads leading to it were absolutely fantastic, full of sharp curves, descending rapidly. Built by the Italians, they were curved to allow comfortable driving at an even pace.

Leaving the high ground behind, descending to the Sea, the climate changed drastically to the intense African heat except here it was also very humid. The road we traveled took us to Massawa, a tiny coastal town. I have never swam in saltier waters than the Red Sea's. Warm, and soft with the high salinity, it would let you float effortlessly for hours. When I dried in the scorching sun, my skin was white with salt crystals. White smooth sand, the thousands of tiny, racing crabs, the palms, the thatched huts strewn haphazardly along the endless deserted beaches, the almost empty resort hotel baking in the sun, all those are clear, beautiful memories I can conjure up whenever I please – as long as I live.

But Africa is also memories of sand storms, of standing in a whirlwind of gritty, blinding particles unable to see even my hand and feeling lost – utterly lost.

Africa is also an unexpected safari and I, making like the big white hunter, shooting birds and whatever came handy, and finally two young, unsuspecting leopards, cornered and shot down without mercy, who found their way into the sleeves of my leopard coat, my long-treasured trophy of that insane adventure. Fortunately, the coat is long gone, the victim of a burglary, but the memory of that brutal, exhibitionistic kid will haunt me forever.

We almost made it to Saudi Arabia – the Holy Land – because some American officers of the forces manning the oil installations saw us and liked us so much they asked King Saud to give special permission for us to come and entertain them. The King denied their request. He must have felt they represented a sufficient number of "intruders" and that the oil concessions were one thing, but the hell with the entertainment. Still, he came to see what it was that prompted the officers to approach him with such an unrealistic request. To me he was just another Arab in caftan and fez.

I was sorry about it though because they'd have flown us there in a military plane reserved for the top-brass and later all the way to Istanbul.

Since the grandiose plan of the American military once again fell through, we took off directly for Istanbul on our own steam, that is, in an ordinary, everyday plane reserved for ordinary everyday people.

But after what seemed like a long time in the Middle East, we were on our way back to Europe.

Although it was just a stopover, Istanbul was important for several reasons. One – it was there that Jonny finally agreed to change his style of costume. We found an excellent English tailor who faithfully followed my design and against all expectations, Jonny was surprised to find the suit was also comfortable to work in.

In Istanbul I also found a sympathetic Austrian Vice-Consul who offered to help me with my studies so I would often travel across the Bosporus to the Asiatic side of Istanbul where the Consulate was located. I loved it. Dr. Vorndran improved on the plan of studies I was assigned and suggested enough reading material to last me for years. It had nothing to do with my studies, but it was a most fascinating list. It was he who encouraged me to read as many books as I could in the original language which is indeed a great way to keep them up.

Istanbul had the kind of romantic quality that appealed to me immensely at the time. There was a small island in the middle of the Bosporus which I used to pass on my way to the Consulate with an ancient, tiny castle where a Sultan kept his daughter to prevent the prediction, that she would be bitten by a snake and die, from coming true. The legend had it that at night her lover would swim across to see his princess. Evidently, a snake had the same idea and the princess died as predicted. Whenever I saw the islet I'd gaze at it with the wistful contemplation of a budding romanticist, and I think I even shed a tear or two for the sad fate of the lovely princess.

The place we appeared at was a huge, modern club which looked like a representative house, beautiful and imposing, situated in the midst of a lovely park filled with bronze statuary. I remember vividly an enormous painting of Kemal Ataturk hanging in the main room which inspired me to start painting again. The victim of this new adventure was the door of my dressing room on which I painted a life-size self portrait and was shattered I couldn't take it along.

The Cassino du Taxim, as the place was called, although no gambling of any kind went on there, was owned by an elderly couple who treated me like the child they never had. Anything I wanted, I could have. I ate mountains of caviar – every single day – and some fantastic mushroom dish the old lady had the cook make up for me whenever I wanted it. Thus my diet, during our entire stay there, consisted of those two dishes exclusively. I never got tired of either. To this day it remains my favorite food and even supersedes dumplings. Come to think of it, caviar and dumplings sounds like a combination worth trying. (The trouble is that the only place I found served good caviar, not that salty mush one finds in those little jars, was Club 21 in New York.)

While in Istanbul, we got an offer to join an Italian Revue heading for Mexico. That, of course, was a tempting offer. Finally, we would be heading toward the American continent. The salary wasn't fantastic but the air transportation, including excess luggage of which there was plenty, was paid. The rest of the company went via boat. My excitement was indescribable.

CHAPTER FIFTEEN

With the visas and everything all set, we flew from Rome to New York where we were to switch planes. The trip was fantastic. The plane we took had berths, somewhat like a couchette on a train, where I spent a few hours of restless sleep, and on boarding all female passengers, me included, were given an orchid and a small vial of perfume. The president line, or something.

In New York we learned that our connecting plane wouldn't depart until the following day. Having only transit visas, we were carefully guarded and escorted to the hotel where we were to spend the night. But once there, we were left on our own, to do as we wished. It made absolutely no sense to me, all the ridiculous precautions at the airport and then leaving us alone – free to do whatever they feared an "alien" in such a situation would be apt to do in the 'land of the free.'

But New York was a gigantic disappointment to me. The city I painted in my imagination with such golden colors was a filthy mess, the lofty skyscrapers intimidating and stifling and the food atrocious. I was actually relieved to leave again.

California! It had to be California – where the sun shone forever and life was free and easy... Someday...

Meanwhile – it was Mexico. The guy who footed the bill and brought the Italian Revue of some 80 people was a rich Mexican of Italian descent who didn't know what else to do with his money. I found that aspect of Mexico appalling. Such wealth and extravagance in face of so much poverty, squalor, and misery.

Anyway, we found the advertisements of the "fresh Italian Imports" splattered all over the city. Mexico City was a mess of placards uglyfying every available wall. In this announcement of the Revue, headed by an impressive line of "stars," we found our names in tiny letters at the bottom of the bill. The memorable occasion was to take place at a lovely old theater, the Esperanza Iris. Today, it's a dilapidated old building ready to fall apart but at the time, it had just the right ring of status and respectability to it. The style was pseudo-baroque, the condition, filthy – but old Oriani was spending money to have it cleaned and freshened up, and it felt like a real honest-to-goodness theater – not a nightclub, and the Revue looked more legit than the usual run-of-the-mill kind. To do it justice, the Italian company was indeed good and would, even today, put many a Las Vegas show to shame – certainly in class and originality. It was indeed class all the way. Good dancers, great costumes and scenery and good choreography.

The whole thing was put together by the wife of the lead dancer who was uncharacteristically straight-looking (for a dancer, that is) and ruggedly handsome, sort of a Richard Burton type. But his wife, obviously the brain of the whole operation, remained in Italy and he took up with the lead singer and made her the star of the show. She was a rather cute petite blonde with a small but disagreeable voice and they put her into the most sumptuous costumes to hide her obvious inefficacy.

The comic, a thoroughly hideous little man suffering from delusions of grandeur, who was promised the starring spot had colic seizures over it. Two of his greatest delusions were that he believed himself to be the world's greatest comic – a genius superseding even Chaplin, and that he was irresistible to women. In that department, however, he didn't do so well with Tina, the singing "star." They were about the same size, he looking like an ugly, skinny leprechaun, and they would stand there yelling at each other gesturing wildly in the typical Italian way. I thought it was rather entertaining on the whole. Actually, as it turned out, not one of the great assemblage of "stars" was content with his or her spot in the show or the size or place of his name on the program. Thus, crisis followed crisis. At one time or another, everyone threatened to walk out of the show. Since we arrived late, no one was quite sure yet what to make of us, and we were contented to be left out of their constant bickering. Jonny didn't even protest all too strenuously about the humblest billing they afforded us.

But immediately after the opening night, all that changed. We were such a hit, everyone was overwhelmed. The audience cheered and gave us a standing ovation. I'd never seen anything like it. But later I learned that that was rather typical in Mexico. When they happen to like you, they go all out. The next day the breathlessly awaited reviews were disappointing to most of the "stars." The show itself however, was a hit and ranged from extravagant praises to: "...And here are the real stars of the show..."

Instantly, we were on everyone's hit-list, particularly since the management immediately changed all the advertisements, ads and programs to comply with the verdict of the press. And the press, who felt they "discovered" us, really got on the bandwagon. The papers were constantly full of pictures, huge layouts and interviews: gossip columns reported regularly on everything I did or did not do, whom we saw, where we went, what we said, whom Jonny was dating, etc. There were constant television appearances, radio interviews, parties in our honor, and of course, lots of benefits for all sorts of "good causes." The movie stars from Maria Felix to Cantinflas were inviting us to all sorts of parties: important business people were vying for our favors and we were frequent guests at the President's villa, on trips in his private yacht, and an airline owner put a private plane at our constant disposal because word got out I liked to swim and where else could I do it better than in Acapulco, right? What can I say? They adored me. I was the "most beautiful," "most talented," the "child-woman" – the intangible something they chose to glorify. I couldn't walk on the street without having a crowd of people gather, often even small, snotty children with big, adoring eyes running after me begging for autographs. Elegant restaurants were hanging my old discarded toe shoes on the walls like some rare trophies. Picture contracts were shoved at me, five, ten-year contracts which Jonny gently, but firmly, refused. The only offers he accepted were for films where we would do nothing but dance.

How I felt about the sudden, unexpected rise to fame? I was not terribly happy. I don't know why – I often wondered why there was a constant, vague gnawing of discontent, an unsettling feeling of something amiss, of something that I still wanted. But I just couldn't find a definite answer anywhere. The offers from the U.S. were coming in and I still wasn't happy.

Part of that discontent, I suppose, were "growing pains." I began to be interested in all the guys constantly eyeing me. But here, "Daddy" was firm. The young son of the man who brought the revue to Mexico was always around. Jonny would allow him to take me out dancing but this always happened under his watchful eye. I was furious. Most often, however, he'd pack me off to sleep "after all, there's a rehearsal tomorrow and you mustn't get overtired," and then he'd go out with one of his many girlfriends and have a ball. I felt it was shitty. Life was a drag and there was no way out for me. I got tired of benefits, or presidential parties, of giving interviews, of smiling my thanks to compliments. Nothing seemed real or genuine. I couldn't go and see anything – there were people everywhere, people that recognized me and wouldn't let me alone. The show went on and on, and I was getting tired of it.

Since we were swamped with offers it was hard to decide where to go. There was New York – Latin Quarter and Radio City Music Hall which we were negotiating with. Then Hollywood – Cocoanut Grove. Havana – Tropicana.

In Acapulco, Teddy Stauffer, suffering from grave financial pains, decided he might as well cash in on our popularity and asked us to come and appear at "La Perla." I took one look at the "stage," which was a balcony hanging over a sheer cliff and said forget it! Not to be deterred, he decided to take over a seaside club for the occasion. I think that was the first deal I negotiated myself. Jonny knew Teddy when he had a band in Switzerland so Teddy tried to use "old friend-ship" as a bargaining ploy. But since I decided to negotiate myself, he had to content himself with me, and I am sure he thought it would be a cinch. "Look honey," he'd say coaxingly, "I know you'll love it here. It'll be like a four week vacation in Acapulco, all expenses paid, the finest hotel and everything, and you'll make some money on top. What do you say, angel?"

"How much?" I said laconically trying to appear bored.

"I'd be willing to go as high as $1,600," he said with a fine, generous flair.

"$4,000," I said never flinching an eyelid.

Both Jonny and Teddy stared at me flabbergasted.

"He'll never pay that much," Jonny hissed in Hungarian. But I was just sick and tired of being constantly told what to do.

"But angel, I'm offering to pay for your vacation," Teddy managed to say reproachfully.

"I don't need a vacation," I declared matter-of-factly. "It's $4,000. Take it or leave it."

He gave me a curious look and said suddenly; "How old are you?"

"Nineteen," I said casually.

He glanced sharply at Jonny. "I heard rumors that she's only thirteen."

"Blodsinn." Jonny came up with his favorite deprecating remark.

But Teddy was looking at me again – peering inquisitively. "And rapidly going on thirty," he added, nodding his head.

And so it was $4,000 and it turned out to be a disaster – a personal disaster, that is.

The club was lovely. The big, round stage jutting out into the ocean was lit by soft spotlights which cast their reflections onto the ripply surface, wide, carpeted stairs led down from the street level and everywhere were lush, tropical plants. A tasteful production number and an excellent orchestra was all he backed us up with. And he sunk everything he had into it figuring it couldn't fail.

Actually, I was indeed happy to be there. I loved the tropics and in those days, Acapulco was a dream. I was also glad to have the opportunity to go on with my water-skiing over which I fought so hard with Jonny. At home I used to ski in the mountains and water-skiing certainly seemed easy enough.

I did very well for almost a week, and so did Teddy. The club was all booked up for weeks ahead.

Then one day, putting on my skis, I remarked to the instructor that the rubber binding seemed too tight. But he just smiled saying it was all right. I wasn't so sure, but then I figured he ought to know what he was talking about. And it did seem fine. For a while anyway. But soon, I got into some heavy waves of a crossing boat and fell. Of course, as I had suspected, my feet didn't slip out and I felt a sharp pull at my ankles and then, as I turned over under water, in my knee.

But finally I managed to get free of the skis and came up. It hurt terribly for a while but then it subsided and I was able to walk fine. But I still felt a little odd so I decided to just swim for a while. Soon it was time for my afternoon rest. That was something I hated but could never argue my way out of it. "You know salt water debilitates your muscles. You need to rest!" Jonny would always say and I had no argument against it. So I had to obey. That was another thing I despised. I could write business letters, negotiate deals but whenever it was convenient, he'd remind me sharply that I was "just a child" and that he was "legally responsible" for me. Bull!

Well, I laid down that day, not to nap, but to read as always. Actually that was the only time I could really stay quiet. After some time I happened to glance at my feet and gasped. My ankles were all blue and swollen and so was my knee. It was only when I tried to get up that I noticed the pain. I couldn't even stand on my feet.

Jonny was furious. I had danced with colds, the flu, and all sorts of aches because "the show must go on" for whatever insane reason, but this time, it seemed I was just not going to make it. Jonny called Teddy and gave him the bit of cheerful news. Teddy was at our hotel in record time and stared with horror at my swollen ankles. He was devastated.

"Perhaps it'll be all right in a few hours?" he suggested hopefully.

I shook my head. "I doubt it."

"Are you sure?" He seemed close to tears. "How can you be sure? Honey, could you at least try? I don't care what you do, but do something... please!"

I was exasperated. Couldn't he see I just couldn't? "I'd like to, but how?"

"Good God! I'm ruined! Ruined! Don't you see that? I'll go bankrupt! I've put everything I've got into this... I've borrowed... This was my last hope..." He was pacing the room in terrible agitation. "Look," he said taking my foot and beginning to rub my ankles. I winced. "Perhaps there is something that can be done. Of course!"

In the next instant he was on the phone calling his doctor. "He'll fix you up, you'll see."

I didn't see it at all, but I didn't say anything. He was completely irrational.

The doctor came, examined my poor limbs and shook his head. "This will take longer to heal than a fracture."

Teddy groaned. "How long?"

"If she stays off her feet, four weeks, perhaps."

Teddy stared. "Isn't there something to kill the pain so she can dance tonight?" But the doctor refused to oblige him and find some miraculous cure. All he did was prescribe some ointment and told me to keep it bandaged. Both Jonny and Teddy were rubbing the smelly stuff on my feet and Teddy kept repeating: "It'll be all right you'll see. You'll be all right..."

The damn thing burned so I hardly felt anything else, and I begged them to stop.

"But don't you see, honey? That's good! That's great!" he yelled enthusiastically. "That way you won't feel the pain."

"Teddy, I'm sorry, but I don't think I..."

"Don't say it..." he looked at me imploringly. "Try honey, won't you at least try? Please! You don't know what this means to me..."

I couldn't stand it. I had no idea how I could do it, but I

agreed to try. Also there was Jonny looking at me with holy wrath and his: "I told you not to do it" look. And I was eager to make up for my transgression.

I spent the rest of the day soaking my feet and applying the ointment. In the evening I thought I was ready to "try" it.

Teddy and Jonny carried me down the steps leading to the club – I just couldn't make it. Steps are the worst thing for sprained ankles. To put my toe shoes on was out of the question. I had to dance in my rehearsal shoes. Over the thick bandages I could barely get them on. When I looked at myself I could have cried. I looked like a race horse and there was no telling the tight bandages would help any-way.

Teddy watched with growing despair. Suddenly he disap-peared and returned shortly with a double Scotch only lightly laced with soda and ice. "Drink it."

I looked at it with distaste. "But I don't drink." I protested.

"Well, you will tonight. It'll help you. Here!"

I sniffed at it and pushed it away. "It smells like medicine."

"That's right, honey, it's medicine."

He made me drink it all. It tasted as bad as it smelled but very soon I was so high I thought I could fly through the act. My ankles no longer bothered me, and I was cheerful and optimistic about the whole thing.

I will never forget that night. I got out on that stage floating – but as soon as I started on the first step, the pain was so excruciating I turned cold sober and tears sprung into my eyes. I really don't know how I finished but it felt like an eternity and when I got into the dress-ing room I wept for hours with the agony of it.

I hobbled through that engagement feeling I was giving the worse performance of my life, but Teddy was presumably 'saved.' It took four months before my ankles were well again – four months before I could dance in toe shoes again.

Today, Teddy is "Mr. Acapulco" and I wonder whether he even remembers it all.

Needless to say, I never skied again – water or snow. I spent the remaining days in Acapulco floating in the pool, or baking my skin to deep tan, eating, reading, anything but walking, preparing myself mentally for the ordeal each evening. I think the club was packed with people, who, seeing me around the pool hobbling like a cripple, were curious to see how I could do it.

CHAPTER SIXTEEN

Earlier, we had accepted an engagement at the Latin Quarter in New York. We had applied for visas and were waiting for them to be granted. (The word was granted, not issued.) It was taking terribly long and whenever I called the American Embassy, the answer was the same: they were still checking on our information. No one can possibly imagine how tedious a procedure it was. The application for visas entailed filling out numerous, lengthy questionnaires, stating all the places one has ever been or lived. One had to turn one's life inside out for the inspection and scrutiny of cool, impersonal government officials.

That is something I've always detested, partly because my mother passed her own fear of authority onto me and partly because it went basically against my grain. Perhaps it also was because as long as I can remember we were tainted with the stigma of being "foreign." In the country I was born, my mother was born, because she happened to have married a foreigner, we were all considered foreign. The absurdity of these things has always struck me as totally irrational and idiotic.

From my father's teachings, his beliefs and convictions, there is one thing I managed to grasp – the feeling of internationality. And that is another important aspect of the Marxist ideology that got lost in its translation into practice. And to my way of thinking, it's probably the one most important, most valuable aspect of it. It makes much more sense to feel allegiance to all of mankind, to the whole planet, rather than to a specific piece of land divided by man-made borders. To me the whole concept was limiting, vision narrowing, restrictive, and, in the final analysis, antihuman. In those days I only knew I hated the meddling of impersonal, unfeeling bureaucrats into one's personal affairs.

After constant calling, inquiring, we nevertheless became quite friendly with one of the officials of the American Embassy in Mexico City. Even he had to finally admit that it was taking unusually long. The date of our debut in the U.S. was approaching rapidly but still no visa. Finally we were told by our friend in all confidence, that someone in the U.S. had gone to the immigration authorities denouncing Jonny as a communist.

Jonny was flabbergasted, but his incredulity soon gave way to a terrible rage. After all the years of painstakingly evading any political involvement, refusing to even think about politics! In his justified anger, he insisted on knowing who the informant was, insisting there had to be an ulterior motive behind such a lie.

At the Embassy they admitted they suspected as much but nevertheless had to carry out an intensive investigation of the matter before granting the visa and that we had better postpone our opening date. And that's all they would tell us. No amount of coaxing could induce them to divulge the source of the information. I thought these rules were very unfair, but there was nothing we could do. But Jonny was determined to find out who was behind it. He had a few Hungarian friends in New York and he immediately wrote letters asking them for the names of people who would be most likely to benefit from our being kept out of the country.

Meanwhile, Lou Walters, the proprietor of the Latin Quarter had to be notified of the delay and we accepted another engagement to tide us over until the matter was cleared up. We chose to accept the offer from the Tropicana in Havana, Cuba. Lou Walters, however, refused to believe the story about the visa, claiming we must have gotten a better offer from the Tropicana and preferred to go there. I was furious and wrote him an indignant letter saying I found his attitude insulting and in view of his insinuations, would not consider appearing in his club at all, and he should therefore forget the whole deal.

Needless to say, I was dreadfully disappointed. My first encounter with the irrationality and paranoia of suspicion, which I until then presumed to be the sole prerogative of my mother and Jonny, left me full of exasperation and helpless anger.

I went to Havana feeling as if I were going into exile. But not for long. The island, with its tropical climate heavy with humidity, rich with lush vegetation, cooled by breezes tasting of the sea, blacks and whites seemingly mixing with great informality and ease, was a storybook place to me. If it wasn't as it seemed at first glance, I never had the chance to find out although I spent there some nine months. My world there consisted of the club and a lovely villa we leased in an exclusive oceanside community, the Marianao. Our reputation preceded us and so the treatment we received there was a continuation of the adulation I enjoyed in Mexico.

The Tropicana, huge, elegant and imaginatively designed, remains the most beautiful club I've ever seen or appeared at. The design was simple and effective. A series of arches of increasing sizes, connected by great, curving spans of plate glass revealing lush, tropical gardens in which the club was built, gave a feeling of spaciousness yet at the same time provided an intimate atmosphere. A gigantic semicircle glass wall enclosing the last, and largest arch, black marble, waterfall cascading down a mountainous rock, a huge tree jutting through the ceiling overgrown with plants, those were the first sights one encountered when entering the showroom. The arches, diminishing to a smaller semicircle of glass which formed the back of the stage, were covered with dark, acoustical spray, in which tiny lights shimmered like stars. Thick red rugs effectively muffled any sound which might destroy the feel of softness and tranquility.

The club also had an outdoor showroom which was used in the summer months. The designer seemed to have worked with utmost care and respect for those old, lovely gardens, taking advantage of the trees and plants rather than disturbing them. Here, the stage was set against a dense wall of ancient trees which spread their gnarled arms over the stage and laced their branches through a gigantic, abstract sculpture of metal bars which was erected behind the stage separating it from the orchestra. When lighted, it resembled a myriad of oddly twisted neon tubes.

Everything about the place was lavish, yet tasteful from the showrooms and the casino to the show itself. During my travels I found that it can be said there is such a thing as a natural character although there is an exception to every rule. The Cubans were warm, friendly people unpretentious and informal. Whatever class distinctions there were, and there had to be many, at first glance they seemed nonexistent. The people were curiously devoid of inhibitions and artifice.

The owners of the club, whom I didn't meet until much later because they were content to let the manager run it without too many interferences as if it was his own place, were simple, good-natured people who were quite contented to stay in the background. The stout, pink-cheeked couple rather resembled someone's favorite aunt and uncle than the owners of a casino. If the place was a marvel, it was because to them, that club was their 'child' and they tended and babied it with all the love and devotion they would have showered on their own offspring had they had any.

We found ourselves headlining a fine show, studded with excellent productions that sparkled with fresh, imaginative ideas. When I saw the show for the first time, before we opened, I was amazed to see the cast project an unusual amount of élan and enthusiasm. This was due, I was told, to the choreographer-producer they were justifiably proud of. I imagined he would have to be a sharp, powerful man, a strong dancer himself, who could inspire the cast to such enthusiastic performances. I was most astonished when I was introduced to an odd little creature who came toward us shuffling on his heels as if he had no toes and spoke with a croaking, strained voice that seemed to fight its way out of worn-out vocal cords, brittle and cracking with the exertion. He was old and ugly, a mere wisp, a ruin of a man, his fingers like gnarled, deformed claws, talons devoid of flesh and only the long, curved nails were sharp-looking and prominent. When he shook my hand, all I could feel was the pressure of those nails. Obviously, the man was sick, but I couldn't discover what it was. Either no one knew, which seemed unlikely, or for some odd reason pretended not to know. Finally someone mentioned that he had had polio but that sounded improbable and, at any rate, evasive.

There was hardly a time when he didn't have at least a couple of band-aids on his fingers. Whatever disease he had, it seemed to be shrinking him.

He was also a homosexual, but in spite of his many obvious handicaps, he never lacked the devotion of a young, good-looking boy friend.

Later, I was asked whether I would participate in a production he would build around me and the act. I was glad Jonny agreed to it. As soon as the press got wind of it, we were swamped with interviews. One newsman covering the event for "Bohemia" wanted pictures of me working with Rodney on the choreography. His photographer was shooting away while Rodney was showing me some Afro-Cuban steps. The pressure of his bony fingers on my bare shoulder was rather unpleasant. Apparently he had no feeling in them because he used his nails to apply pressure. I felt pain and knew he must have broken the skin. I didn't want to say anything but I was glad when it was over. After Rodney had left, the newsman insisted on putting some disinfectant on it. It wasn't anything much and I was sorry I had mentioned it. I was puzzled by the conscientiousness with which he attended to so insignificant a scratch rubbing it with alcohol and mercurochrome with great care and vigor. It was then that he told us that Rodney had leprosy. I was horrified. Rodney, the brilliant choreographer-producer was a queer leper! I remembered with horror how often I shook his hand, felt the strangely unpleasant clasp of his bandaged fingers. I shuddered. Those band-aids were holding together disintegrating flesh! And now this! Why didn't someone tell me sooner! The newsman, still rubbing the scratch, assured me it wasn't contagious as it had been contained by some serum. It didn't cure it, he said, but it arrested the disease in the state it was.

"So what are you doing that for!" I wanted to know. He bore my challenging stare with a confident grin. An unnecessary precaution, and to prevent a minor infection. Not daring to trust him, we discussed the matter with a doctor and were reassured that I had absolutely nothing to fear.

And the preparation for the production went on. Rodney's specialty was African, or Afro-Cuban type of productions which he structured like a primitive ballet. As such, each had its own abstract kind of story.

The production, or I should say ballet, which he had in mind for me, was based on the voodoo rites still in wide use throughout Cuba. In African, or Afro-Cuban dancing, the main thing is the rhythm. Before beginning to set one single step, Rodney took me to an authentic voodoo ritual. They used to be held in great secrecy, attended only by the 'initiated,' or the 'regulars.'

We drove to the outskirts of the city, to the slums of Havana. But even here, the people had the same carefree spirit which seemed the one unifying aspect of the Cuban character in general and reminded me so much of Africa.

The place we went to was someone's home and the gathering was congregated in a large room almost devoid of any furniture. When we arrived the meeting was already under way. Three half-naked blacks, their skins glistening with sweat, were at the congas – their eyes closed – beating the taut skins with entranced persistency. The room was packed with people of various ages and shapes sitting on the floor, swaying gently with the rhythm. It sounded very African and reminded me of the bush men I saw dancing in the African desert.

The floor around the congas was crowded with plates of food that I had trouble identifying. Each new arrival contributed something, then laid down on the floor, touched the floor with one hip, then the other, finally with his lips and taking a morsel of food, got up to find a place to sit. There were fewer and fewer places to find. All the windows were open and I could see the darkening sky through the slits in the bamboo shades billowing in the breeze. But it did little to relieve the heat in the room intensifying with each new arrival.

At first, I insisted on standing, even though I was dressed

casually, as Rodney had suggested, but later, getting tired and hot, I knelt to sit down on my heels. The floor was stone and felt pleasantly cool. I glanced at the people around me. Everyone swayed and chanted, eyes closed, completely absorbed in the rhythm of the beat. The chant consisted of some erratic, improvised, but curiously blending shouts, staccato jabbering and deep humming. I tried to penetrate into the sound and it felt curiously soothing and at the same time exhilarating. Gradually the drums and chant were getting louder and faster, as if gathering momentum – the persistent, hypnotic beat seemed to echo in some remote part of my brain – diminishing to a tiny point which rose to the very top of my skull battering away at it – threatening to break right through. I was pushing it away, trying to broaden it – I opened my eyes, and it was only then that I became aware I was swaying with the rest.

The volume of the sounds around me was still growing until it reached a frantic, feverish pitch and suddenly I heard a terrific shriek – a scream that shook the whole room – and I saw a fat Negro woman thrashing on the floor amidst the swaying bodies. She screamed again and again as if in mortal agony while the chant, drums and everything flowed together until it was a roar in my ears like some gigantic waterfall – interrupted only by the woman's horrible screams. I shook my head like a wet poodle – trying to clear my head. Then I felt the pressure of Rodney's bony hand on my shoulder.

"Vamonos, muneca..."

I got up and staggered out of there feeling strangely incomplete as if I had failed to finish something. Still there was also a feeling of lightness and strange peace. For the moment I had the feeling that the irksome, persistent drive, that powerful something within me urging me on and on was stilled for a while and I could breathe freer.

Years later, when I came across a book extolling the virtues of screaming as the basis for a 'new, miraculous' therapy promising to cure all mental disorders 'discovered' by a trumper-player-turned-psychologist, I would remember the screaming woman and realize that what I had witnessed there was an ancient, primitive form of psychotherapy practiced by Africans since who knows when. Apparently, nothing is ever really new. Who knows how many things today, assumed to be someone's brilliant, new revolutionary discovery are in reality ancient practices or remedies – rediscovered, restated, only slightly improved upon, if at all.

At that time, however, I had no way of figuring out just what the whole thing was all about. Even the few vague, intuitive feelings I came away with were diluted by my overriding concern of how it could be translated into a ballet and how the hell I would ever be able to duplicate that scream.

It's been only lately that I've come to realize how much more inhibited – uptight, ego-centered – the white race is and therefore more neurotic. We just don't have the capacity to let go like that and rid ourselves of the restrictive mental hang-ups.

Driving back, I sat next to Rodney – silent – absorbed in my thoughts. But the memory of those people back there kept coming back – how content and relaxed they seemed – accepting their lot with such serenity – the serenity of poverty? Can there really be such a thing? Years later Bob Dylan would write: When you got nothing – you got nothing to lose. They indeed had nothing – but whatever they did have, they gladly shared. They lived from hand to mouth – but it seemed to bother them little. I never saw such peace in the eyes of the rich people I met. I found these thoughts disconcerting, bristling with more and more questions for which I could find no answers. And there was no one to ask.

"It will work fine," I heard Rodney say confidently and glancing at him I saw his satisfied grin. "I think you really got the feel of it – right down in your gut – that's where it counts."

I was still dazed. "What happened to the woman?" I wanted to know.

"She was taken by the spirit – later it has to be shaken out of her."

The spirit? I thought. She looked psychotic.

"Words, what do words mean? – Spirit? Psychotic? – What does it matter? She will be cleansed and feel much better afterwards."

"I see..." I said not really seeing at all. Rodney sat there with his eyes closed clucking to himself contentedly. Jonny, sitting up front next to our driver, threw an amused grin in my direction and shrugged his shoulders.

"The story will be of a white girl belonging to a voodoo sect," Rodney croaked suddenly, spinning his tale behind his closed eyes. "In the midst of all the blacks there'll be this white, fragile thing, dressed like a queen and before it's over, she'll be reduced to a shrieking, raving madwoman. It'll be the best thing I've ever done."

Great, I thought. I was to yell and scream like that woman back there? But soon, certain possibilities began to hit me. The process of thrashing about and shaking out the spirit, could be turned into a stunning, wild dance full of lifts and we could use the boys and have them toss me back and forth – then into various lifts and so on. It occurred to me that we might be able to put that sculpture to some interesting use.

But my fantasies were one thing and reality another. I hadn't even begun to cope with the major problem. Being raised by my mother, and now by Jonny who in many ways was even more restrictive than her, in spite of my self-assured, confident, grown-up front, I was a pretty inhibited kid and I kept worrying about the screaming part of it. Just thinking about it filled me with the hot, unpleasant flush of embarrassment. No – I just couldn't see myself being able to do that. It seemed too silly and I was convinced I didn't have acting talent worth a bean. I argued with myself that ballet was indeed acting as well – still pantomiming a dying swan was a far cry from the kind of yelling I would have to come up with. But there was no turning back. I was committed. Besides, I wouldn't have admitted what was bothering me for the world.

However, Rodney was right about one thing. I did get the feel of that rhythm. In fact, I felt as if I had just experienced the very essence of all rhythm. It's simply the capacity to push all rational thought and inhibition aside and resign your whole being to that mesmerizing beat and letting your body do whatever that rhythm seems to convey. Once you get adjusted to it, the rest is easy.

The transformation of the primitive, basic steps (which too reminded me of the bushmen's) through the already instinctive technique of the classical dance to ritualistic steps is then automatic and almost unconscious. Rodney actually knew very little about ballet, and next to nothing about its basic rules and techniques. But he had an instinctive feel for the dynamics of dance and a natural understanding and talent for the structure and development of a danced 'story.' Handicapped as he was, for his toes were as shrunken, unfeeling and therefore useless as his fingers, he attacked the problem with such energy and persistence that even a perfectly healthy individual would find hard to maintain. He would hop around on his heels, demonstrating what he wanted the dancers to do, and cracked instructions in that hoarse, sandpaper voice of his and everyone was ready to work till exhaustion. I soon learned to take his basic idea and transform it to my own style.

All through the rehearsals, I only marked the part where I had to do the screaming. I was still unable to get into it. But I knew, and I knew Rodney knew, and he knew that I knew that he knew – (to be quite specific) that this was my weak point and that I had serious doubts whether I could ever make myself do it. But he said nothing. He was accepting my ploy with nothing more than an occasional glance. But that fleeting, probing glance was enough. I knew he was waiting. For on that one single thing depended the success of the entire production. Could I really act out convincingly the part of that crazed woman I saw writhing on the cold stone floor? I didn't know – and I was afraid to find out.

We had the whole thing all set and it was still a big question. Since I obviously didn't have the necessary faith in myself, I couldn't see why Rodney should. I could see how important this production was to him. He really did look at it as the high point of his career. He felt it was the most audacious thing he'd ever tried.

The whole production, which he called, "El Omelenco," lasted over half an hour which is very long for a nightclub production. He hired the same conga players we had seen at the voodoo meeting and used many melodies and rhythms which were considered sacred or something and using them commercially was looked upon as a terrible trespass if not sacrilege. I thought it was just superstitious nonsense but the conga players cast doubtful, apprehensive glances at the proceedings while beating the hell out of those drums. Considering their misgivings, I don't know what Rodney did to persuade them to work there. Undoubtedly their needs must have been greater than their fear.

The last part of the ballet – I could never think of it as anything other than a bizarre, primitive ballet – was up to me. Jonny chose four of the strongest and ablest dancers and under Rodney's watchful eye, I put together a wild, surrealistic kind of dance. I was tossed up and tossed down, swung and spun and pulled at in a dramatization of 'shaking out the spirit.' In the final stage, I climbed the twenty-five foot tall sculpture until I reached a platform rigged up in the crown of the trees. Once there, a sharp, white spot would hit me and, waking up from the trance and realizing where I was, I would scream and throw myself down where Jonny would presumably catch me, assisted by the boys. It all worked fine – but I still hadn't uttered a peep. I took a neat dive from the twenty-five foot platform without a moment's hesitation – feeling no fear – but I was reluctant, or afraid, to give out a good, healthy scream. I used every excuse from sore throat to laryngitis.

Then there was the evening of the 'full' rehearsal. I stood there staring at the clear, starlit Cuban skies and the black silhouettes of the towering trees wondering...

Well, this was it – the moment of truth... but I panicked, literally panicked and once again managed to finagle my way out of doing it 'for real.' Having run out of excuses having to do with my throat – I developed terrible cramps and insisted it was an ulcer. I could fake that okay – why couldn't I fake a few screams? But no, there I had 'integrity.' It had to be good – it had to be 'real.'

Then, all of a sudden, it was opening night and I wondered where all the time had gone. But there it was – and there was I racking my brain, searching for some rationale to hang on to – I felt I needed one in order to do it. I was convinced that to do anything effectively and convincingly, one must have a reason for doing it – no matter how nebulous or far-fetched – it had to make some sort of sense. To be 'possessed by a spirit' was simply too abstract for me to grasp much less to relate to. So, I just had to find an alternative. The show was already under way and I still couldn't think of any.

I watched the beginning – the cast milling about, carrying

fruit, platters of food and small animals – the sacrifices offered – thought it looked damn good. The rhythm section came in.

> Me puede falter el pan, i no tener que comer,
> pero no me pue' falter, l'alegria de mi ritmo...
> (I can do without bread, without anything to
> eat, but I can't do without the joy of my
> rhythm...)

Rodney indeed had a fine sense for originality and his translation of the gathering of the crowd into dance was an exciting collage of vibrant colors and movement. Nothing looked too staged or repetitious, nothing out of place. Every touch fitted perfectly. The animals, the old man hobbling around chanting wildly – I was only hoping the animals wouldn't shit on the stage.

All these thoughts were distracting me from my objective – I still hadn't come up with anything.

Then I was on. I laid down in front of those drums and went through the whole business trying not to appear distracted or absent-minded, but my brain was racing. Just one – one single, plausible reason to scream!

Anger, rage? At what? No, that wouldn't do... Fear? Of what?... Suddenly I thought of Asmara and 'my attack of nerves,' or hysteria, or whatever it was. Of course, that was it! When the pressures, anxieties and stresses become too much – wham! The release valve goes off. Suddenly it was crystal clear how I would do it. The mere thought of it brought the distant but well remembered exasperation – the feeling of bottled-up despair – rising like a suffocating wave of nausea that had to be spat out...

I grabbed at it and held it – nurturing it. The maddening staccato of the drums increased the tension driving it to new heights and its inevitable end. That's what the woman must have felt – the mounting tension – the insane need to vomit out all the shit one has to take, the urge to be rid of the bitter taste of swallowed anger, tears and frustration. The need to let it build up until you don't give a damn until the "I," rebelling against all restrictive, suffocating shit heaped upon us every day, forgets itself and lets the fury erupt uncensored – uncaring – exploding all the muck – sending it in great, engulfing, yet liberating waves, shooting out – screaming out with all the fury of pent-up centuries of resentment and pain.

I screamed and screamed, and this time, mercifully, no one was putting ice on my forehead, no one was calming me down – it felt fantastic! I was on the floor relishing to the fullest the great, total release. As if through a haze, I saw the white, startled faces of the people sitting close – frozen into awesome immobility. Each face was a mirror of awe and wonder, apprehension tottering on the brink of appreciation.

My second observing "I" seemed to be guiding me through the routine parts. I slipped automatically from the improvised part into the set routine, maintaining the steps – the tempo.

Lying limply – spent for the moment – I was carried about high in Jonny's hands. I caught a glimpse of the conga players – their eyes wide with fear... I saw them upside down, but I could see, or rather, feel their fright. Well, the hell with your superstition, I thought – it's almost over, mi negritos...

I slid down and snaked my way to the sculpture and began to climb up the fine, luminous metal bars, delicate and fragile, looking like long tubes of cold, blue light stretching up high.

The idea was that they couldn't shake out the spirit, and the possessed – that is I – trying to elude them, climbed up into the trees – and to her death.

I climbed with such realistic laboriousness that it seemed a real chore to make it up there although it was usually a breeze. I had ways to make it appear as if I were really falling and I used every one. I could hear the audience gasp as I let go and slid down a few paces.

Getting up there finally, I stared aghast at the scene below. It looked like a snake-pit and somehow much higher than I remembered it. But – my God – I'd made it!

The spot hit me and I screamed my last scream and dove.

Those bastards! Instead of helping Jonny catch me, as it was rehearsed, they crouched and covered their cowardly heads. Although Jonny caught me all right, my back hit their bodies and it knocked the air out of me. There was no way I could get up. I lay there, gasping for breath like a fish out of water and my back felt broken. Jonny, with a fine presence of mind, instead of letting me slide to the floor where I was to lie till the blackout and then scoot out, carried me in his arms, my body dangling lifeless close to the floor.

Then, blackout – and screaming – except this time it was the audience. They yelled and cheered while Jonny, having whisked me out of there, was rubbing my back while I attempted to get my breath back.

"Can you make it?"

I took a few shuddering breaths and nodded.

God, how can anyone describe the triumph! I felt half-dead, that sound was sweet music to my ears. I looked down at the enraptured faces that only a short while ago registered such shock and incredulity, and took another bow.

Christ! With all the shit, the traveling and packing and living in countless, faceless hotel rooms, never having a spot to call home, with all that – it was worth it. It was well worth it – at that moment anyway.

CHAPTER SEVENTEEN

Only my father – my father never saw me dance except that one performance so long ago – he never really saw the best of me – and that,
by God, was one of those times. What the hell are we doing these
things for anyway? I want to know!

My back was killing me and the blacks were nodding knowingly. Didn't they say so? There are some things one should leave
alone.

What idiocy, I thought, but I was furious. In all the time I'd
worked with Jonny, I hadn't been hurt – not once. And now, just
because of those morons...

But the following night something else happened. During the
final part, one dancer, Miguel, was carrying me across his shoulder.
Two others, Henry and Cayetano, were to take my hands and feet and
Miguel would then throw me off his shoulder and I'd go into a swing.
Henry and Cayetano would swing me a couple of times more and then
toss me full force, sending me flying in a wide arch to land with my
back in Jonny's hand.

Well, there I am, dangling across Miguel's shoulder and he's
strutting across the stage in some wild step. I see Henry and Cayetano

are nowhere near, let alone having a firm hold of my limbs – but I feel Miguels' hand already sneaking beneath my back to toss me off. NO! NOOO!! I am screaming but, of course, he can't hear me in all the racket, and if he could, he'd think I'm into my raving act, and so he gives a smart heave.

I am falling, again on my back – but being arched, fortunately it's my head that takes the brunt of the fall and since I have a thick braid coiled around my long, flaring hair, it acts as a cushion and absorbs the power of the impact. As it is, my already sore back protests vehemently and I see a fine burst of stars in front of my vision. Henry and Cayetano stare at me flabbergasted. I reach out and they quickly comprehend they are to pick me up off the floor. One wide swing, then another and I'm flying... The audience roars, completely unaware they've witnessed another disaster.

Now the conga players are really spooked-out. They whisper furtively while fingering their beads.

But it's the third night that turns into the disaster. There is a part where Miguel, Cayetano and Henry are tossing me from one to the other and finally to Jonny who tosses me back, and I wind up lying in the arms of Henry and Miguel. Jonny takes my feet, they give a heave, and I am standing in Jonny's outstretched arms high above his head. There I twist and sway before he tosses me back to them. Well I am up there – about a little over seven feet it must be – and I feel him give a powerful heave and I'm flying, sideways – I see their upturned faces and their outstretched, waiting arms – nowhere near where I am about to land. Miguel, standing opposite with his back to the audience, sees what's about to happen and comes rushing in. He breaks the fall only slightly – I land with a crashing, horrible crunch on my hip. Thousand arrows of sharp pain shoot through me, but I twist and turn and keep on dancing. Good God! What kind of weird animals are we? What dark, terrible forces keep us going? I could be half dead, but I am intent upon keeping up the illusion that nothing has happened. Heaven forbid that the audience should realize something's gone wrong! And, of course, they didn't! "How realistic it is..." they will say later with appreciation.

I finish – I know not how – my hip feels like it's on fire burning until no feeling's left.

Backstage I gingerly peel off the tiny piece of brightly colored wisps of silk that's my costume and discover an angry red, swollen mark, the size, shape and color of a piece of raw steak. It's hard as a rock and hurts like hell!

Jonny is in a terrible rage. He's ready to kill them. A doctor is called in to comment on the steak on my hip.

I wind up with a lot of ice on my hip and it hurts so I can't even feel its scorching coldness. The thick, meaty piece there feels like something foreign – something that can't be part of me. My lovely, silken body deformed! Slightly narcissistic? You bet your life! I am ready to cry and sob – not so much for the pain of it – but the gross disfiguration of my beautiful, slender hip.

Needless to say, I danced the next night. If I danced with sprained ankles and knee, a steak on my hip was of little concern.

Before the show on the fourth night, the three conga players came to my dressing room bringing a carefully wrapped little box. Their faces were solemn and grave. When I opened it, I found a string of beads not unlike the ones they wore. "Voodoo beads – sacred..." they informed me nodding seriously. "Now nothing will happen to you anymore. You must wear them all the time."

I thanked them never showing my skepticism. But, just to be sure, I braided them into my hair. And from then on, everything went as smooth as can be. Apropos, I still have the beads today.

El Omelenco was a success beyond the most optimistic expectations. The papers were filled with raves and Rodney's blotchy, ugly face shone with pride. Suddenly we had our own TV show, bars were serving El Omelenco cocktails, and for the first time since the Tropicana opened, the showroom was pulling in more money than the casino. The place was packed every night. American tourists vied for seats with Havana's finest, including high officials of the Batista government and Panchin, Batista's inscrutable, morose brother would sit there almost every night with his entourage consuming a lot of champagne.

But the ones most impressed were the blacks. "No white dancer had ever been able to do that... Chiquita has a black soul, claro!" they whispered with satisfaction. "Nuestra Chiquitica, verdad? Ella es Chiquita La Grande! La unica!" They would say and nod with a certain pride of ownership. After all, they saved me... they knew...

I listened to all the extravagant praises with a bewildering, unsettling mixture of glee, satisfaction, and the kind of embarrassment that goes with a display of fake modesty which is considered 'good breeding.' Hell, if I did something well, why should I feel weird and embarrassed when people told me so? And why did I really need to hear it anyway? God, how superficial it all seems now! How can these things ever mean so much? How little must one think of oneself to need so much attention and constant reassurance? Yet no amount of praise and compliments can compensate for lack of self-esteem simply because whatever you get goes to the front you've created, that artificial, cultivated facade, and the real thing, the essence of one's being is crouching behind that facade, forgotten, useless and lonely. So it doesn't really matter how many people crowd around, looking at you... admiring you – look – there she is – that's her...

But all the compliments, flatteries and attention remain vaguely disturbing and leave you empty, unfulfilled. Yet you have to smile your thanks – you smile and nod and smile again – thank you, thank you – you look at faces you can't possibly give a good damn about, what they think, how they feel – faces you'll probably never see again – as long as you live, but that phony, unsatiable facade laps it up and you have to smile until the smile is a painful mask you fear will crack – disintegrate and reveal the child beneath begging for attention.

Somehow, the real human creature is lost – drowned in the shallowness of every gesture – every thought. My God, where was I – what happened to the thing that's really ME?!

How plainly I see the destructiveness of that drive or ambition or whatever you want to call it that prevented me from really enjoying anything. It's like an endless ladder. There is always the next rung that has to be climbed. Yet, I love dancing and I should have been able to enjoy it – really and fully enjoyed it instead of the recognition it brought. When the reward means more than the 'doing' itself, it's got to be wrong. It's neurotic. It's like when being alive means more than actually living. That something that is really me, may have had a better chance to enjoy that part of my life – the 'real' part of it – the dancing, the 'doing' – and not allowed it to dissipate into meaninglessness by the fame and adulation desperately needed to feed the monkey on my back driving me on to 'new and better things' – never satisfied – never fulfilled.

Looking back, how I wish I would have had the capacity to enjoy it then because although I've done many other ballets and productions after that, several even with Rodney, none had quite the same emotional impact as El Omelenco – on me or the audience.

A couple of years later in Hollywood, I saw a production at the Moulin Rouge that was lifted – pardon me, inspired – by El Omelenco. But unfortunately the choreographer hoked it up with some 'African safari' nonsense, ala Hollywood B-movies, with the girl in the inevitable 'safari' uniform, the khaki outfit, complete with the hideous hat that no respectable 'safari girl' would be caught dead without (according to Hollywood, that is) and all the rest of the paraphernalia as seen on Vera Ralston, etc. in countless Republic productions that still pollute the airwaves on many a late night. To spice up the finale of the production, he had the bright idea to have her throw herself into a fire. A real 'sharp' improvement on the original. Understandably, no one went berserk over that one. But not knowing when to quit, the good man took it one step further and applied the same idea to another production, this time in Las Vegas, but replaced the girl with a half nude, and a muscular, well-oiled, terribly gay dancer who strutted through the part swaying his bare buns provocatively. Oh well, you can stretch a good thing too far... and get a lot of shit.

As far as I am concerned, just give me the gay, old leper any day, and he'll outdo them all! But the tormented genius of a man died a few years ago – away from the golden island of his triumph. Finding little outlet for his genius in the post-revolutionary Castro Cuba, he followed the trend and went to Miami. But there too, lacking the proper patronage, he could accomplish little. And so, El Omelenco remained a success he never surpassed. And for me, the first three days notwithstanding, it was one of the most satisfying things I've done.

CHAPTER EIGHTEEN

I don't really know when I began to wonder just why I had this drive to succeed and conquer – to be famous. All I know is that I found out pretty soon that being popular and admired wasn't as much fun as I imagined it would be. In fact, at times, it was a real drag. It wasn't until years later that I began to suspect, after much mind-expanding and prying into the thing we call our psyche, that if one isn't happy, even after accomplishing a much desired goal, it may not have been one's own, real need but a cultivated one – or one passed on by our elders. But realizing that and actually divorcing one's self from this cultivated need, is another matter. The gnawing, disquieting drive that took someone years to cultivate isn't that easily discarded. It hangs like an albatross around our necks – plaguing us onto death.

You can see sixty, seventy year old men – still struggling, fighting, trying to fulfill someone's wishes and fantasies – long after that someone is dead and gone and they've long forgotten why they keep plodding on – or what it really is that is driving them! Can we ever see it? Accept it? Can we ever say enough! I'm through! Leave me alone with your crazy expectations and grandiose plans! I'm tired of fulfilling your ambitions – your dreams and killing myself in the process. Let me be myself!

As much time as I've spent making myself into something I thought would please them – I've spent almost as much time trying to discover why I did it. I've dissolved my ego – died a thousand times. Turned my unconscious inside out – and there were still remnants of them that I had to struggle with.

Somewhere in these interim years, my mother had remarried and together with my sister and stepfather, they had left Czechoslovakia and found refuge for a while in an immigration camp in Germany, hoping to immigrate from there to the U.S. Actually, they were expecting just as I had, that I'd be there already and would arrange for them to join me. As there was no foreseeable date when I would be able to do that, I wanted to get them to Cuba, at least my mother and sister. I knew it wouldn't be easy. Mother, after her divorce, lost the right to an Austrian passport and my stepfather was Czechoslovakian so they had to flee across the border. Since she hadn't any kind of traveling documents, I didn't know how I would be able to accomplish that. But I was determined to get them to Cuba somehow. The very thought of their coming filled me with excitement. Finally, my mother would see how famous and terrific I'd become! My stepfather decided to wait it out there and go straight to the States if he could. Meanwhile, I was busy scheming how to get the visa.

While performing for Batista, I took the opportunity and asked him to arrange for my mother and sister to come to Cuba. And again, something that must have been an important moment in my life remains but a blur, a simple fact – the details of which are as faded as the faceless blur of a man that made it possible. Surprisingly, it turned out to be simple. Passport or no passport, they were sent the visa, I sent the tickets, and waited impatiently for their arrival.

The press made a lot of it, and I thought how pleased mother would be seeing all the commotion her arrival was causing. I could hardly wait to see Kay. I thought often of the promise I made to her the day I ran away from home. The night before they were to arrive, I could hardly sleep.

Finally, I stood at the airport, surrounded by newsmen, watching the plane settle to a halt. It took ages before the passengers began disembarking. My eyes searched frantically for a thin, little figure and a head full of long, golden ringlets. Then I saw this tall, wan looking thing and my heart sank. Kay, twelve-year-old Kay, looked taller than I. Her long locks were cut shorter and the gold had tarnished to ash and pale copper. My mother looked strangely self-conscious, but she walked down those stairs – her body stiffly straight, the head held high and proud, just as I remembered her. As always, she was dressed well and with immaculate taste. To her, clothes were always on top of her list of priorities. I noticed with a shock that Kay's front was bulging quite impressively for her age. I could have cried. I was hoping, quite irrationally, of course, to see the same little girl I had left, what seemed so long ago, who refused to be pushed out of my memory by this thin, leggy kid with a tired child's face and swollen chest.

The reunion was understandably constrained and self-conscious. The newsmen milling about asking questions snapping pictures didn't help matters any. Mother's eyes were glistening with suppressed tears but the cool barrier without which I couldn't even imagine her was still there. Except now, for the first time, I recognized it for what it was. I used to think she was merely strict.

It's all because of the newsmen, I kept telling myself. We need to get reacquainted, get used to each other all over again.

But it was a strange situation. There we were living all together in the large, breezy villa by the sea – and drove each other crazy. Mother disliked Jonny because to her he was 'your father's friend' and she couldn't forget nor forgive him for that. She never said to Kay 'your' father this, or that.

She kept her reserve and I could never tell whether she was proud of me or what. Later after she became more familiar with everything and began to feel at home around me, she started complaining about my work being 'too dangerous,' that I should cut out the lifts, that Jonny hated her, that I should start painting again and so on. I was bewildered and hurt. I had hoped she would be pleased and proud of me. But she took it all in stride, as if it didn't mean much. It took a lot of probing and racking my brain over the recent years trying to remember whether she'd ever said anything nice or flattering

CHIQUITA AND JOHNSON

Erna a few months old

Erna on toes at 5

*A "Chiquita & Johnson" publicity photo with
Jonny in Prague, 1947 – Erna's 9*

*"Chiquita & Johnson" performing at
Auberge Des Pyramids, Cairo, 1949*

Beirut, Lebanon,1949

Damascus, Syria,1949

Auberge Des Pyramids, Cairo, 1949

Erna & Jonny at the
Casino Municipal de Taxi,
Istanbul, Turkey, 1950

Erna and Jonny in Beirut

Chiquita in Mexico, 1950

Erna, Mexico City Airport, 1950

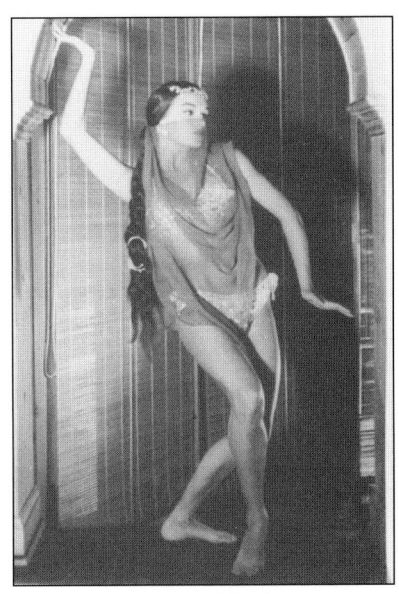

Erna in Mexico

*Chiquita and Johnson
on stage, Mexico City*

Publicity photo in Mexico

*El Patio Marquee,
Mexico City, 1950*

Chiquita & Johnson performing at El Patio, Mexico City

EL PATIO

Presenta hoy a la mejor pareja del mundo de baile clásico acrobático

CHIQUITA AND JOHNSON

CHIQUITA

JOHNSON

servac

HOY

GRAN TEATRO
ESPERANZA

IRIS

ATRACCIONES
INTERNACIONALES

TRIUNFO CLAMOROSO
DE LA
COLOSAL PAREJA

CHIQUITA
y
JOHNSON

CON UNA NUEVA y SENSACIONAL MODALIDAD

MODA
3 P.M

NOCHE
10 P.M

A Newspaper rendering of Chiquita
& Johnson in Mexico

Performing in the Plaza de Toros bullring, Mexico City

Marquee at the Tropicana Nightclub, Havana, Cuba, 1952

Performing at the Tropicana, Havana, Cuba

Two Hand, handstand, Tropicana

"Air-spin," publicity photo, Cuba

Chiquita & Rodney, the choreographer of "El Omelenco," Tropicana

Rehearsal of Voodoo production

Conga players, rehearsing for "El Omelenco" production

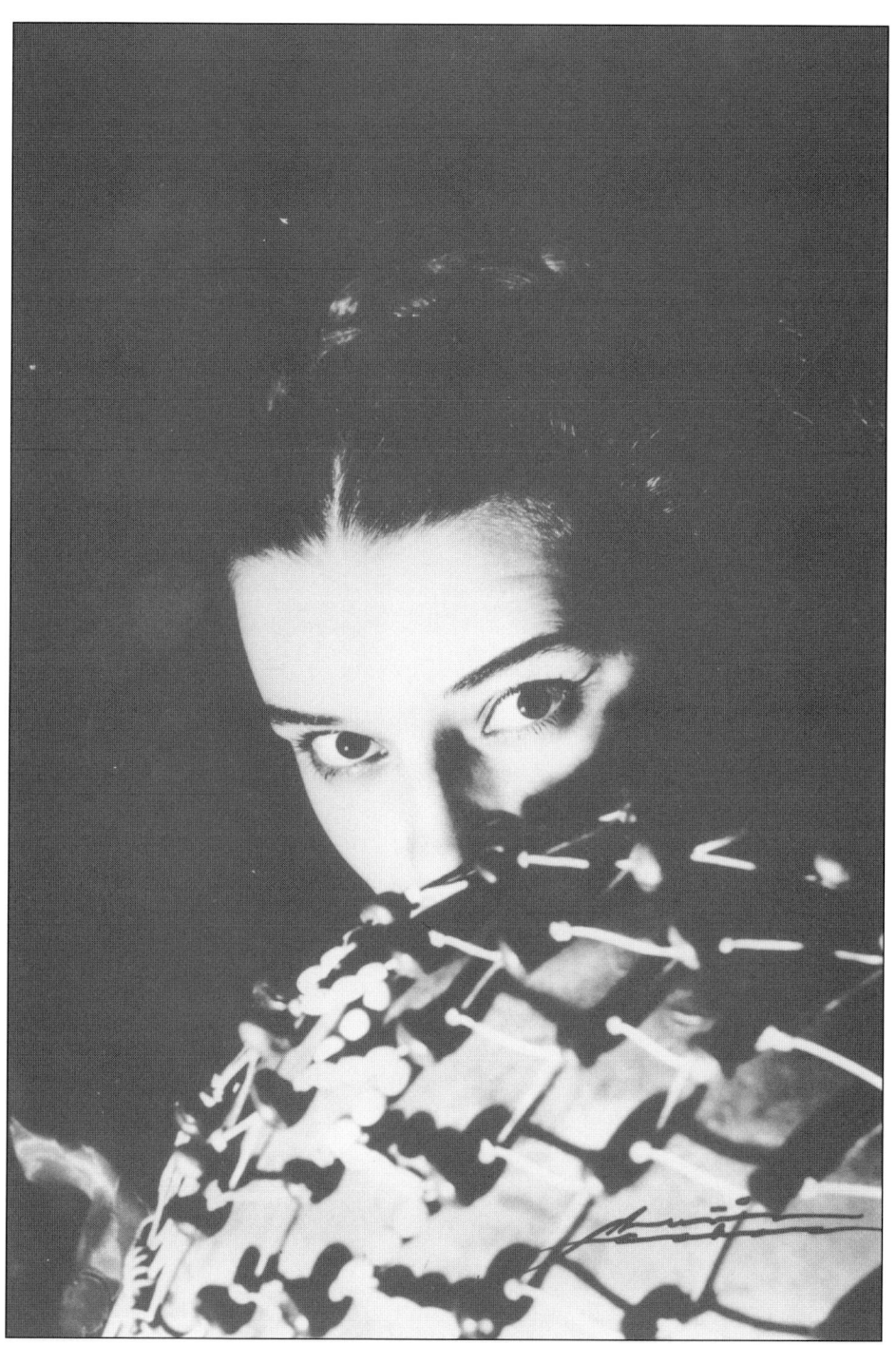

"El Omelenco" publicity photo

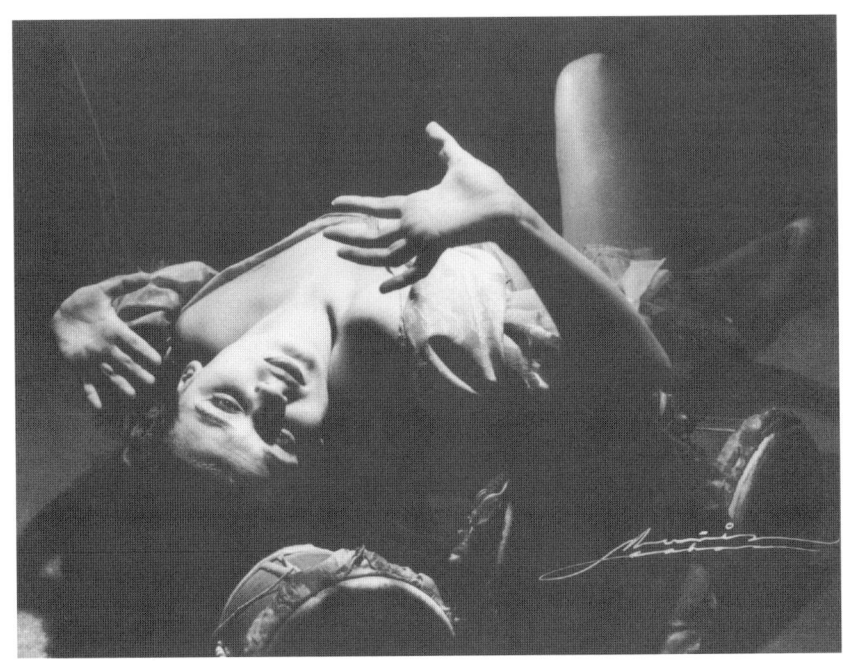

Another publicity photo at Tropicana

*Chiquita's famous leap at the climax of the "El Omelenco" production,
Tropicana Nightclub*

Erna behind the wheel of a Cadillac convertible,
with Jonny in Havana, 1953

Variety ad announcing Chiquita & Johnson's arrival in the USA

America Greets:

CHIQUITA
and
JOHNSON

Arriving Triumphantly in New York,
Thursday, August 27th,
Making Their American Debut as
Guest Stars on

Ed Sullivan's
"TOAST OF THE TOWN"
CBS-TV
Sunday Night, August 30th, 8 P.M.

After having just concluded
A most successful eleven-month
Starring engagement at
The world famous "TROPICANA" Night Club, Havana,
This brilliant acrobatic dance team
Has thrilled audiences for eight months
At the exclusive "EL PATIO," Mexico City, and
THE COPACABANA, Rio de Janeiro.
They have appeared in Rome, Paris, Cairo,
London, Athens and Turkey.

Chiquita & Johnson
headlining the show at
Radio City Music Hall,
New York, U.S.A.

Chiquita & Johnson take top billing at Radio City Music Hall alongside Clark Gable and Ava Gardner in the movie, "Mogambo"

Chiquita & Johnson performing at Radio City Music Hall with another amazing leap into Jonny's arms.

Publicity photo and Variety review of Chiquita & Johnson at Radio City Music Hall, 1953

December, 1953 cover story & photo of Chiquita & Johnson for "This Week in Los Angeles" announcing their upcoming engagement at Hollywood's famous Moulin Rouge

*Frank Sennes Moulin Rouge, Hollywood
with 10 foot high cutout of
Chiquita & Johnson, 1954*

*Chiquita & Johnson publicity shots
for their introduction into
Hollywood*

Chiquita & Johnson performing on stage at the Moulin Rouge, Hollywood

Chiquita publicity photo, Hollywood

★ NIGHT CLUB REVIEWS ★

Cocoanut Grove, Hollywood
The Hollywood Reporter, 1955

COCOANUT GROVE

Headliner on the current bill at the Ambassador's Cocoanut Grove is Connie Russell, and this looker can warble, but we can't think of many night club performers who could steal the play away from Chiquita & Johnson and it's too much to ask for Connie who must necessarily suffer from the handicap of having to perform with her clothes on. This is not one of Chiquita's problems. She twirls high in the air, spins on the floor and leaps toward the cocoanut palms dressed in sheer black lace that has male ringsiders in sheer ecstasy. Outside of Las Vegas, we can't remember seeing an entertainer of Chiquita's proportions dressed so daringly. Her partner, through much subtlety and strength, manages to keep the attention always centered on his doll, and we'll bet there are very few first-nighters who could tell us if he had a mustache or not. Incidentally, their acro-ballets are tops.

Connie Russell is a great singing personality with a fine, resonant voice who is on her way up. She is responsible for a colorful, imaginative act. "That's What a Rainy Day Is For," done with umbrella and tinsel to represent rain, is a good number, as is her "Magnificent Matador," done in matador costume (Hollywood style). She sings a teary sad number, too, like "Lonely Town," effectively. Her only mistake was coming in with Chiquita & Johnson.

Freddy Martin dissolves Liszt in an opening concert with his "Second Hungarian Mambo" and backs up the show and dancing with verve. This was Hawaiian night, too, and a South Seas revue entertained well during the wait for the main drag. **— Leo Guild.**

The GIRL On Yesterday's Back Cover!

Chiquita

of the

World-famous Acro-Ballet Dance Team

Chiquita and Johnson

Just Closed
COCOANUT GROVE
Ambassador Hotel

 ★

★

Guesting Sunday, June 26th
"COLGATE VARIETY HOUR"

Chiquita just completed a starring role in "JAGUAR" — her first American motion picture

Ad on the back of Variety which prompted Howard Hughes' office to call.
Ad announces completion of "Jaguar" Chiquita's starring role with Sabu.

Sabu, Maurice Duke, "Jaguar" producer and Chiquita

Chiquita & Johnson reviews from the Latin Quarter, New York

From "Scheherazade" production

Chiquita from "Scheherazade" production

Chiquita publicity photo

*Chiquita & Johnson with Henny Youngman at the Empire Room
at the Statler Hilton, Dallas, 1956*

Henny Youngman, Chiquita and Jonny in a lighter moment

*Chiquita
publicity photo*

Marquee of Chiquita & Johnson with Jerry Lewis at the RKO Palace, New York, 1957

A letter from Jerry Lewis to Chiquita & Johnson following their engagement at the Palace

Jerry Lewis
PACIFIC PALISADES
CALIFORNIA

Essex House, NY
March 4, 1957

CHIQUITA & JOHNSON
Palace Theatre
47th St. & Broadway
New York, N. Y.

Dear Chiquita & Johnny:

When I signed to play the Palace, I was given the right to choose the acts to be with me on the bill. I chose you ... and this is just a note to say how delighted I am with that choice!

You didn't disappoint me ... never let me down for a minute ... in fact, you enhanced me greatly. So, on behalf of my company and myself, may I say THANK YOU for a wonderful job.

You both helped to make my stay at the Palace one of the happiest and most rewarding events of my life. I sincerely look forward to working with you very soon again.

Affectionately,

JL/eg

Performing on stage at the Palace, Chiquita standing on her toe in Jonny's palm.

Jerry Lewis with Chiquita & Jonny

Chiquita doing a one arm handstand, balanced on Jonny's arm.
On stage at the Palace.

Los Angeles Herald & Express

Monday, June 24, 1957

By LOUELLA O. PARSONS

Add Chiquita and Johnson, the thrilling dancers, and, believe me, this act is one of the tops! I'll tell you more about the ... swank Coral ... of the Dis...

Cobina Wright

...ed a gay pa...
an exciting mambo with club owner, Steven Peck ... ...ing raves at Flamingo Hotel in Las Vegas with Jack Benny are Chiquita and Johnson, that wonderful dance team who stopped show after show at Moulin Rouge for so long

JUNE 8, 1957

...lwa... ...espe... ...ience. An extra added attraction CHIQUITA and JOHNSON America's favorite acrobatic dance duos in showbiz. They ballet dancers, are one of the most spectacular dance duos in showbiz. They combine breathtaking precision lifts and dizzy spins with a wealth of imaginative and flawlessly executed routines. They are at all times poised and graceful and nowhere will you find two more gracious performers. CHIQUITA and JOHNSON are accompanied by talented organist KAY GRABLER.

KAY GRABLER, who plays the wonderful organ music for CHIQUITA and JOHNSON ballet numbers, will do a "solo" on the ED SULLIVAN Show August 4th. KAY is CHIQUITA'S younger sister ...

VARIETY

Terp team of Chiquita & Johnson display showmanship impact with smooth leaps and spins. The shapely Chiquita is a looker who does difficult contortions and balancing tricks which are rewarded with enthusiastic audience response.
... production number held over from

Wednesday, May 29, 1957

More reviews

THE *Hollywood* REPORTER

Chiquita, Johnson Guest

like...
Chiquita and Johnson guest star on
Jack Benny's "Shower of Stars" tonight.

January 9, 1958

Bill Kennedy

PUT ON turban and went to Arabian Room at Dunes for dinner. Lied about my age and stayed for Minsky's "Treats of Paris." Haven't seen so much white space on showgals since ladies night at Vic Tanny's.

Hit of show was dance team, Chiquita & Johnson, who will appear on Jack Benny's "Shower of Stars" next Thursday. Fell real hard for Chiquita. She real doll who dances up a sandstorm.

Tuesday, January 7, 1958

"...

The other ayem, we watched CHI-QUITA and JOHNSON rehearse, after three shows at the DUNES HOTEL. They were running through the number prepared for their starring spot on JACK BENNY'S "Shower of Stars," January 9th. Although the routine takes three and one-half minutes of TViewing time, Chiquita & Johnson had put in many weeks of arduous rehearsal. Couple strive for Perfection! ..."

By LES DEVOR

Chiquita & Johnson, Minsky show-stoppers in "Treats of Paris" at the Dunes, Las Vegas, into Los Angeles for rehearsals ... Getting set for Jack Benny's Shower of Stars TV show, Jan. 9. Chiquita's the most fetching little lass ever you did see, hazza style all her own.

...Journal

TONIGHT!
from Hollywood

JACK BENNY in
"*Shower of Stars*"

starring
TOMMY SANDS
JO STAFFORD
PAUL WESTON
CHIQUITA and JOHNSON
and special guest star
ED WYNN

and introducing the piano artistry of
JONATHAN EDWARDS and DARLENE EDWARDS

8:30 Channel ② ⑧
with your host BILL LUNDIGAN for
CHRYSLER CORPORATION
THE FORWARD LOOK

TV

Announcing the Jack Benny "Shower of Stars" with Chiquita & Johnson

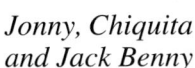

Jonny, Chiquita and Jack Benny

Steve Lawrence and Eydie Gorme with Chiquita & Johnson

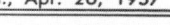

Fri., Apr. 26, 1957 — DAILY **VARIETY**

COCOANUT GROVE
(Cover, $2, $2.50)

What may well be the most beautiful nitery room in the country was unveiled to a name-dropper's-delight-audience Wednesday night when the new Cocoanut Grove opened its doors. It was a strictly invitational preview crowd, with Schine Enterprises picking up the entire tab to launch the new version of its world-famed rendezvous. From a party standpoint, it was a smashing success; but it was something less than that as an entertainment offering and the management would have been better advised to run the preview as a private affair, restricting the press to the public bow last night.

Admittedly, for the preview, much of the buildup to the actual show can't be charged against the layout. And the "welcoming" speeches by Don Wilson, G. David Schine and J. Meyer Schine were in keeping with the general atmosphere of the evening. But the show that followed seemed to be a ragged first rehearsal, with missed lighting cues and a faulty sound system lending to the confusion. Too, top-billed Tony Martin essayed little that was new in his stint marking the re-opening of this top room, and his 52-minute chore was much too long for that time of night. A portion of the audience departed long before he swung into the home stretch.

As a package, show has all the elements for top appeal and in all probability Gus Lampe is whipping them into shape to make the offering match the elegance and charm of the new room for paying guests. It opens with an excellent Freddy Martin overture of tunes he has introduced in past Grove stands, a melange that is a blend of the hit parades of the last two decades. It was marred, as was the usual good Martin dance beat, by a blaring sound system—a fault that also lent an untoward stridency to Tony Martin's vocalizing. Overture was followed by the top-drawer adagio turn of Chiquita and Johnson. They're utilizing their standard routine, replete with skilful spins, splits and whirls and highlighted by a pulse-pounding somersault drop to command ringside attention.

As always Tony Martin leans heavily on his trademarked tunes, some of them undergoing slight change via new arrangements by Al Sendry, who also accompanies and conducts for the singer. Songs like "Manhattan," "There's No

Time," all delivered with the Martin salesmanship and personality. For this type of an opening, however, Martin should have concentrated more on an act than a standup singing chore. *Kap.*

THE Hollywood REPORTER
Friday, April 26, 1957
COCOANUT GROVE

Opening dance act of Chiquita and Johnson was a fitting one for the splendor of the room because they're the best act of their kind on the circuit . . . Chiquita is refreshingly beautiful with a body that deserves display in the Museum of Art . . . Tony Martin for the . . .

Los Angeles Times
BY EDWIN SCHALLERT — FRI., APRIL 26, 1957

. . . club history . . . even a missed . . . or so didn't handicap the splendiferous . . . Chiquita and Johnson performed brilliantly . . . Chiquita and Johnson will be the one of four feminine outlaws . . . "The Dalton Girls," Bel-Air production to be made . . . Aubrey Schenck and . . . rd Koch . . .

Los Angeles Herald & Express — Friday, April 26, 1957
Cafes, Nite Spots

. . . The exciting . . . almost impossible antics of a . . . dance team Chiquita and Johnson always the best, was . . . again great. . . . Freddy Martin . . .

extra added attraction
CHIQUITA and JOHNSON
international dance stars

Cocoanut Grove reviews with Tony Martin

Hollywood publicity shots

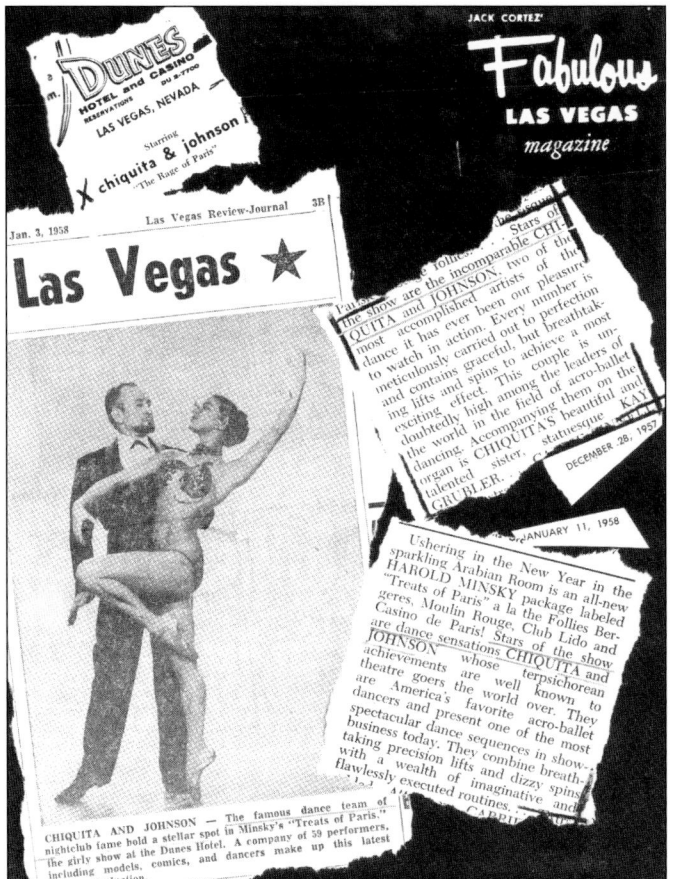

The Dunes Hotel, Las Vegas, 1958, announces the world famous Chiquita & Johnson in "Treats of Paris" show.

Opening Harrah's Nightclub in Tahoe with Red Skelton
Christmas, 1959

Chiquita and Jonny with Red Skelton and friends

In support of President Kennedy's program to attract "tourist bundles for America" from abroad, the British commercial network, ITN, sent newscaster Tom Barry and crew to Miami Beach and the Carillon Hotel to film a sound feature.

Barry, Britain's Chet Huntley, chatted with poolsiders as the camera rolled. Being interviewed is bikini clad Chiquita of 'Chiquita and Johnson,' the exciting dance team now starring in Lou Walters French Revue at the hotel. Said Barry, understandingly delighted with his assignment, "What Britons love about Florida is the sunshine, something we lack most of the time. Chiquita's beautiful tan should attract many visitors from back home."

(Lou Walters in the dark glasses, 1961)

The White House Correspondents' Association

IN APPRECIATION

of the invaluable assistance of

Erna Grabler

TO THE WHITE HOUSE CORRESPONDENTS' ASSOCIATION

ON THE OCCASION OF ITS ANNUAL DINNER

IN HONOR OF THE PRESIDENT OF THE UNITED STATES,

HOTEL STATLER, WASHINGTON, D. C., MARCH 5, 1955

ENTERTAINMENT
COMMITTEE

Jack Doherty

PRESIDENT

A certificate presented to Erna in appreciation of her part in a gala performance for the President of the United States. Personally signed by President Eisenhower, 1955

ROTARY INTERNATIONAL CONVENTION
Los Angeles, California, U.S.A.
Hollywood Bowl
7:30 p.m.
SUNDAY, 3 JUNE, 1962

Organ Music
SPENCER BROWNE

Welcome
DOANE R. FARR
Chairman, 1962 Convention Committee, R.I.
Clinton, Oklahoma, U.S.A.

Silent Invocation

Presentation of Flags
VISA STUDENTS

Address
JOSEPH A. ABEY
President, R.I.
Reading, Pennsylvania, U.S.A.

HOLLYWOOD UNDER THE STARS
Produced and Directed by C. P. MacGregor

Master of Ceremonies
RONALD REAGAN

Hollywood Television and Recording Orchestra
BASIL ADLAM, Guest Conductor

JOSE GRECO AND COMPANY

ATTILA GALAMB

CHIQUITA & JOHNSON

VIVIENNE DELLA CHIESA

JOHN CRAIG

GENE SHELDON

MORMON CHOIR OF SOUTHERN CALIFORNIA
FREDERICK DAVIS, Conductor

Chiquita and Johnson perform at a Rotary International event with master of ceremonies, Ronald Reagan, Hollywood Bowl, 1962

Chiquita & Johnson on stage, Teatro Blanquita, Mexico City, 1961

Chiquita publicity photo, Mexico, Teatro Blanquita

*Teatro Blanquita, Chiquita in another
production featuring the gong.*

*Erna and Jonny preparing for
their Mexico City performance*

On stage in Mexico City

Correspondents banquet honoring Cantinflas.
Chiquita is the only woman there.

Cantinflas (Mario Moreno),
his note to Chiquita saying
she's the most enchanting
woman in the world.

Caracas, Venezuela – TV production finale

Erna - self portrait, pencil sketch, 1962

Erna – Chiquita

about my dancing. When I finally realized that she hadn't, when I managed to recall all that I'd pushed out of my mind and reevaluated it, I began to understand at last why my success could never make her happy. She transferred her own unfulfilled drives to her child and cultivated in me her own ambitions to excel – to succeed. But of course no matter what I did, what I'd become, it could never satisfy her. Only her own accomplishment could have done that – and it was too late for that.

I resented her trying to run my life again and refused to let her do it. So there was constant friction.

Kay seemed apathetic. She did whatever mother told her with quiet, resigned compliance. On the surface anyway. Was I too late? Was the spirit I remembered being there stomped out by mother's heavy-handed, irrational methods of upbringing?

I felt that, somehow, I'd failed her. It was indeed too late... She looked at me with uncertainty – the gap created by the long absence was hard to fill. How often I had cried when I remembered locking her into that drawer and tormenting her so viciously. Now she was with me, but I didn't know how to make up for it.

And mother – mother had grown only older – but not wiser. She never learned that you've got to live and let live. Her incapacity to find peace within herself and to live in peace with others, filled me with pity and hopelessness. I was longing to leave – to be far away from her again.

One evening after the performance, the manager came to tell us we had a visitor. It turned out to be a short, rotund American with a bright cherub face. His bald, round head shone in the dim lights of the club as he got up and introduced himself as Mr. Loew, the owner of the Latin Quarter, and said he came all the way from New York to talk to us. I was surprised because I assumed Lou Walters owned it. He smiled saying most people thought so but that he didn't mind. He rarely interfered with the business but now he felt he had to.

I knew immediately what was on his mind. I felt flattered but I wasn't about to make it easy for him. I went into the whole thing again, reiterating how incensed I was about Walters' attitude, etc., how terribly unfair it was particularly in view of the fact that we still didn't have the visa so indeed there was nothing to talk about.

I was really a strange kid. If anyone dared to cross me, I'd take an offense and refuse to forgive or forget – or perhaps I simply enjoyed being in the driver's seat and being a bitch about it.

Loew argued patiently that he didn't do anything to insult us and since it was his club, what did Walters matter? Why should he be deprived of 'our talents' since it was Lou who wrote the letter?

I decided it was time to start giving in so I said I would reconsider, providing the 'conditions' were persuasive enough. For a moment he looked startled, then nodded quickly saying, "whatever you want" – and then started laughing so hard he was gasping for air and tears started running down his round cheeks. At the same time he was leaning back so far in his chair to give his fat, heaving belly some room, that the chair fell over and he went down with it. He stopped abruptly and looked terribly surprised to find himself on the floor, but then broke into fresh peals of convulsive laughter without making the slightest effort to get up. I had to laugh myself seeing him lying there like a fat little dumpling, in spasms of uncontrollable laughter.

In spite of my promise, however, the Latin Quarter was not the first place in the U.S. that we appeared. It was the Ed Sullivan Show and Sullivan himself phoned us in Havana to arrange the deal. Needless to say, I was thrilled to receive a call from the States. But instantly, I began to worry. Who was Ed Sullivan? Was his show any good? Was it worthy of us! It wasn't until much later that I learned the whole thing was a result of careful preparation and planning executed meticulously by a man who called himself Bill Taub.

It was only a few weeks earlier that we had received a letter from an American 'personal manager,' as the elegant stationary informed us. William Taub wrote that he had heard of us and would like to represent us in the States and if we were at all interested in the proposition, he would fly out to Havana – unless we were already committed to someone else. Not only were we not committed, we didn't even have the visas yet.

Well, Bill Taub flew in as swift as the sea breeze – eager to negotiate. I was rather distressed. The Mr. American – personal manager – turned out to be a pasty-looking, frail man with an unbecoming twisted smile and a big, protruding chin and forehead. It gave him a certain unwholesome appearance. Even the discreet elegance of his dress and manner seemed unreal, like an elaborate front behind which lurked something unsavory. His voice had an unpleasant lilt to it that further reinforced the initial impression.

He was thrilled when he saw the show and even more eager to sign us up. He would clear up the visa situation immediately, he assured us with confidence. After all, he had also arranged the visa for Maurice Chevalier who really had a problem since he had worked for the German forces during the war and was considered a 'collaborator,' and consequently denied entry. But he – little Bill Taub – did what no one else could do. He had arranged the visa for him. He didn't really brag about it, it was said in careful, subtle tones but the message was there nevertheless. Bill Taub was an 'influential' man. The soft, modest tone, didn't quite disguise the boastful note of self-importance. I was afraid to trust him, and hesitant not to.

When he left, he had every reason to believe we would sign the contract he was going to send us. And we did. By sheer coincidence, Taub didn't have to do anything about our visas. Just one day after we had signed the contract, our man at the Embassy called to tell us our visas had been granted. It seemed they finally established that the accusation that Jonny was a communist was a deliberate lie – and the reason behind it, 'ulterior motives.' We didn't press them to tell us who it was. We already knew.

Before our departure from Cuba, there were homages, dinners in our honor, gala shows which attracted top performers eager to participate and lend their talents. The proceeds went to all sorts of worthy causes.

The last and biggest 'gala performance' packing Havana's largest theater the "Blanquita," was organized by and for the press. The high moment of it was when the governor of Havana came up to the stage to present us with a gold medal 'for all we have done for the Cuban people.' I suppose that should have been a high point in my life. Yet I have no clear, sharp recollection of that moment – there is very little to remind me of how I felt or reacted when accepting the medal. All I know is that it was reduced to the function of gracing my key chain which is the only reason I recall the inscription on one side and the Cuban landscape, palms and all, engraved on the other.

And then we were off, heading to the country of our ultimate destination. We kept the villa in Marianao for my mother and sister's use until the time I would arrange for them to join me.

I have found, very often in life, that I should trust my intuition more often. But unfortunately, I've never been able to do that.

In Bill Taub's case, I had every reason to be suspicious which we didn't find out until later.

CHAPTER NINETEEN

At the beginning, Taub made excellent moves and had he devoted all his energies to represent his clients to the best of his ability, which was considerable, he'd have done very well indeed.

He got Sullivan to book us, sight unseen, for a relatively low salary with the understanding that Ed would double it if the act turned out to be all he promised. Ed did double our salary after just watching one rehearsal. This was, of course, picked up by the press and helped our prestige. It was no doubt a great maneuver. Unfortunately, he had others up his sleeve.

Arriving in New York, we found newsmen waiting, snapping pictures and all the jazz that meant so much at the time. Our days were filled with radio, TV and press interviews, luncheons and, of course, rehearsals.

Taub set us up in sumptuous suites at the Ritz Towers which cost a fortune but he assured us it was important, and I was running around Fifth Avenue buying clothes I didn't need but which Bill insisted I should have. He was quick to point out we were to give him all our receipts since he would be making out our income tax returns.

Even before we had arrived in the States, papers carried

blurbs about us. I was surprised to read about my 'escape' from behind the Iron Curtain. It didn't seem to matter that we had simply taken a train – it was better this way... I complied readily and even got very good at it. I was full of marvelous little statements such as: You Americans don't know how valuable freedom is! You don't know how to appreciate something you've always had. Or – After the 'oppression' in Czechoslovakia, (I wasn't sure what the word meant but it sounded good) arriving in America, I understand for the first time what freedom really means... and similar stuff. I thought it sounded super and even got all choked up, I was so good.

One of the first reporters to interview us was Dorothy Kilgallan. I laid it on thick and was surprised to see a thin, bitter line form around her mouth and the chin recede even further. No matter how complimentary I was about her country, she didn't seem to react to it. It took many years before I began to understand and by that time she was dead.

I thought she was a very nice woman, and I was most astonished and disconcerted at the possibility that she actually wasn't crazy about me. There was one thing she said that bothered me for a long time. "You think this is so much better than the Bolshoi? – I hope you'll always feel you've made the right choice."

The Sullivan show was an interesting experience – one we were to repeat several times in the future. The studio was so much larger than the one in Havana, not to mention the potential audience. But even after I realized Ed's show was the top variety program in the country, I still wasn't nervous about it. To me, doing a TV show was rather like a dress rehearsal. I was hardly aware of the audience in the back of all the cameras and lights, and the fact that the probing eyes of the camera lenses represented millions of people just wouldn't register. I could see myself in the monitors and was pleased I photographed so well and that everyone commented on it. It was a shock to see how different I looked once they put all the make-up on me which they insisted on doing in spite of my protestations. Until then, I never used to put anything on my face except eye make-up and sometimes lipstick. Now the thick cake make-up gave me a vapid doll-face look which I despised. Before the show, however, I went back to my dressing room, took the goop off and started all over again.

The show turned out very well, and Taub instantly got all sorts of offers for us. The first date he decided we should accept was a four week engagement at the Radio City Music Hall. Taub succeeded in getting for us equal billing with the stars of the film which was never done before. Across the entire marquee of Radio City Music Hall there we were in the company of such distinguished stars – Clark Gable, Ava Gardner, Chiquita and Johnson. Not bad at all. The salary wasn't what we had agreed on with Bill, but he said it was an important date and therefore well worth it. Since it wasn't the salary he guaranteed us in the contract, he made us sign a waiver.

To me it simply meant four shows a day which is a hell of a lot of work. Leon Leonodoff produced the show. He too saw El Omelenco and had the bright idea I should jump off of something. It turned out to be an eighteen foot ice cooler with a champagne bottle in it which he had built especially for me. The bottle opened and, as expected – I popped out and went flying down. Our grandiose presentation included a hot steam curtain which shot out of a perforated steel strip a foot or so in front of the footlights. Then out of the steaming mist the damn champagne bottle and cooler came rolling out.

Two stagehands had to hold it securely in place so that it wouldn't move when I took the leap. They never did manage to keep it steady and Jonny had to be really on his toes. Even a one inch give meant a yard shorter dive than anticipated. The dive didn't really hurt me, but doing it four times a day gradually bruised my ribs and they began to hurt. When ribs hurt, it's a little hard to breathe, if you know what I mean.

Four shows may not seem like much in view of the fact that our performance took a little over seven minutes. But I expended a tremendous amount of energy in those seven minutes. Also, a lot of time was spent in warming-up, rehearsals, etc. With all that, the engagement felt like real drudgery and I was glad when it was over.

There was no time to go anywhere or to see anything in New York. I remember being taken to a nightclub once, the shortly-to-be-closed-and-torn-down, "Riviera." Bill Taub said one of the top singers in the country was appearing there and that we should see him. His name was Frank Sinatra. We wound up sitting with Bill Miller, the owner of the club, which turned out to be a big mistake.

I didn't like the sleek, smart, but cold style of the line of girls which opened the show, nor Sinatra. I thought he sang well, but I took an instant dislike to his style. I guess, arrogant and condescending would be an adequate description of it. Those qualities are something I can't stand in a performer to this day, and being forced to sit through one hour and thirty minutes of it was almost more than I could bear. As far as I was concerned, he overstayed by about one hour and twenty-five minutes.

But, as I was told, Ava Gardner sat in the audience, and he couldn't be scraped off. I had this mad impulse to take my chair and throw it at him. And when the audience broke into applause after he announced a song and mentioned its composer with his back to the audience and turned back abruptly saying coldly: "I didn't write that..." I could have really punched him in the face. I guess you can tell I am not exactly crazy about the guy.

Later, when being on a TV show with him in Hollywood, I still felt the same way and found it difficult to overcome my aversion. During a run-through rehearsal, Sinatra, who was watching us and obviously enjoying it, began to applaud. I gave him a cold stare and proceeded to ignore him. I knew it was stupid, but I just couldn't help myself. The man had certainly no idea why I should dislike him and I saw clearly the puzzlement and wonder on his face.

I can't remember which TV show it was but even there someone decided to have me dive off something. This time it turned out to be a twenty foot mockup of a medieval castle. Just as I was about to go on, standing atop the structure behind the drawn curtain, I saw Sinatra walk by slowly, hunched over ever so slightly. No one else was in sight. Suddenly he stopped and looked up holding out his arms. "How about it Chiquita? Want to jump?" I realized it was the last gesture of friendliness. Again I looked at him coldly saying humorlessly: "When I want to die, I'll call on you."

He said nothing – absolutely nothing – he just stood there staring at me totally bewildered, his face a big question mark. What have I done to you? it seemed to say. There was a hurt expression in his eyes and then I saw it – the one need unifying us all – the need to be liked – by everyone. I never knew then how much we had in common.

Before we finished the four grueling weeks at Radio City, we had an engagement all set in Hollywood to open and star in Frank Sennes' Moulin Rouge – the old Earl Carroll theater on Sunset near Vine – remodeled. It was then that AGVA (American Guild of Variety Artists) stepped into the picture informing us that Taub was receiving more money from us than he told us which constituted some 30% of the gross. This was against their rules since a personal manager had no right to take more than 15%. Consequently, they didn't consider our contract with Taub, which wasn't a standard AGVA contract, as binding. The trouble was that the courts (AGVA rules or not) did. However, there were other minor complications such as fraud, etc.

We were flabbergasted. Taub's defense was – he was entitled to do it since it was HE who paid our hotel bills, paid for my wardrobe, etc., for which he had receipts in his possession. Fortunately, Jonny had saved the little note he sent us requesting all our receipts for tax purposes. Still, it was quite a hassle, tedious court procedures, our engagement at the Moulin Rouge was in jeopardy; he said he would exercise his right to veto it and so forth. At this point AGVA was very 'helpful' and supplied us with their attorney, at the cost of a mere $1,200 – for telling us we had better settle. The settlement turned out to be $7,000 – in cash!

I am sure the lawyer, an obese, kindly man by the name of Henry Katz sincerely believed he was arranging for us the best deal possible. We were told, however, no doubt to make our ordeal more bearable, that Taub extracted $10,000 the same way out of Charles Trenet and $15,000 out of Maurice Chevalier (without ever having arranged for his visa, by the way.) At least we were in good company. But things like that were quite apropos for the crafty little man. He was foolish enough to tell us his modus operandi in acquiring the furnishings for his sumptuous Park Ave. apartment and office.

He would order the most expensive rug in a special shade stressing it had to match something or other. After the rug was installed, instead of paying for it, he'd turn around and sue the company for having come up with the wrong shade, causing him untold troubles, delays, etc., etc. The company, eager to hush up the whole case which soon began to assume gigantic dimensions with blurbs in the papers, etc. offered to leave the rug there free of charge if he would make up his mind to live with the shade and drop the charges. In a similar manner, he acquired everything else.

Before we left New York, Henry Katz gave me a thick volume of Webster's dictionary as a gift with an inscription I was never to forget: "Make use of the power of words." Little Bill Taub knew!

I never studied English, but I never stopped reading – books, magazines, papers, whatever, and swore I'd never let myself be taken that way again – a promise I found hard to keep for there are too many bullshit artists in this world just itching to get their hands into someone else's pocket.

My days in New York were incredibly busy and hectic and all the excitement, constant activity, and having to portray an image that seemed expected of me kept me from stopping long enough to sort out my impressions and decide how I felt about being in the 'country of my dreams.'

CHAPTER TWENTY

And then there was Hollywood. Hollywood! Who could escape the magic of that word and all that it implied? And who could escape the dismal disappointment when actually seeing it for what it was – and still is – a gaudy little section of a city that never was. Looking for the city of Los Angeles was a futile attempt. To me, Los Angeles looked like an insane mirage of communities, scattered, distant, as if trying to escape from each other. The tremendous contrast between the mess of gaudy shops, loud signs and ostentatious movie houses lining Hollywood Boulevard, and the sumptuous, green elegance of park-like suburbs such as Beverly Hills and Bel-Air was an absurdity I thought every newly arriving European must find difficult to comprehend – let alone get adjusted to.

The buildings, looking as if they were never meant to last, imparted a sense of impermanence and I longed for the old, solid structures of the European cities and the feeling of security and permanency they tend to instill in their dwellers. It took me a whole year before I stopped being homesick for Europe.

But the most regrettable thing about the built-in obsolescence in evidence everywhere, was that somehow, I saw it reflected in the people and their attitudes, not only toward life, but even toward themselves. It seemed to have spread from each inanimate object infesting every human being with its nihilistic poison. The results were staggering. I hadn't seen anywhere else such disdain and fear of old age. Things such as dignity of old age, or respect for it, appeared to be concepts totally alien to the culture I found myself in.

Slowly, I began to realize that as a building, which would be considered new in Europe, is torn down and quickly replaced by a larger and even flimsier one, or a car discarded in a few years, so the human being, as soon as he begins to age and wrinkle and stops looking fresh and appetizing, is pushed aside, ignored, preferably locked away in rest homes so that he shouldn't remind the rest of humanity of its own perishability.

In view of this, the fact that all the old senile politicians I saw being reelected and allowed to run the country seemed, at first, incongruous I soon realized it was perfectly in keeping with the ever-present spirit of absurdity and irrationality I was met with everywhere. However, the saddest aspect of this built-in obsolescence, accepted as something essential to the American way of living, was that it seemed to have drastically changed people's values.

I felt it most keenly during that first year. I realized everything was viewed in terms of dollars. I saw the people as cold, calculating individuals motivated primarily by materialistic considerations. I felt I wasn't valued as a human being but rather as a commodity – an ornament, or asset – a potential sell. People liked to be 'friends' because I was 'that girl on the ten foot picture atop the Moulin Rouge.' They thought it added to their prestige to be seen in our company. We were fair game for unscrupulous salesmen eager to take advantage of our ignorance of the American facts of life and to push the "status trip" on us.

People had the most disconcertingly obvious 'covert' ways of trying to learn – how much we were 'worth,' or rather, how much we were 'good for.' This was followed by attempts to familiarize us with the 'musts' of the star-status. Cadillacs, ostentatious clothes, huge parties full of celebrities, etc., etc. And I am afraid we swallowed it all, hook, line and sinker. When I think back to those years I wonder whatever became of ME? Where was I keeping the real me? And what became of the mad, impetuous time we call puberty? – The girlish crushes, puppy loves and all the erratic, irresponsible, wonderful behavior accompanying that stage.

While still at home, I remember being envious of the older girls, smart and grownup looking, flirting casually with boys. My puberty was swallowed up by a lot of work, obligations, duties, and a whole set of strict, puritanical rules, imposed by my 'warden,' that crushed my spirit as effectively as a straightjacket.

Jonny could be marvelous, fatherly, a close, warm friend, someone to share my dreams and ambitions with, but he could also be an unbending, inexorable, puritanical bigot, a tyrant, whenever I dared to even contemplate devoting time, or even a thought, to anything other than our mutual goals. Whatever puppy loves I may have had, were crushed by his rigid attitude, strict rules and watchful eyes. My 'affairs' consisted of a furtive look, touch of the hand, a whispered word, a sad head shake. And all the dreams of glory, all the fame, applause and adulation couldn't make up for the tears on countless sterile hotel pillows, shed for who knows what, and the need of an understanding mother to explain it all away.

I was in a strange country, among strange people with customs and ways that were alien to me, with a man I didn't understand, whose often erratic, irrational attitude I feared – yet being wholly dependent on him, unable to escape his total domination nor the contradicting influences of his behavior. There were times when I really liked him – times when we planned, mapped out our career – dreamt up new ways of improving our art. But then there were those times when my own individual needs – needs for freedom, self-expression came to the fore enraging him and turning him into that cold, wary stranger I detested and was afraid to even speak to.

One important taboo was money. It was not up to me to ask, to know, to care how much we spent, for what and why. I could get anything, buy anything I wanted – but how we were doing financially, whether we were saving anything, etc. – was none of my business. I was a child, a minor, he was my guardian – responsible for me – he was doing what was expected of him – and that was that. Any question directed at money, no matter how guarded or discreet, threw him into a rage and reduced me to the role of a hireling, unimportant, dispensable – and confused the hell out of me.

Physically, I was growing up nicely. Mentally, of course, I was a mess. My trademark became a costume, designed by Jonny, which was a flimsy business of skintight flesh-colored mesh, graceful, flowery designs of shimmering sequins and stones artfully covering 'strategic areas,' and wisps of silky chiffon – the barest indication of a tutu. Looking at pictures I realize I was a knockout, but in those days, although I wasn't bothered by showing a lot of skin as long as the 'vital parts' were covered, if anyone dared to say I looked 'sexy,' I became most indignant thinking it the worst insult in the world. All references in news columns or articles to my costume or any fabricated romantic insinuations such as Walter Winchell's suggesting Panchin Batista followed me to New York and similar nonsense, filled me with helpless anger and frustration. Naturally, in view of the crazy upbringing I received, I could have hardly reacted differently as far as such things were concerned. However, I also disliked the sensational journalistic type of reporting which I felt lacked style and finesse. Even the reviews, and they never failed to be enthusiastic raves, were written in the flashy, brash style I so disliked. Only Ann Barzel wrote sensitive, good reviews that I truly appreciated. She mainly reviewed legit things, but she came to see us and wrote a beautiful, objective review showing a fine understanding of ballet and how I tried to use it. I kept the review for a long time.

The opening of the Moulin Rouge was a big affair and we became 'Hollywood celebrities' practically overnight. Being sans agent, due to the Taub disaster, we had agencies vying for us. Frank Sennes, whose brother ran a small theatrical agency, every week before handing us our paycheck pushed a management contract at us to sign. But no amount of persuasion could make us sign. I liked Frank, but it seemed rather unethical to be employing as our agent the man who was employing us, his brother fronting notwithstanding. Besides, there was some sort of an AGVA rule against it and we'd had enough hassle to last us for quite awhile.

After much romancing, we finally agreed to sign with William Morris. At that point we really didn't need an agency because we were booked-up for the entire year but were finally convinced by well-meaning 'advisors' that that was the thing to do. Thus William Morris made a handsome sum in commissions for doing practically nothing. The same was true later when we switched to MCA. But that was all 'par for the course' – the 'American way' which we were learning so much about.

The show at the Moulin Rouge was a smart, high-class revue somewhat like the current Las Vegas productions. A big cast, sumptuous costumes and all the accouterments belonging to the American concept of a successful show. Nothing original, mind you, but a lot of brass and fanfare.

The production preceding our presentation was intended to be, presumably, the 'coup d' resistance.' The Moulin Rouge had a revolving stage and an independently revolving outer ring some four feet in width. On this narrow strip of stage, eight lanterns came rolling out beneath which the corresponding number of couples sensuously twisted and slid around each other to some funky, bluesy number. When they were done with that, the strip obligingly disappeared and with it the shimmering curtain immediately behind revealing an all pink stage for the all pink production. There were all sorts of clever little things such as a rain screen gushing into low metal containers which had rolled in on the heels of the lanterns, and the pink dancers blithely skipping through their routines behind it. When they were finished, the stage revolved exposing another all pink set. Pink columns upon pink steps surrounded by pink clouds, showgirls in pink, shimmering gowns and big, befeathered pink hats stood in frozen poses grouped around the columns. Dominating the scene – a pink pedestal and on it, draped from head to toe in yards of pink chiffon, standing like a statue – me.

With the opening chords of my introduction reverberating in the hush, from somewhere above the pink clouds a mob of doves spread their pink wings and flew around and across the stage and startled audience, and headed toward some spot near the lights in the back of the room prearranged by their trainer. There were always two things on my mind at that moment. Why they had to dye those poor birds pink and whether they'd ever shit on anyone and hoping that it wouldn't be me. I thought they rather over did the whole bit, but since it was done with respect and pomp they felt was due to our newfound 'status,' I'd have been hard put to complain or to criticize it. Besides, however corny I may have thought it, the audience seemed to eat it up. The only minor problem with the whole thing, one which I knew was bound to end in disaster, was that one of the frozen showgirls had what might be loosely termed as birdophobia! When those damn doves took off and the wild fluttering of dozens of wings mingled with the opening chords of my introduction, the girl stood there – eyes shut tight, teeth clenched – a perfect picture of petrified terror – except for the slight tremor in the stiff, outstretched arms. I used to watch her with passive curiosity, waiting for the inevitable. Was the money she was receiving every week worth the daily torment? Then one day it happened. A dove flew straight at her finally settling on her head. The terrified girl started screaming fearfully and ran off stage as fast as the narrow skirt of her gown would permit. Well, that's show biz !

But every time the whole scene appeared, birds and all, I must say the audience sat spellbound – and when the 'statue' – that is, I came to life, so to speak, and the chiffon slid off settling into a pink, graceful mound around the pedestal revealing my "scantily dressed exquisite figure" "as perfect as chiseled marble" (to quote a few newsmen), the audience never failed to emit an enchanted sigh. And when I extended my pink-shoed toes and stepped daintily into my partner's capable palm to be borne through the air as light as the breeze, as graceful as the swan, they thought I was a living doll, a talented, effervescent beguiling "charmer" (another word I hate) and they came to see again and again.

And so it went for ten long, yet short, months, all of which blended into a carefree monotony punctuated by frequent bouts of homesickness, TV appearances, benefits, parties, hordes of 'friends,' adoring men I couldn't do a damn thing about and gritting my teeth in helpless frustration continuing to play the part of the unattainable enchantress – the pure, innocent thing that just looked sexy but was above it all – the perennial cock tease. Shit – that was one hell of a life I embarked upon!

No, the United States of America was not all that I had hoped it would be. But then whose fault was it really? I think it's the unfortunate part of human nature (or at least certainly mine) to expect too much, to want everything to come out in the same bright colors our imagination uses when painting the quaint little pictures in our minds.

No matter how alien a style of living, attitudes, or values, when living in it long enough, it begins to rub off on you. Predisposed as I was to wanting, needing always more, never being satisfied with the status quo, I found I soon began to absorb that cold, calculating way of looking at things and evaluating people the same way they evaluated me. The disadvantage of this trait is that whenever you meet someone new, since you don't evaluate each other on the human level, every encounter becomes a contest for supremacy which immediately rules out the chance of establishing a true friendship. In such a highly competitive world people find themselves very much alone and the struggle toward bigger, and still bigger goals is constant and nerve depleting but hardly compensates for the loss.

All I knew at the time was that I was very dissatisfied. I was torn between two worlds and although I knew instinctively which one was more real, my neurotic drive and ambition always pulled me the other way. That in turn caused deep dissatisfaction and a sense of something being definitely amiss.

In the U.S. success came easily to us. Since we started at the top, there seemed no place to go – everything was simply more of the same. Engagement after engagement, city after city, it all blended into a chain of identical events.

A long, steady stream of successes can be as monotonous as a long, steady stream of failures. The only difference is – you have money. Money means status, power and the need to show it – to 'flaunt it' preferably on ostentatious, conspicuous things.

I seriously contemplated buying a custom-made car I saw at an auto show called the Golden Sahara. It came with a TV set, stereo, bar and all the chrome was gold-plated. The whole thing cost $50,000. I was going to settle for chrome without the gold-plate

because that seemed just a touch too ostentatious as well as too tempting to steal. Sans gold, at $25,000 it seemed a bargain!

At that time, however, Jonny came up with an uncharacteristically sane alternate plan where to put some money – real estate. I
agreed, and he started investing in land. But that didn't provide the
necessary security either.

What remained the most persistent objective on my mind, one
which I hoped would fulfill all my desires and needs, was to be of age
and free already. Free from Jonny's tight, suffocating hold, free from
his domination, free to do as I pleased. The need was so strong it felt
like a great irritating sore someone was constantly picking. Freedom
to me was utopia and the fact that the time when I would reach what
is called the legal age still seemed a million years away, made it as
unattainable as the moon. Meanwhile Jonny was busy working on my
tender, vulnerable psyche. His objective was to convince me he was
indispensable and there was nothing I could do or be without him.

As was to be expected I had the usual amount of film offers.
Once there was even a call from Howard Hughes, or his office anyway, after a particularly attractive picture of me appeared in the
trades. All of that, however, was subtly, but most effectively, discour-
aged and rejected by my venerable partner. Today, I realize it was his
own insecurity which prompted him to do that. Whatever came up –
there were always 'intervening contracts' which had to be fulfilled –
or else! Someone was always threatening lawsuits at the mere
prospect of our breaking a contract because of some film. And so I
lost out on a few interesting things, one of which I would have really
like to have done – the part of Anne Frank. Still, I must admit I didn't
fight too strenuously for it. The prospect of becoming an actress did-
n't especially appeal to me. It's only attraction seemed a vague possibility it might offer a bit more freedom than I had. But knowing
Jonny, I wasn't all too sure of that. I might have enjoyed acting and
would have probably been good at it. But there were aspects to it
which were definitely undesirable – as Jonny was quick to point out.
In my genre, I was unique. No one else in the country did quite the
same thing, and those who subsequently tried to copy our style, were
nowhere near as successful at it. Had I gone into acting, I'd have been

one of the many actresses fighting for their existence in a declining business. Since I had to excel, this possibility was unacceptable. No – there was no way out for me.

CHAPTER TWENTY-ONE

And our career continued. Barely a year after arriving in the States, we were asked to perform at the White House. It took three months before we were cleared by the F.B.I. We were at the Latin Quarter in New York at the time (finally) and got time off to do it. The occasion was the White House News correspondents' dinner and was attended by newsmen, congressmen, senators and of course – the President.

For TV appearances I used to wear a more 'conservative' costume and in view of the 'sterling quality' of the audience, I suggested to whomever was running the program, that I would wear one of those. I was surprised by the quick negative response. "Better wear the net thing. Let's give the old boys some fun."

I resented the comment but said nothing. Just before the performance, everyone backstage was searched by the F.B.I. Naturally, I wasn't. (Whatever they thought they had to look for could have hardly been hidden in that costume unless I'd have stuck it up my ass!)

I was a bit nervous because I couldn't see one single woman among the audience, and except for Mary Ford, I was the only female on the show. At that age, anyone over twenty was positively ancient so I didn't even count her. In any event, her presence gave me little, if any, reassurance. Why I should have needed any, is beyond me.

The show consisted of Duke Ellington, Tennessee Ernie Ford, Peter Lind Hayes and Mary Ford and us. I thought the audience would be extremely conservative and the reception would be most dignified if not cool due to that damn costume and I worried about it no end and wished I hadn't asked anyone for suggestions and worn what I considered proper. But it was too late, and I was soon to find out how wrong I'd been.

We were on. The first chords of my introduction sounded as if they reverberated in an empty hall, it was so quiet. However, as soon as I appeared on stage I was greeted with such a raucous of whistles, cheers and yells that I couldn't hear one single note of the orchestra right behind me. The MC had to come out and try to keep the noise down and the orchestra had to start the introduction twice before I could make out what I was to dance to. Being very young, naive and idealistic, I was shocked beyond belief. I had expected the men running the greatest country in the world to behave according to their status and certainly their age – there wasn't one, I suspected, who couldn't have easily been my grandfather – but the reception I received, however flattering, beat even the raucous I used to hear during our USO tour of Germany. However, by the time we finished, I was glad to see the exuberant tone of the applause had changed to one of respect and appreciation and ended with a standing ovation. At that point I was glad to see that my costume was all but forgotten.

After the show there was a party and we were to meet President Eisenhower and receive some sort of certificate of appreciation with his signature, etc. I met so many representatives of the government that the faces and names all blurred into nothing. I haven't a clear recollection of anyone. I only have a vague recollection of Charles Wilson who kept insisting he was fifty years ahead of his time in car designing. Interesting how people tend to live under such grandiose delusions. Had he really been 50 years ahead of his time, General Motors would now be putting out totally pollution-free cars, not to mention safer and more durable ones.

Next I remember being introduced to Milton Eisenhower and speaking with him. Then there was the President himself. I saw the familiar face in the flesh – the facile smile close-up – and it was curiously anticlimactic. We spoke for a moment, I think he even said a few words in German – I heard the usual words of praise and congratulations, took the scroll of paper bearing his signature which he handed to me, shook his hand again – and that was that.

And so, the much anticipated, 'monumental' event was over – the excitement that never lived up to its expectation, (as is always the case) subsided and life went on as usual. Actually, not quite – if anything, it seemed even more monotonous. For after 'conquering' the government, where can you go from there?

At the age of 16 I felt my career, if not my life, had reached its peak. I saw no place to progress toward – nothing to look forward to – no new sights to hang my hopes and drives on.

But everyone else seemed to have an entirely different idea. We were sought after by the so-called 'super stars' eager to round out their show with attractions which were sure to go over big. There's nothing worse than having to follow a mediocre performer who bores the audience stiff. It takes a long time then to pull them up again and many of these super stars can't do that. Many are actors who take the job because of the money. They are offered the money because it's expected they'll draw the audience but often they cannot put across a solid, truly entertaining performance. Live performances are very different from acting in front of the film of TV camera.

But being good has its drawbacks as well. Whenever the press reported we were a hit while someone else who was supposed to be one, wasn't, it tended to get a bit hairy.

One of many such experiences took place at the Eden Roc Hotel in Miami Beach. There was Lena Horne, Jimmy Komak and us. The reviews were fantastic both for Lena and us. But Jimmy didn't do so well. The reviewer was rather unkind. After showering praises on us he started on Jimmy with: "As far as Jimmy Komak is concerned, he might as well have played to the Grand Canyon for all the effect he had on the audience..."

Jimmy was livid and his initial friendliness became rather strained. But then something unforeseen happened. Jonny had a great system of advertising. Our PR man would take the review, multiply it and send copies to the various theater and club managers. Such things keeps them properly impressed, particularly if they see you're not so easily available, which was always our case. By some coincidence the beginning of Jimmy's review, although marked up with a thick red pen, was still legible.

Jimmy, who was becoming progressively less amicable, really blew his top after discovering that little mishap. He hollered and threatened and was generally a nuisance. I could see his point, however, and the PR man was instructed to redo the reprint and to be more careful in the future. However, it didn't seem to hurt Jimmy in the long run as he eventually gave up his career as a standup comic and put together the successful TV series, "The Courtship of Eddie's Father."

But sometimes people resorted to all sorts of underhanded methods in order to repair an injured ego.

We were to open with Tony Martin the completely remodeled Cocoanut Grove in Los Angeles. Before, there was no elevated stage and the palms looked a bit frumpy after years of drooping over the great constellation of stars reputed to have considered the shade of their artificial, glittering leaves the place to be seen. But the whole room was actually a disaster. Being long and narrow with the floor in the middle, most of the audience got a side view of the show and the performer faced a few rows of people and a wall. I was rather looking forward to the 'new look' and the promise of an elevated stage which was to roll out from beneath the orchestra podium. Unfortunately, there wasn't a damn thing they could do about the shape of the room. Still, at least they gave it a try. The management arranged a preview night for the press and flew in over 700 newsmen from all over the country.

Arriving for the rehearsal I was shocked to see the 'stage' turned out to be a tiny affair barely ten feet in depth. It rolled out only to about the middle of the dance floor. To top it all, both the stage and the floor were stained black and with the spotlight on, it was impossible to see the edge of the stage, and I worried about falling off. I couldn't believe the stupidity of the design. Didn't anyone ever consider the needs of a performer? I asked Gus Lampe, the manager, why they hadn't consulted with various performers about it since it was, after all, built for their convenience – or supposed to be. But as the thing was done, there was nothing to do but to try and make the best of a bad situation.

During rehearsals Tony Martin was friendly and pleasant. But the preview night for the press, which unfortunately turned out to be a disaster, changed all that. First of all, the program was poorly paced. The show kept being interrupted by self-congratulatory speeches which broke up the continuity and by the time Tony came on, everyone was tired and ready to go home. We were on early and thus scored another hit. After Tony's third song people were leaving in droves. Many, such as Mitzi Gaynor and friends, stopped backstage just long enough to say hello and congratulate us and they were off while Tony was still in the middle of his repertoire mournfully watching his audience go by.

The next day, I couldn't believe the reviews. As usual we got raves while Tony was either panned or not even mentioned. I must say I thought it was unfair and even felt sorry about it.

In the evening, arriving at the Grove for the 'official' opening night, I stared aghast at the stage. One third of it was taken up by a piano – a baby grand at that.

In those days I was a holy terror. It might have been a way of overcompensating for being repressed and bossed around by Jonny. In any event, I was prone to say exactly what I thought, what was bothering me and to complain a lot whenever anything was not exactly as it should be. Usually it was the orchestra which bore the brunt of it. Jonny, having little sense for the right tempo, always left the orchestra rehearsal to me. Our musical arrangements were never simple, but neither so complicated that a halfway competent orchestra wouldn't be able to do a decent job of it. However, there were several abrupt changes in tempo and style and sudden stops and these had to be just right. I always took as much time as I needed or until they had it down pat. I knew every single note of every arrangement we had and if a conductor made the mistake of trying to treat me as if I didn't know what I was talking about, I simply conducted the orchestra myself. This usually convinced him I knew what I was doing and I'd get no further argument. This and the fact that I heard and could identify every wrong note which I never failed to point out to the perpetrator of the goof, earned me the title: The Bitch. "What a bitch – but what a body" was the musicians' general opinion of me. I didn't mind it in the least - as long as I got the results I wanted – as near a perfect accompaniment as possible. But at the Grove, I never had a problem with the orchestra nor its leader Freddy Martin.

Having this propensity toward defending and demanding what I felt was due us, as soon as I saw the monster of a piano standing where it had no business being, making the already small stage positively ridiculous and certainly unfunctional, I lost no time in confronting Gus and demanded to know how they expected us to work now and whose bright idea it was to put the piano there. Gus looked rather sheepish. "Tony says he needs it."

I stared. "What for?" I wanted to know. "There are two pianos already."

Gus, a small, balding man sporting a middle-age paunch and self-important, confident manner, seemed ill at ease and I knew something wasn't quite right. "Well, he insisted on it..."

"Great. Then you'll have a one act show tonight. I can't dance there."

Gus looked startled. "But you have to go on..."

"How? With that piano there, it's physically impossible. Can't you see that?" I could almost see his brain struggling with the problem.

"But there's no way of getting it off now. The place is packed already."

At that point Tony sauntered in all dressed for the show in a fancy suit and lots of ruffles. His face was a picture of innocence as he looked at me with what was presumably intended to be concern. "Will the piano bother you there?"

I was seething. "Will it?! I should say!"

His face lit up with satisfaction and he actually rubbed his hands together. "Good!"

At least there was no pretense. I took a deep breath. "You miserable son-of-a-bitch. You did it on purpose!"

His eyes opened wide with surprise and rolled from me to Gus. "Did you hear what she called me?!"

Gus stood there in the middle of it, totally at a loss what to do or say. To top it all we were both signed with the same agency (it must have been MCA or William Morris at the time) and the agent was also there looking much like Gus – not knowing what stand to take.

"How could you let him do it? Of all the low-down, under-handed tricks..." I was talking to Gus. We arrived quickly at the point where we were talking to each other through those bewildered men. "He knew damn well I wouldn't be able to dance on it." Jonny, whose English wasn't good enough at the time to argue such things out – stood there knowing what it was all about but saying nothing. But his mere presence was a support to me – had I really needed it.

"Can't you cut out some things?" Gus was suggesting hope-fully.

"That's all right, Gus," Tony offered eagerly. "I can do the show alone. Let's pay them out and they can quit." At that point Gus livened up and became more decisive.

"That's out of the question. We need them in the show."

"I don't need them," Tony insisted stubbornly.

But there Gus was firm. "No. They'll stay in the show."

"But you heard her. She can't work this way and I need the piano there."

"Can't you try it honey?" The agent suggested hopefully.

"With the piano there? How?!"

"But he needs it..."

I turned at the agent snapping testily, "What he needs he ain't got!"

Tony turned scarlet. I knew it was terribly mean but as enraged as I was I cared little what I said.

Tony's anger was being replaced by a hurt look and his calf eyes looked at me reproachfully.

"Look, I really need the piano there."

"Don't give my any of that shit. We both know what it's all about. You know damn well how hard it was for me to dance there even without the piano."

"Oh, come on," Tony interrupted bitterly. "Look at the reviews you got!"

"Aha!"

I turned to Gus and the agent triumphantly.

"You hear that?! Isn't it all clear now?!"

"But there's no way of removing the piano until tomorrow." Gus reiterated hopelessly.

"Then I'll go on tomorrow or whenever the piano is removed." And I stalked out of there dropping a sharp: "Bastard!" as I passed Tony.

On the way to our hotel rooms the whole thing flashed in front of my mind with painful clarity. I just couldn't believe I had said all those things. I couldn't remember a time when I was as angry at anyone. In a way I was sorry about it all and felt I shouldn't have allowed myself to be provoked into such a dreadful argument. But Jonny was well-pleased with it all.

Naturally, we did not go on that night – but the following night, when we came back – the piano was gone and Tony was as apologetic as could be. I chose to ignore his attempts to be friendly. But no matter what I did, no matter how rudely I behaved, he kept at it. Every time I came off the stage, Tony would be there helping me into my robe and handing me whatever I had to take back to the room. I used to give him a look of disgust which he never seemed to notice. Did he have no pride? Wasn't there anything I could do that would make him say enough! I've humbled myself sufficiently for my blunder!

Much later, when I finally decided to quit playing the injured part, he said he used to stand there watching me dance thinking to himself: Could that lovely, innocent thing have really called me a son-of-a-bitch? A bastard?

That experience taught me that the worse you treat someone, the more they'll try to get you to like them – the more challenging it becomes to turn you into a friend. But that, of course, is a characteristic typical of the 'stage personality.' Why else would we be there? My greatest joy used to be to see the hard, closed faces of women, particularly older women, who, turned off by my youth, my costume, would cast suspicious glances at their husbands, gradually relax into expressions of delight and joy. Then I felt I really succeeded in accomplishing something. Often these women who glared at me with open animosity at the beginning and made obvious, offensive noises, were the ones who came up to me later with bright smiles and showered me with compliments.

I think that was the most enjoyable part of my work. To see the closest faces, settled into rigid masks of worry, guardedness, apprehension and distrust relax for a while and forget the things that carve deep lines into our faces. Gradually, it became clear to me just why people not only like, but need, entertainment. It makes them forget – at least for a while all the fears and anxieties they have to grapple with every day. Anything that can take you 'out of yourself' seems attractive and worth pursuing. I don't think we do it consciously – it's something instinctive, an unconscious awareness of the need to view ourselves from a distance, objectively, so that we may see ourselves clearer – the same way we step back from a painting to see it as a whole – clearly, objectively – in order to evaluate it fairly.

But we manage to accomplish that only rarely which is all too evident in every aspect of our existence.

Having lived in this country for the past 18 years, having actually grown up here, I've had plenty of opportunity to observe the dismal results of this fact. I've seen the narrow-mindedness, selfishness and self-righteousness slowly eroding the noble principles on which this country has been founded. I've seen America slowly topple from the mighty pedestal the world elevated it to – and I've seen how mindlessly and readily everyone helped it along.

This led me to wonder about many things. I've come to wonder about the viability of the whole democratic system (or rather what it has deteriorated into) as much as I do about the communist system. I've observed how with every election the politicians lose more and more dignity as they turn into performers, actors, even comics in their effort to impress the electorate – and together with the endless, stultifying TV and press coverage and the carnival atmosphere and vicious competitiveness of the ever-increasing amount of primaries, the whole thing has turned into a fierce, bizarre game – the greatest game of them all – a contest to see who'll win this time – whose turn it'll be to rip off the people for the next term or two.

If all it takes to win is money, as is becoming increasingly obvious to everyone, do people really have a choice? Do they have the chance to elect the candidate they really want and need? Aren't they rather electing a candidate that's being forced down their throats by the mind-boggling propaganda which few can resist? Is it then still a democratic system run 'by the people, for the people?' Isn't it in reality 'money' that determines who will govern the country? Something as ridiculously abstract as printed pieces of paper and cheap metal coins intended merely as a bargaining commodity assumed an all powerful, all-dominating place in our society superseding even God!

If, as I believe, these conclusions are so clear and logical that any child can figure it out after a bit of simple, objective analysis, why then don't people do something about it? Unfortunately, by far the most distressing aspect of human ambitions and greed is that in our drives to accumulate wealth – to gain power and recognition, we arc totally blind to the fact that these drives are ultimately self-destructive. Perhaps it is here that we find the seed of self-destruction present in us all. The unconscious self-annihilating mechanism we don't know how to turn off. As childishly simple and clear as it may appear, it is consistently overlooked by the world's greatest financiers and statesmen alike. We are forgetting that every action has a reaction. We are forgetting that greed and lack of concern and compassion for the next guy is at the bottom of all the ills of our society. I've come to realize that no matter how long I'll live, no matter how many examples of this I'll see, I know there'll always be new ones added to the awesome numbers of stupid, irrational acts committed because of blind greed.

It was greed that fostered communism – when we carefully examine all the circumstances, analyze all the facts, it will still come down to that – and this in turn plagues and terrifies us because we cannot see it for what it is. A reaction to our action. As Giuliano de Medici warned his brother Lorenzo: By wanting too much, you may lose all. And now, five centuries later – we still cannot see the truth of it. How blind can we get?

Bankers, financiers, greedy to make more and more money, by employing more mechanized power are forgetting that the people they are thus depriving of work and income are the buyers of those products they are so eager to make as cheaply and flimsily as possible.

Politicians, spouting expedient rhetoric instead of something they really believe, are forgetting that ultimately the credibility of all politicians will suffer to a point where people won't believe anything any politician says and the entire governmental system will become obsolete.

Industrialists reluctant to do something about the pollutants they pour into the environment – 'because it would be costly and cut into their profits' – are blind to the fact that they cannot breathe, drink, or eat the money they save by refusing to act while there is still time.

Is this blindness something inherent in the human mentality, or is it a sign of a deep, universal mental disturbance that knows no political, ideological, cultural or social boundaries? And why are we so afraid to even consider such a possibility? Is it all part of the built-in seed of self-destruction which cannot be rooted out?

But at the time I was busy enchanting the audiences, such thoughts were still far from my mind. I was much too busy struggling with my own guilt feelings and gratifying my ambitions to worry about the fate of mankind.

CHAPTER TWENTY-TWO

To quench my unquenchable guilt feelings, I did everything in my power to get my mother and sister to the U.S. and my efforts were rewarded. Since my stepfather had meanwhile managed to obtain an immigrant's visa and had moved to Chicago, that's where they went. I contributed to the down payment on an apartment house for them but if I thought that this would alleviate the ever-present guilt complex so carefully cultivated by my mother, I was wrong again. Even all the expensive gifts I kept sending didn't wipe it away. Perhaps they were meant to convince mother I was indeed a success. Whatever they were intended to accomplish, which wasn't clear even in my own mind, they never did.

Meanwhile, I was being taught 'the facts of life' – show biz style – and no matter how hard Jonny tried to shield me from the 'corruptive influences' of that environment – I kept learning all sorts of 'inappropriate' things just the same. As it was, for someone who was spending such important formative years in the world of entertainment, I was still amazingly naive and innocent. Whatever Jonny may have thought of showgirls and dancers, I didn't learn as much from them as I did from the stars.

At one time or another, we worked with every significant performer in the business. I saw people drink, flirt, act superior, make asses and saints of themselves. I learned that behind every rumor there is a little bit of truth. I saw that often people were even eager to keep these rumors alive. Those reputed to be Casanovas did their best to live up to that reputation and chased after every, more or less, available female. Those reputed to be tightfisted bargained and cried a lot when working out the salary; those supposed to be lushes hung around backstage dutifully brandishing a drink; the 'far out' ones wore the perpetually stoned, distant gaze.

At the Latin Quarter I always knew when the musicians were stoned because their tempo was all off and I was ready to brain them.

The Latin Quarter was as strange as I once thought its venerable Lou Walters to be. But Lou, after a brief, discordant beginning and exchange of rationalizations for our respective attitudes, turned out to be a decent sort and we got along rather well. His wife, a very pleasant, mother-type of a lady treated me like a member of the family. They had two daughters, Jackie and Barbara. It was obvious Barbara was the apple of her mother's eye – to use an old cliché. She would talk about her incessantly. Perhaps it was up to Barbara to make up for Jackie who stuttered and at 30 was still 'the baby' in the family and totally dependent on her mother. Obviously, Barbara did an excellent job of it, because today she is the most reputable woman reporter in the country. It's been only lately that I became aware of how shabbily 'enlightened' America treats its women. Never having experienced discrimination as a woman, since I found it nonexistent in the performing arts, it took a long time before I began to understand what it was all about. In view of that, Barbara's accomplishment is even more remarkable.

If anyone had told me what the Latin Quarter would be like when I was still in Cuba, I'd have never believed it. When I finally saw it I was flabbergasted. The decor was a cross between pseudo-whorehouse and third-rate dance hall. The ceiling was draped with limp waves of ancient fabric of some dark, unspecified color which rippled tiredly in the breeze from the air-conditioners and did little to dispel the musty smell of stale smoke and other undefinable odors.

The floor was transparent – big squares of frosted glass, each lit with a different color of light – real sharp. It felt like dancing on slippery cement.

The dressing rooms were tiny, dilapidated cubicles that looked as if they were built for Vietnamese refugees. The cardboard walls didn't stifle one single sound. And those were the star's dressing rooms!

From Julius La Rosa, the matinee idol of the time, I heard things like: "If the fucking jerk (whoever it was) won't quit fucking around, I'll throw his fucking ass out and hire someone else!"

In fact, every noun he uttered was prefaced by some juicy participle or adjective most of which I didn't even understand. This definitely being my puritanical period, I was appalled by such language. But I waited till the engagement was over before I told him I was thoroughly disgusted by the filthy language he was crude enough to expose me to. (Today, I wouldn't give a fuck!)

There were many people I shared the forced intimacy of those dressing rooms with. Johnnie Ray was another one. Off-stage he was a rather quiet, gentle soul and I rarely heard him say anything nasty to anyone. One of the big effects of his performance was that he perspired a lot which seemed to go well with his dramatically turgid, intense style and made the audience think he really worked hard. This, as I found out, was achieved by a great consumption of beer just before the show. I'd constantly hear the popping sound of the can opener and watch with amazement the rapidly diminishing stacks of beer packs in the hallway. I couldn't imagine how he kept so skinny. But his records had been my favorites long before I came to the States, and I was pleased to work with him.

Another interesting experience was Mae West. At the time she was to open at the Latin Quarter, we had just spent about six months working without one single day off – that's another part of show biz: you work seven days a week – and we had succeeded in getting a vacation during the month she was to appear there.

I was thrilled. A whole month of freedom and leisure – of nothing to do in the evening except perhaps a movie, a dinner in some nice restaurant at the time other 'normal' people have dinner. That was a rare treat indeed! Since I could never dance after a meal, I'd usually have dinner at two in the morning. That's glamorous show biz for you.

On Mae West's opening night, Lou invited us to dinner and to see the show. I wasn't particularly keen on going, but we went. It wasn't until later that I realized we'd have been better off not to have gone.

It started out well, however, and felt like a celebration. I could hardly believe it. For once I was actually the spectator instead of performer. It was great. Of course I was curious to see the grand ole dame of the American cinema and her show. It turned out to be a strange melange of risqué songs and sketches rather like a burlesque show. Her 'line' consisted of six or eight musclemen of various shapes and sizes dressed in draped skirts, somewhat like miniskirts, which looked positively ridiculous on those grotesquely muscled bodies. To top it all, some genius had set up a perfectly god-awful choreography for them which consisted of small, mincing steps and made them look like a line of trained elephants.

Mae West herself appeared sitting on a settee of cream satin in the middle of the stage looking every inch like a prizefighter in drag. Her bulging body straightjacketed into what looked like a damn solid corset, she sat there trying to appear seductive and was obviously convinced she succeeded. One by one, her musclemen would appear draped in voluminous capes, turn their backs to the audience and open the cape so that only Mae could see what treasures lay hidden within. Mae, keeping her eyes on the level of their crotch, would utter various kinds of appreciative sounds. It must have been intended to be funny but it wasn't. At that stage of my development, I guess a lack of appreciation of such a 'presentation' was to be expected. However, the audience didn't find it funny or entertaining either. There were very few laughs – and forced ones at that.

The show wasn't even over yet, when Lou joined us looking anything but happy. I didn't like the looks of it and sensed a coming danger. He lost no time getting to the point, saying he felt she couldn't carry the show and that he hated to deprive us of our vacation but he needed us back. I was shattered. But that wasn't all. He wanted us to do the second show that same night.

Well, that took care of the 'peaceful, quiet month' I was looking forward to. But Mae was a fascinating person. In spite of what she may have looked like to me – those musclemen, and they were all young, even good-looking guys – were busily, and seemingly earnestly, vying for her favors. One of those musclemen was Mickey Hargitay who, during an actual fist fight over the lady, wound up being knocked down by a much smaller and lighter specimen. Thus 'defeated,' insulted, but still resilient, Mickey sought solace elsewhere.

At that time Jane Mansfield was being 'discovered' in "Sweet Smell of Success" which was running then on Broadway. Mickey began dating her, the new would-be carbon copy of Monroe seemed to have lost her head over him and the rest is Hollywood history.

There was one thing that gave me a brief insight into the makings of a personality like Mickey's. Since, like Jonny, he was Hungarian, they became fast friends. Sometime later he came to visit us at the house we bought in Malibu, bringing Jane and her daughter Janie. I caught Janie – who couldn't have been more than six or seven at the time – give her future stepfather the most hateful, nasty and surprisingly grownup glare accompanied by a deep-felt, "You... you schmuck!..." Mickey smiled nervously and patted her head. Later, when he stood near the edge of the cliff looking out over the great span of Pacific Ocean lying beneath us, his gaze became wistful and full of yearning. "...In a place like this..." he said quietly. "A man can feel like a king..."

How strange, I thought, the place never affected me that way however much I loved the ocean. But the house, which I bought without really liking it, had only just begun growing on me.

That day I gave Jane one of the kittens born to the first pet I'd had since our pet duck Lida. It was a lovely Siamese cat I called Kazi and I used to take her with me wherever I went. She was even an uninvited and certainly unwelcome guest at the Fontainebleau Hotel in Miami Beach where she made a shambles of an elegant, powder-blue brocade sofa.

I had already promised I'd let Jane have it but when I saw little Janie holding the poor kitten as if she were resolved to strangle it, I felt like taking it back. Instead I told Jane to make sure the girl wouldn't mistreat it. Not at all pacified by Jane's assurances, I watched them depart wondering what fate was awaiting my Kazi's 7th offspring.

The next time I met Jane was at the Melodyland Theater in Anaheim where we worked together in "Gentlemen Prefer Blondes." Jane was already divorced from Mickey, had a new baby girl by her new husband and Mickey's two towheaded boys aged four and six were running around peddling their mother's nude pinup photos.

The show was a disaster. Jane seemed forever drunk or something and Dick Foran, who played opposite her, kept complaining he had to hold her up on stage and of the tufts of fake hair that would continually come off her hairpiece and stick to his clothing and make the audience laugh. It really was a riot. Anyone who'd come in contact with her would leave the stage covered with those blonde, dull strands of hair. It was surprising any of it was left on her. It was really hard not to laugh, Dick's anger notwithstanding. Everyone was wondering about the qualifications of the 'hairdresser' she had with her all the time. Her hair forever looked as if it hadn't been combed in days. I had the feeling the work made her nervous and insecure for she needed constant reassurance. Several times I heard her say to her husband just before having to venture on that stage: "Talk to me dirty... Tell me something really dirty, baby..." while she was pressing against him. I guess we all need something.

The change in Jane since I first met her was indeed startling. But by far the most disagreeable thing about her was that she seemed to have given up things like personal hygiene. She'd come to the theater with traces of the pervious night's make-up and proceed to add to it a new layer. She looked unwashed, unkempt, full of black and blue marks and exuded a strange odor – somewhat like an old washcloth. The theater was forever in an uproar over some rumor or scandal connected with Jane. She stayed with her entourage in a nearby motel from where they were thrown out because of the racket they made. Then there was a big mess about unpaid bills and such. Jane had indeed changed since I first met her.

The next time I heard about Jane was in 1967 in London. I was just entering Westminster Abbey when I spotted the headlines: JANE MANSFIELD DEAD IN AUTO CRASH. Her short, tormented life was over. I was sad, as I am sad for anyone who can't shed the maddening, destructive drive to excel above all people.

CHAPTER TWENTY-THREE

At the Latin Quarter in New York, we worked exclusively in the spring or fall. The rest of the time we were busy either in Miami Beach or the western part of the country. I rather liked Miami Beach in spite of the high humidity and the plastic quality of its clientele. There used to be a Latin Quarter in Miami on Palm Island, one of the lush, emerald green gems of suburban havens accessible by way of the MacArthur Causeway, a neat, slim ribbon of pavement cutting across the blue ocean connecting Miami with Miami Beach.

I loved it. I was always far happier in warmer climates. Even though I was born in a city which abounds with snow every winter, I quickly felt at home in the tropics. Already as a child I remember looking forward to the summer months and these would pass all too quickly.

Life on Palm Island was great. We would live in a large, rented house near the water and from its expansive lawn I could see the deck of the Latin Quarter which was near enough to swim to. All through the day the island was peaceful and quiet – as if miles away from the hustle and bustle of the city and the beach area.

Later on, the Latin Quarter was closed and we would appear

either at the Eden Roc or the Fontainebleau Hotel.

Life in those big hotels was nowhere near as pleasant as on Palm Island. There a performer, except when sleeping, was constantly in the midst of his audience. There was always someone staring or trying to chat. For some perverse reason the showroom would inevitably be on the far end of the huge lobby which had to be crossed to reach the elevators. No matter how hard you'd try, you couldn't evade the well wishers nor the curious stares. During the day, unless you were willing to spend it in the cool, ostentatious elegance of the $100 a day (minimum) room (fortunately our rooms were always free), there wasn't the remotest chance of having a leisurely, undisturbed time around the pool or the beach for that matter.

But I loved to observe the people. As I provided for their entertainment at night, they obligingly and unwittingly provided for mine during the day. The only difference was, they didn't get paid for it. They certainly were a strange, transparent conglomerate of humanity consisting mainly of wealthy New Yorkers most of whom had specific objectives set for their one or two week vacation. I watched them come and go and they always seemed the same. The most common objectives wcre, either to burn their aging skins to a deep leathery tan to impress their less fortunate city-dwellers, for everyone knew that kind of tan in the middle of winter had to cost plenty, or to 'unveil' marriageable daughters in the rich, fertile environment they assumed to be crawling with the most desirable, eligible bachelors. However, there weren't as many as they would have liked to believe and the few 'catches' weren't easily snared. You could see young, pretty girls in exquisite bathing suits, coifed and made-up so that it was perfectly clear they hadn't the remotest inclination to do what they presumably were there for – to enjoy the water and the sun. Instead, they would parade around as if the pool deck was the runway at a beauty pageant while their mothers kept a sharp eye out for any promising-looking oglers. The only problem that I could see, was that most of the young, good-looking guys were there for similar reasons. They were after older, wealthy women or young divorcees with attractive alimonies.

The intrigues that went on were unbelievable. I was amazed to see how much effort people were willing to expend in their search for easy money. But in a place where each is bent on hyping the other, the pickings are slim indeed and I saw many, who arrived full of hopes and anticipation, depart without having made one single stride toward their dubious goals.

Being in the midst of it was like watching an interminable silent movie. I would have never suspected there were as many variations on the same theme. What struck me as being odd and rather senseless already then, although at the time I didn't see myself as being part of it, was the realization that everyone's main concern was how they appeared to other people. Whether they impressed and pleased them – or, best of all, aroused their envy.

In the evening the well-rouged matrons wore their minks or chinchillas in spite of the oppressive heat and humidity and their aging, wrinkled necks and hands were laden with jewels. Even when they were around the pool, their restless fingers glittered with diamonds and gold. At first I thought the only ones unconcerned about what kind of impression they made were the old, decrepit providers of all the display of finery, sitting around card tables in the shade of the awnings of their cabanas doggedly maintaining their pallor. Later I realized that having a cabana was a status symbol as well. They'd sit there scowling at their cards from beneath the rims of their straw hats adorned with shells and similar nonsense, never caring how ridiculous they looked in their baggy, flowered bathing trunks that rarely tasted the salinity of the ocean nor the sharply smelling chlorinated waters of the sparkling pool. They all looked the same. Shriveled muscle and skin, sunken, hairy chests, bulging potbellies, intent poker-faces that fooled no one. Most often they'd blow on cards as much as their wives and daughters blew on clothes, furs and jewels and liked to boast about how much they won or lost. Both seemed to be status symbols and something worth bragging about.

I felt strange and out of place in that environment and glad of it. What a field-day Renoir would have had there – what gems of poignant stories his brush would have told, that a thousand words cannot accomplish.

If it hadn't been for the ocean and the warm, tropical climate I was so fond of, I couldn't have stood it. But Miami Beach had other compensations as well.

During one of our many visits to that resort town of New York's 'idle rich,' I had the opportunity to see and meet Lenny Bruce. We'd been hearing much about him and so Jonny decided we'd try to catch his late show. He worked in a tiny club somewhere on the Beach. Unfortunately, at the time, his style and type of satire was beyond my limited understanding. And it wasn't just a question of the language. I understood what he was saying well enough but the deeper meaning of his satiric style, full of biting sarcasm totally escaped me, and I hadn't the vaguest notion what people were laughing about. However, neither did Jonny's girlfriend and she was American. But then, she wasn't too keen on Milton Berle either.

Knowing us by reputation and seeing us there, Lenny joined us after the show. I was surprised to see how completely different he seemed off stage. He was gentle, soft-spoken and I had a feeling he was genuinely interested in anything I had to say. We spoke of Malibu, I told him how I was beginning to feel at home there and how much I missed it. I thought he really understood how I felt. Unlike so many people who listen without hearing, say sympathetic things without empathizing or even meaning it, Lenny had the rare gift of being truly concerned about other people. He was easy to talk to – to open up to and I was amazed to find myself telling him things I wouldn't have discussed with close friends. Gradually I began to have the unsettling feeling I was betraying more about myself than I had intended. But the almost instant rapport was difficult to resist. I felt we communicated on a truly human level. Not as one performer with another or even a male and female but simply as two human beings.

Even Jonny, usually suspect of anyone who talked to me, especially if it was a fellow entertainer and a male to boot, sat there perfectly relaxed, chatting with his girl, hardly listening to what we were talking about.

Just before we left, Lenny mentioned having just finished reading a novel which dealt with Malibu in detail and offered to let me have it. I thanked him half suspecting he'd forget.

The next day, however, a package was delivered at the hotel and I was amazed to find it was the promised book. Somehow, Lenny even found time to underline the passages which referred to Malibu and to jot down some remarks.

I never saw him again, but I never forgot that one casual meeting, nor his kindness.

In the years that followed, I saw Lenny go from one tragedy to another. And all he was really doing was to follow his conscience as he tried to explain to me that night. If indeed the artist's role in society is to be its conscience – to use his art as an entertaining, but truthful, mirror in which the society can take a good look at itself, then Lenny was fulfilling his function. His only crime was to dig a little too deep beneath the surface of America's collective unconscious and stir up all the muck and hypocrisy. Here, the recent words of one of the really great filmmakers of today come to mind: "Totalitarian regimes of today tolerate protests only as long as they don't feel seriously threatened by them. And this tolerance is basically all that remains of good old democracy."

Lenny didn't fit into the category of harmless, or inoffensive, protesters, so he was hunted down, broken, destroyed. Lenny was a kind, noble soul, with a deeply humanistic spirit that wouldn't be silenced – even after his death.

It wasn't until years later that I came across a book of his routines – a book full of the sharp, witty, uncompromising sarcasm that was his trademark and began to understand what Lenny was all about. Lenny used the tools he had at his disposal to get at the human spirit hidden beneath the hardened facade of everyone of us. It may not seem like much – but that's what he had – and he used it well – perhaps too well.

It's amazing how close-knit the world of entertainment really is in spite of the jealousies and highly competitive spirit overshadowing all else. You may be in a totally strange city but you can be sure that after hours the performers get together somewhere, somehow. In places such as Miami Beach or Las Vegas there are always parties and all sorts of events taking place which bring everyone together.

On one such occasion a wealthy Tennessee Williams fan opened his sumptuous home in Coral Gables to a star-studded gathering celebrating Tullulah Bankhead's opening in Williams' play. All through the night, guests, drunk or stoned on various intoxicants or self-importance or both, were staggering around the great indoor pool gleaming with dozens of gardenia blossoms whose intoxicating scent mingled with the smell of cigarette smoke, stale perfume and food. But that's how things usually turned out.

The Fontainebleau's owner, Ben Novak and his lovely European wife, also took great pains to make sure the entertaining stars were properly 'entertained' during their stay there.

It was in Miami that I met Judy Garland and her husband at the time, Freddie Fields. I felt the almost tangible aura of doom surrounding the woman – I heard the yearning, wistful tone in her voice when she spoke of her daughter. We had just met and sat together at the table and she readily poured out her frustration to the first sympathetic stranger. Then she got drunk and never made the next show.

In all the years of my career, I've seen so much misery and frustration hidden behind the glamorous facade of fame and success I had to eventually realize that we were all striving toward some nonexistent or unattainable goal. There was no satisfaction in realizing 'a dream.' A dream tends to hide hard, cold facts we don't really want to face. Attaining it means having to face them – having to realize that behind each dream there is nothing but a new one – a never ending string of yearnings, dreams, and each one attained represents a new disappointment. Yes, the real losers are the winners because they learn the bitter lesson that behind every dream there's only you – often a very insecure, frightened you that wouldn't know what to do or be without the maddening drives and ambitions. And years bring only more insecurity. Aging stars desperately try to cling to their youth, charm, magnetism. I've seen aging actors, singers, even comics, act as if every female had no choice but to succumb to – to what? Surely not their manly charm?! And yet they'd persist. They must have been aware that any success was due only to what they represented. Why then? Masochism?

In my days of ignorant innocence I had experienced many 'rude awakenings.' Some were even quite unintentional or accidental.

Once we appeared in Las Vegas with an aging comedian – in

this instance I won't tell his name in order to protect the innocent, namely myself, from the guilty party's outrage over simple truth. I should add that this particular engagement in Las Vegas wasn't our first nor last and that we worked with a long string of comics – there and elsewhere. To me, except for the very first time, Las Vegas was a real drag. Except for gambling, which I couldn't do being a minor and wasn't interested in anyway, there was nothing for me to do but read. I've never read anywhere as much as in Las Vegas. I'd go through two, three books a week, easily. As soon as I finished dancing, I'd settle in my dressing room and read, while Jonny tore out into the casino as if his life depended on it.

Before each show I'd spend about forty-five minutes to an hour warming up and rehearsing on the stage. On my way back to the dressing room I had to pass the comic's dressing room which was adjacent to mine. His door was always wide open and he'd sit there in his shorts and T-shirt applying make-up to his wrinkles. He'd always smile at me and try to chat for a while. One day while hurrying from the stage to continue reading a particularly fascinating chapter, I was surprised to see his door almost closed. When walking by I caught a glimpse of the interior. It's peculiar how even the briefest glimpse registers and leaves a clear, detailed picture in our mental eye and only the mind – subjective, conditioned – distorts what we've actually seen. Since I'd never seen or even knew that what I had just seen existed, or could possibly exist, I immediately doubted I'd seen correctly. What I 'seemed' to have seen gave me such a shock that I stopped in my tracks and stood there as if petrified. To test the accuracy of my vision I finally managed to take a step back to have another look.

No – my eyes had not deceived me – although my senses were ready to leave me. In the first fraction of a moment I saw the man, dressed as usual, standing in his famous pose, stomach slightly protruding surveying himself speculatively in the mirror. In the next fraction of the moment's glimpse, the rest registered. His shorts were down around his ankles and a cute blonde dancer was on her knees in front of him sucking on his limp, rubbery cock as if trying to breathe some life into it. For another instant I stood there horrified, and then fled.

I thought it was the most disgusting thing I'd ever seen and even later when I heard that it was an activity practiced quite frequently by many people, I still thought it disgusting. To top it all, the girl was one of the nicest and sweetest girls I'd ever met and I had resented Jonny's constant reminders I was to stay away from her as well as all the other dancers and showgirls. I knew she was having an affair with one of the black singers in the show who was a very nice sort and certainly much younger and better looking than our famous comic, and always treated her with great affection and respect, paid for her apartment, etc. In view of all that, I just couldn't imagine why she'd want to suck on anything so revolting as an old, shriveled prick even though it belonged to a celebrated star. (But I have changed considerably since. Today, some of my best friends are cocksuckers and many aren't even females.)

CHAPTER TWENTY-FOUR

Las Vegas – the mecca of entertainment is the perfect example of the old saying that 'not everything that glitters is gold.' Unfortunately, it is also true that if you say something often enough, people will start believing it. And so Las Vegas does conjure up an image of a fun-town, glamorous, enticing, 'the playground of the stars,' and indeed 'the entertainment capital of the world.' But I always found it hard to swallow that what was shown on its stages was the best the world had to offer by way of entertainment. I thought the Las Vegas 'extrava-ganzas' were excellent examples of how to compensate for lack of imagination and inventiveness: spend a lot of money on the trim-mings. Every new show tried to outdo the previous one in the lavish-ness of costumes and sets – but a really innovative, original idea was seen only too rarely. Why they never even once found an interesting rationale for showing nude showgirls, I will never know. It's always been a line of beautifully denuded, tall girls slowly slinking across the stage, exhibiting their pneumatic wares – more often than not rein-forced by silicone shots or implants. It may seem frivolous and silly but often it was simply tragic, and hardly worth the easy money it earned.

While headlining the show at the Dunes Hotel, I got to know one of these nude show girls fairly well – in spite of Jonny's objections. She was a very thin girl with a shapeless, awkward figure, a sad, pathetic face and a downtrodden look in her vapid eyes. But she had a pair of brand-new knockers – some plastic surgeon's 'work of art' and to her these things were more important than money in the bank.

I never saw her rap with the other girls who seemed to look down on her or at best ignore her, but for some odd reason she would always seek me out and try to talk. I am sure I never gave her any encouragement to do so, still she persisted. Mindful of Jonny's strict prohibitions, I'd try to evade her but she'd always find me and continue from where she had broken off the last time, usually as a result of my spotting Jonny and taking flight. But she seemed determined to relate her entire life history to me and there was nothing I could do to stop her short of being outright rude which I didn't have the heart to do.

She was never aggressive or chatty. She'd always amble toward me on her long, skinny legs, and watch for an opportune moment to start talking. (The nudes at the Dunes used to wear a plastic snap, a kind of semicircle that fitted around their crotch and ass, hugging it securely. This eliminated the old G-string. The end in the back would be adorned with feathers or similar junk, the front with designs of pearls and so on. On their heads they'd wear these incredible creations laden with more feathers and things that looked as if they'd topple any minute. The most ridiculous outfit I saw on any nude was a transparent helmet like some out-of-space creature with nothing else on except that crotch snap adorned with beads and a couple of sparklers up her ass.)

Anyway she would amble toward where I was rehearsing and begin talking to me quietly, haltingly as usual, in the dead monotone that was her style. She had no one. Her mother was an alcoholic, her father raped her when she was nine. She said it matter-of-factly as if it was the most natural thing for a father to do. When I asked her whether it had affected her psychologically, she stared at me dumbfounded. She didn't seem to have a boyfriend, or any friends for that matter. At least I never saw her talk to anyone. To her, the two hundred dollars a week she was getting for showing the tits she acquired with such difficulty, was more than she'd ever hoped to earn. Unfortunately, one of the incisions refused to heal. It was infected and kept on ulcerating. I thought she looked strangely unaffected when she told me the doctor said the silicone implants would have to come out.

One evening before the show, I saw her dressed – obviously she wasn't doing the show. Her thin shoulders were hunched over, trembling and she staggered drunkenly. When she came up to me I saw she was crying. Her face, free of the heavy make-up she always wore for the show and without which I never saw her, looked unusually expressive and vulnerable.

She looked devastated and pathetic. She looked at me through the tears that kept welling up in her frightened eyes and said she wouldn't be doing the show. After a moment's hesitation she offered her hand – I shook it trying to give it a reassuring squeeze. It was cold and skinny like the rest of her. Then she actually smiled at me – or tried to anyway and said, "Thank you – thank you for everything... Good-bye..." Then she was staggering away. A nude went by, looked after her and shrugged her shoulders disparagingly. "Drunk, no doubt..." she said and pranced on. I had a strange feeling as I looked after her. I would have liked to have said a few reassuring words – something, anything, but I didn't know what – and besides I could see Jonny looking for me.

The next day she was found dead – drove her car off an embankment a few miles outside of Vegas.

Yes, Las Vegas was a lot of fun. To escape it, I buried myself in books. To me books were like drugs. They took me to marvelous, strange places where the present dissolved like a dream. I used to love science fiction – particularly stories about fantastic, utopian societies somewhere in far-off galaxies – societies of far nobler creatures than mankind. The only problem was I always had to come back and face reality. Sometimes I felt like living between two worlds – the one I tried to escape and the one I liked to explore. This gave me the feeling that I didn't really belong into the madness, that somehow I was outside of it – that it couldn't touch me. I guess I was neurotic as hell.

At the Tropicana where we shared the bill with Carol Channing, I would read in my dressing room with the intercom turned very low and although I hadn't a conscious recollection of having ever heard her act, after three months, I discovered, to my utter astonishment, that I knew her entire act by heart. I always thought Carol was a rather strange person. I never could decide whether she was totally spontaneous and therefore sincere – or well rehearsed and slightly batty.

In Chicago at the Palmer House were we again worked together, I got to know her a little better because we shared the single dressing room the Palmer House had to offer. I used to warm-up and get dressed in my room so I'd come down in my coat all ready to go. But Carol did her whole bit in that dressing room. It's amazing how everyone has his own way of preparing for a performance. A dancer does the bar exercises, pulls and yanks at her limbs to get the extensions and contorts in all kinds of strange ways – singers work diligently on their vocal cords, tuning, toning them, emitting strange, mysterious sounds – and Carol – Carol had her album. The absent-minded procedure of her getting dressed was constantly being interrupted by her bending over her album and studying with utmost concentration the pictures of people she would be impersonating in her act. Whenever I would come in, there she would be, half-naked, bent over the album, her nose almost touching the pages crammed with pictures of Sophie Tucker, and she would be mumbling something in Sophie's abrasive beer-baritone. I was amazed to see the door was always wide open and the musicians and busboys that were strolling by peering at Carol's tits. But I didn't see that it was any of my business – so I said nothing. I've met plenty of strange people with even stranger habits and if Carol got some vicarious kick out of showing herself naked, that was fine with me. Seeing her peer so close at the pictures I realized she was half-blind.

One day as I sat there watching her go through her antics which were by far funnier than anything she did on stage, she turned around and squinted at the door. Then she walked up close, bent as if stalking a prey, squinting and groping for the door. Finding an empty space instead, she squealed and fled into the deeper recesses of the dressing room. "My God," she said in that slow, moronic voice of hers and turned her huge staring eyes in my direction. "I didn't realize the door is open."

"Yes, it is open," I concurred never adding that it's been that way for the past week or so.

"I figured, if I can't see that far out, they can't see that far in..." she explained seriously in the inimitable Carol-logic, batting her enormous fake lashes at me.

I realized Carol was a genuine, serious caricature of herself – whether consciously or unwittingly, I was never able to determine. Strangely unapproachable, distant, yet also very warm and friendly in an unreal, detached way that to me was Carol.

Actually it was because of this engagement that Muriel Abbott, the dragon lady of the Palmer House threatened to sue if we were to break the contract because of a film.

But I wouldn't have missed it for the world. At last, I would be dancing in the city where my mother now lived. Evidently, I was ready for another try. But my mother was more anxious to see Nelson Eddie, the idol of her youth who was just closing there, than us. Of course I took her to see him and although she was a bit disappointed to see an aging man shuffling around as if afraid he'd break one of his stiff, brittle bones and the once heralded voice was showing signs of wear. Mother forgave and excused it all because he brought her memories of her youth and she sat there looking at him with tears and nostalgia in her eyes.

But all in all, Palmer House was great. For one thing, it was closed on Sunday. Since we rarely had a day off, this in itself was terrific. No such thing ever happened in Las Vegas where we often had as many as three shows a night.

It was on one such occasion that we agreed to appear with Jack Benny on his TV special – "The Shower of Stars." I thought we'd fly into L.A. once to do the show and that would be it. However, we had to fly over three times in succession which meant I had to do without sleep for three nights. As soon as we had finished the last show, we would take a flight to L.A., have a couple of hours to rest or change before going to the studio for a whole day's rehearsal, then take a flight back and arrive in Las Vegas in time for the first show. It was totally insane. I had to get my doctor to prescribe some uppers or else I would have never made it. By the end of the third day, I was near physical and mental collapse.

We did two sketches with Jack, all ancient 'tried and true' gags he did ages ago with Gracie and George Burns. Jack was very careful never to try anything fresh and new – or 'untried.' The trouble with the whole thing was that Jonny had most of the lines and besides speaking a lousy English, couldn't memorize a thing. After countless, unsuccessful tries, his lines were written on his cuffs and handker-chief. As it was, he kept saying "as a matter of fucked," instead of fact but when I tried to correct him, Mary Livingston, Jack's 'better half,' quickly stopped me, saying I should let him say it his way.

We danced to "Ebbtide" so they had rigged up a beautiful, expensive set of a deserted beach and even brought yards of real turf rolled up like a rug. The set itself cost a thousand dollars. Amazing that they should have assumed I would be able to dance on grass in toe shoes. Anyway, I had them take it away and leave only the sand and rocks in the background.

Later, Jack asked us to join him in his first Miami Beach engagement and after some haggling over money which the Morris agency should have taken care of but didn't, we went.

The Fontainebleau went all out for the occasion. To celebrate what must have been Jack's twentieth thirty-ninth birthday, they flew in Jim Garner whose sole function was to roll an enormous birthday cake onto the stage. Then we all stood there and looked rather silly waiting for Jack to deliver his golden lines. Oddly enough, whenever I just stood around, I felt rather naked in that costume.

Georgie Jessel, who seemed to pop up at the oddest times, was at hand, eager to jump in and upstage his old buddy. He ran as fast as his little legs would carry him, climbed onto the stage and ignoring Jack, he raced toward me, pulled me into a bear hug and yelled: "I always wanted to meet Mr. Johnson." Of course, the audi-ence roared. Jonny, who displayed an extraordinary presence of mind in such situations, retorted readily while shaking his hand: "I am glad to meet you too," and brought the house down. I was glad to find myself finally released. Jessel was never one of my favorite people.

I found that most comics are strange creatures. They act as if they had a monopoly on jokes and whenever anyone happened to say anything funny they looked surprised and vaguely disturbed. I discovered there are two kinds of comics. Those who are very humble and quiet off stage and those who are 'on' all the time. The former are very rare. The latter are difficult to take. Jack Carter belongs into the latter category as well as Don Rickles and Milton Berle. In a way, I rather liked Berle. In New York, after the show, we would inevitably wind up at Lindy's for dinner. We were always with a whole bunch of people including the Wiere Bros., three funny little men somewhat like the Marx Brothers, who worked with us at the Latin Quarter. I think they came along mainly because Jonny always insisted on paying for everybody. I don't think they paid once in all the months we used to go there together. Jonny was also a great tipper, and no matter how many performers or Broadway stars would be standing there waiting, there was always a table reserved for us. Berle, who liked to pass around cigars instead of tips used to sit with us while waiting for his table grumbling about never getting the table he wanted. No one can tell me there's anything that beats the buck in this country.

Comics are a strange breed to be sure. The only other time we appeared in Washington was in concert at the Carter Baron amphitheater with Red Skelton. David Rose conducted the huge, excellent orchestra. It is an entirely different feeling dancing to a really good accompaniment and I felt I always did a much better job when that was the case.

The Carter amphitheater was a big, outdoor theater situated in a lovely section of Washington in the midst of acres of woody park land and apple orchards. It was late summer, the apples were ripening and the air was warm and laced with fragrance drifting in from the nearby woods. I loved to wander about, eating apples off the trees and lie in the meadows streaked with wild flowers. It was one of the most enjoyable engagements ever.

Red was a very gentle, softhearted man who loved to tell jokes except when his wife Georgia was present. He could be in the middle of the most interesting joke and obviously enjoying telling it, but he'd drop it the moment he saw, or sensed her approaching. Georgia was friendly and pleasant but there was the unmistakable aura of superiority and self-importance displayed by so many wives of popular men. I guess they have to overcome a certain feeling of inferiority because they aren't really a part of it. They really can and want to be nice but something keeps getting in the way. Perhaps they feel if they really let go they'd lose prestige or importance or whatever it is they feel they must maintain – hang on to no matter what.

The next time we worked with Red was in Lake Tahoe. We were opening the Harrah's Club. It was Christmas and Tahoe was at its best – shrouded in mountains of snow. I liked nothing better than to work in resort towns and, as far as I was concerned, Lake Tahoe was the best, especially in winter. There was something magical – even mystical about that place in winter – when every sound was hushed by the thick carpet of snow, every contour softened by the cushions of cold whiteness shimmering in the sun or lighting the moonlit darkness with a subtle, ethereal glow. I loved to walk across the snow-packed walks, all bundled up, warm and secure and listen for the soft crunch of my footsteps. At such a time Lake Tahoe was the most enchanting place to be.

When we arrived, the club looked as if it were never meant to open at the scheduled time. Wherever I turned I was tripping over workmen busy as ants; carpet layers, struggling with huge rolls of deep plush rug, carpenters working feverishly on the bar that looked as if it wouldn't be ready for weeks and everywhere were tall ladders with electricians on top mounting fixtures. It was a veritable madhouse and we were supposed to rehearse the orchestra. It looked like an exercise in futility but miraculously, as these things usually happen, the place opened exactly as scheduled. It turned out to be a lovely club – all pink and crimson, good stage and good orchestra. But I forgot all about the altitude and that we should have gotten there earlier to get used to it. The opening night I felt as if my chest would burst and when I came off stage, promptly passed out. But they must have been counting on such things because there were oxygen tanks all ready as well as a doctor. I thought I would get used to it, but as it turned out, I was out cold after almost every performance and so was Red who, as I, had a slight case of anemia.

It's amazing how a club owner's personality reflects in the establishment. Old Bill Harrah had a great respect for artists and this was obvious everywhere. All the facilities for the performers were as luxurious as the club itself. The dressing rooms were large and comfortable, the stars' dressing rooms were elegant miniature suites equipped with every convenience imaginable, and Mr. Harrah was forever inquiring if anyone needed anything. He even provided small Christmas trees for the dressing rooms, perhaps to bring some feeling of the holiday spirit to those who never have a chance to celebrate the most important of all holidays. For at the time everyone else has vacations to spend these days with one's family, for the performer, this is the busiest time.

On New Years, at which time all the clubs put on one show usually, the Club was so busy and so many people who couldn't get in for the dinner show clamored for another one, Harrah decided to accommodate them. To soften the blow, he sent cases of champagne backstage and everyone was getting drunk. I never drank much, let alone before the show, but this time, before that second show I had a couple of glasses of champagne and went out there slightly intoxicated but happy and confident I wasn't that drunk that I couldn't maintain my balance. However, I was soon to learn that all the pirouettes and activity I went through tended to increase the high and by the time I was in the middle of the act, I was so drunk I began laughing without having the faintest idea why, and kept it up throughout the remainder of the act. It was a riot, but I could have easily gotten hurt. As it was – I was lucky and it turned out to be one of my best performances.

At Harrah's we were having fantastic audiences and standing ovations were quiet frequent. Naturally, as every performer, I was exhilarated, even touched by a standing ovation, but I was amazed by Red's reaction to it. The opening night I saw he was so moved he stood there gazing at the audience with tears of gratitude in his eyes and when he came off stage he walked slowly as if dazed and really wept.

"Did you see them?" he asked in a reverently overwhelmed little boy's voice and shook his head as if to clear the awe. "My God... They all stood..."

When he staggered back to take another bow, he still wore that wistful look of a little boy overwhelmed by their generosity. I was so touched by his humility I could have cried myself. Then the next night after another standing ovation, the same thing happened. And then the next night, and the next, again and again. I soon began to realize that Red had a bit of ham in him and enjoyed his tears as much as he enjoyed the applause. Perhaps that was the whole secret of it – he made every audience feel as if they were the first to award him with the greatest prize ever.

There was only one problem backstage. The dressing rooms were one floor beneath the stage and the steps leading down were wide, steel reinforced cement steps that made me wish I'd never trip and fall for several broken bones was the best one could hope for. Once, when I thought I was overcoming my fainting spells and the altitude since I didn't pass out immediately after leaving the stage, I almost fell down that flight of stairs. I began to feel faint only when I was about to descend and saw the steps swimming in front of me in a bottomless void of deepening hues of crimson – then I passed out – just barely missing a head-on crash down those steep steps. From then on, Mr. Harrah put a man at my disposal whose sole job was to escort me and Red down those steps. This, being a rather boring, uneventful job, after the initial novelty wore off, the man filled his spare time with boozing and often, I wasn't sure who was helping whom down those steps. Eventually, they were carpeted and the danger eliminated.

But that engagement at Harrah's remains one of the nicest I can remember. I always liked to work with comics because at the time I was under the delusion – that they were less egocentric than, for example, singers. But then I met a few which dispelled that delusion.

CHAPTER TWENTY-FIVE

When Jerry Lewis was scheduled to appear at the Palace in New York with his own show, the ninety minutes was set up so that the first half was filled up by top headliners headed by us, Eydie Gorme and the Wiere Brothers. The second half was all Jerry. The first half got raves, Jerry was panned but – the place was packed every night. On the other hand, Liberace, who followed us in, got raves, but small audiences. Nothing's ever perfect it seems.

Jerry struck me immediately as a friendly and likable, but at the same time, strangely petulant and childish individual. For a comic, he took himself extremely seriously and took great offense if anyone tried to be even the tiniest bit funny, as if that was his sole prerogative. Yet Jerry was indeed a very capable and talented guy. Some of his routines were extremely funny, even brilliant but I felt a part of his personality was at odds with the rest. It was as if he were fighting himself – trying to be so much that he was destroying what he had. For one, Jerry was a frustrated singer, and seemed determined to show the world he could make it in that field as well. He never had a sufficient amount of self-criticism to realize he just didn't have it, to accept it and stick to what he was really good at. He cut an album –

all serious songs – which was one of the worst things I've ever heard. The only reason I have it is because he gave it to me, unsolicited. There was hardly anything left to do when he offered it to me but to accept. He even offered to autograph it, but I said I was in a hurry.

Another part of his act consisted of poking savage fun at the audience – ala Don Rickles. Some of it was in such bad taste and so crude it was embarrassing even to watch. It lacked Rickles' talent and the underlying good-naturedness that took the sting away which enabled him to pull it off successfully. Coming from Jerry, it was offensive. Actually, Jerry's friendliness was often diluted by a certain amount of brusque, offensive aggressiveness and conceit which probably stemmed from inner insecurity and feelings of inferiority. Up to this day, whenever I see Jerry anywhere, he is always on, he must have the last word, he must always talk everyone down. I guess he never realized he really does have a great deal of talent and doesn't need to be rude and offensive to prove it to others, as well as himself.

When we worked together on that date – in fact it was the only time we did work together – he was extremely pleasant and friendly, joking around, making fun, parodying my warm-up exercises and so on. Although even then I felt a certain underlying guardedness and reserve, I took it all as intended – in fun.

I used to do a fair imitation of his singing and got a big kick out of breaking-up people. Once, however, while clowning around backstage and doing a takeoff on one of his songs, I had a startling experience which showed me how thin-skinned Jerry really was. There I was, doing my bit, when I noticed the laughter ebbing away and a few kids seemed to be looking beyond me. I turned around and there stood Jerry trying to suppress a scowl. No – he certainly didn't appreciate that but he made a halfhearted attempt at laughing it off. It rang false and I knew he was mad. I'd touched upon the sorest spot – his singing. Ever since then, he never joked around or made fun of me anymore. Well, we all have our hang-ups I suppose.

As much as I disliked being told what to do and when to do it and having decisions made for me, there was also a certain kind of security in it, and even a peculiar sort of satisfaction. Everyone knew Jonny was my guardian, some even thought my father – and a very protective one at that. This created an aura of inaccessibility and exclusivity around me which made me look even more attractive and desirable. Naturally, I enjoyed all the attention and even – to a degree – the seclusion I was forced into. Thus, when finally the time came for me to act independently, I was terrified. If I fancied myself using psychology to achieve what I wanted in our work, Jonny must have been doing his own scheming. However much I contributed or thought I did, Jonny never failed to remind me – he was responsible for everything – our success, even my own accomplishments.

When one day he suddenly stopped regulating my life, I was in a panic. I felt utterly lost and abandoned. (People can indeed get used to anything.) I remember a peculiar discussion we had in New York during which he told me that since I was eighteen – legally of age – I could do as I wished – he was no longer required to act as my guardian. I was shattered. I didn't know what to do. The door of the cage was suddenly, unexpectedly opened, but I was afraid to fly out. Whether Jonny anticipated my confusion, even counted on it, I could never be sure. But it would seem reasonably logical that he must have known what he was doing. In any event he seemed perfectly calm and casual when he suggested that if I wanted him to continue looking after me, taking care of me he would do it. He reminded me again of the business being full of unscrupulous people just waiting to take advantage of me.

I nodded eagerly. He looked very matter-of-fact and businesslike when he suggested that if we were to get married, I'd never ever have to worry about those things – he'd always look after me. Somehow I instinctively understood what was on his mind. With Jonny, the first and foremost thing had always been his work and since I was an integral part of it, what better way to secure and protect his investment, his future?

It's difficult to say today what went on in my head. I know I wanted to be free more than anything else. But I was also afraid. Being free meant having to break up everything, and I just wasn't ready to do that. Also for some obscure, unimaginable reason the idea of marriage brought the thought of divorce and divorce had something marvelously liberating and final about it. So – I agreed. I may have been afraid not to. Also, it had occurred to me that being married would give me greater freedom. After all, one doesn't guard a wife as much. But I was dead wrong.

Another motivating factor was that we had already bought a house in Malibu as an investment and – I knew mother would be absolutely devastated. What better reasons could anyone want? Furthermore, Kay had just run away from home and mother, having no idea how to get her back and control her again, finally agreed to let her live with me. Kay was studying music so Jonny decided to put her to work as our accompanist. Since the piano seemed too mundane to him, he decided an electric organ would be best. We picked up Kay in Chicago and headed for L.A.

In Los Angeles, the whole affair was arranged quickly and efficiently. We were married in the city hall and our witness was the court clerk. There wasn't one single person we knew. I remember feeling very strange about the whole thing – as if I was committing myself to some temporary arrangement that was practical and would benefit everyone. I remember vividly the judge – Ida Mae Adams, an ancient lady with a face like a prune and a tired old wig full of tight blonde curls. As she read the marriage vows in her cracking, abrasive voice, she kept poking a pencil under the wig and scratching her head. I could have screamed with laughter. Somehow it all seemed to fit – and was indicative of what the whole deal was all about. It was an arrangement. And I knew we each had our own plan – which conflicted with the other's. And as I ran down the steps of the city hall, I knew I'd be back there soon – and I was.

Meanwhile, life proceeded as usual, with very minor differences. I found sex very uninteresting, unexciting and generally a waste of time. But I got used to the inevitability of 'suffering' through it which was as rarely as possible – and to make it more bearable, I'd read a book. That just goes to show you again that not everything that glitters is gold. Or to put it more succinctly – often the sexiest looking girls are the worst fucks.

God, it's incredible what people are capable of turning their children into in their stupid, puritanical, irrational way of thinking. Why should we look at one of the most basic, natural human needs as something dirty and perverted – something that no self-respecting person would be caught dead doing?

This shitty attitude reflects in every aspect of our existence even our religions. Why is it necessary to dream up fantastic tales about guys being born of immaculate conception before we make them into deities? Could we accept a god who was conceived the usual way? How low we must think of ourselves in view of the fact that we came about as a result of an activity we regard as sinful and dirty! Is that perhaps why we tolerate so many intolerable situations without caring how detrimental they may be to us?

Why should we have this need to feel guilty for doing something enjoyable? Where did all the guilt begin? Why must we destroy the most enjoyable part of the human existence by infecting it with guilt?

I could cry when I think of all the years of enjoyment I had wasted – when I think of all the years of torment, of painful self-analysis – of probing, exploring of new states of awareness, the soul-searching it took to just begin to conquer all the nonsensical guilt complexes heaped upon me by my screwed-up elders.

I am indeed glad to see a new generation emerging that isn't buying all that shit. Maybe that's why there seems to be a dislike by the older generation for the young generation. What right do those damn kids have not to be as guilt-ridden as we were?! Sounds fantastic, far-fetched and absurd, doesn't it? But let's think about it a little anyway.

But in those years I thought life wasn't so bad after all. I was hopelessly fucked-up by my mother and Jonny's puritanical upbringing but since I didn't know any better, it seemed all right. I had my work, all sorts of interests to keep me busy and then there was the prospect of finally moving into a house of my own.

CHAPTER TWENTY-SIX

A few years earlier we had looked a long time for something else to buy besides land. At first, it was agreed we would invest in income property. But driving around suburban L.A., I was fascinated with the idea of owning a house – I wanted to have a place – a home to come back to between engagements. I wanted to have a garden and plant things. It's amazing how hard it is to escape one's past, the conditioning, the influences – good and bad – which we are exposed to during our childhood. It's all there, motivating our behavior, attitudes, likes and dislikes – everything. The happiest years of my life were those I spent at grandmother's – so I wanted to find a place that would give me the same feeling. Of course, at the time I didn't know what I was after. I had that gnawing, disquieting feeling I needed something but I had no idea what it was.

After searching for a long time, I fell in love with a house in Pacific Palisades, in a secluded area overgrown with sycamores and pines called the Uplifters Ranch. The house stood on an acre of sloping land full of pines and shrubs, alabaster benches and secret little hiding places beneath willowy trees. The house itself, built like a hunting lodge of rough logs without and within, could have just as well stood in the midst of a deep, European forest.

It was huge and exquisite. There were beautifully marked hardwood floors of some rare, imported wood; a loft supported by tree trunks; the balustrades and even beds in the four bedrooms were of branches; each window had its own individual, asymmetric shape which lent it a mystical fairy-tale book quality and all drapes and upholstery were of rawhide. It had two huge, luxurious marble and mosaic bathrooms, a fantastic fireplace made of enormous boulders – complete with a big witches kettle. Outside was a bar made of the same boulders which extended into a 20 foot waterfall. Chief Justice Earl Warren, when Governor of California, supposedly lived there for nine years. But that wasn't what made it appealing to me. In California I found that every old house had some kind of fascinating past. What I liked best about it was that it had its own very special feel – a scent of antiquity and solidity. Those were always the things I looked for the most. It was built by someone who obviously spared no expense or effort to make it into something unique.

The man who was selling it was dying and we made a deal with his wife and his attorney. After all the papers had been signed, the down payment made, the whole thing was in escrow, the man recovered sufficiently to decide he wanted an extra point of interest. I wanted them to stick to the original deal. They wanted to renegotiate it. I was so mad I canceled the deal saying that under the circumstances I wouldn't want the house even if they gave it to me.

What's more, I predicted it would take a very long time before they'd sell it. But my anger, indignation and wishing on them all sorts of miserable things, didn't make me feel any better. I wept for three days, but nothing could induce me to reconsider. Jonny kept telling me that if I liked it that much I should pay the extra point, what did it matter? But I wouldn't. I have no idea what I was trying to prove. Looking at it today, I realize I was indeed screwed up. But as it turned out, the house we wound up buying was a much better choice in the long run, and I was right about one thing. It took four years before they sold that house.

Three days later, after I calmed down a bit, I began looking again at houses – if only halfheartedly. By that time I had grown to hate real estate agents and their pushy, hard-selling ways and I would-n't even look at a house that was still occupied. I loved to roam through empty, deserted houses and inspect every corner, every nook and cranny.

One day I stopped to look at an open house in Brentwood. The old man sitting there couldn't have looked less like a real estate agent. He barely glanced at us and continued reading his paper and let me roam around undisturbed. When I was through he got up, folded his paper and said quietly: "I don't think this house is what you want."

I stared at him flabbergasted.

"I'd like to show you something you might like. It's a big home – five bedrooms, four baths. Three acres on a hillside overlook-ing the ocean, private beach..."

I didn't like the beaches in California. Being used to the crys-tal clear, blue, warm water of tropical beaches, I was spoiled. What's more, the house was still occupied. Ordinarily, I wouldn't have even bothered to look at it but I rather liked the old man and also I was curious to see what he considered more suitable for us. He was Dutch and spoke German which helped considerably.

The next day, since I hadn't heard from him all morning, I decided to call him. Just as I was about to pick up the receiver, the phone rang. It was Van Dyke, our Dutch real estate man saying we could see the house that afternoon.

He picked us up and we headed west. The closer we got to the beach, the foggier it got, and the more disappointed I was getting. I began to be sorry I had agreed to see it. We drove along the Pacific Coast for what seemed an eternity. The hills looked dry and barren, and I couldn't imagine I'd ever want to live in such an area. Then I saw a smaller hill covered with big old palms and eucalyptus trees and I thought, how nice it would be if it were at least the hill.

Just then, Van Dyke pointed to it saying: "See that green hill? That's it!" I was cheered by that bit of news but hardly reassured.

The narrow, private road he turned onto was lined with old cypress trees, oleanders and century cactuses and reminded me vague-ly of the Riviera. But reaching the hilltop and the house, I was disappointed again. The place was big, but both the gardens and the house, a big, rambling California Spanish structure, were terribly neglected. To top it all, the interior was painted a horrid dark green which made the house even more depressing. But we made an offer on it – $10,000 less than the asking price. Van Dyke was so sure they would never consider it he didn't even want to make the offer.

"I don't care if they don't accept it," I informed him readily, "I don't like the house anyway."

"But how can I possibly offer that?"

"Tell them I'm crazy or something. – I don't care..."

He finally agreed to write out the offer. Subsequently there must have been about a dozen counter offers but I stuck to my price and finally they accepted as I knew they would. The owner, K.T. Stevens Marlowe, the daughter of Sam Wood, was very anxious to move back into the city. Her husband, Hugh Marlowe, was heartbroken about it because I could see he really loved the place, but she seemed resolved to get rid of it.

After we bought it, we didn't see the place again for at least a year. The Marlowes lived there for another six months, then moved to Brentwood.

On the road, thinking of it and looking at all the pictures we took, I began to see ways of improving it. I still thought it was an awful house, but I decided to make it into something really beautiful. I used to fly in from Las Vegas to supervise the remodeling and building of the pool, and slowly, I began to feel better about it.

But it wasn't until we started living there that I stopped mourning for the Warren house. Unfortunately, we never spent more than a couple of months at 'home' – most often much less. And what was originally meant to be 'a place to come back to between engagements,' became 'the only place to live.' Gradually, the house insinuated itself into my life and assumed a very important role. It became an entity in itself – like a living thing – an integral part of me. And I took it with me wherever I went. I had innumerable pictures of it taken with a stereo camera and whenever I'd get 'homesick' I'd plug in the viewer and look at the slides. It looked so real it felt as if I were actually there. I realized how deep my need for a stable environment was and however neurotic the whole thing may have been, there was little I could do about it.

I wanted to know everything about the house; I pumped everyone I could for information. From the Marlowes, and the date in toilet tanks, I learned it was built in 1928 by a California Supreme Court Justice, Judge Joseph Call who died there. He was the father of Asa Call who was very influential in California politics. Call's widow sold it to Sam Wood, (K.T.'s father), a film director who did many of the Harlow and early Garland films and also worked on "Gone With The Wind." (He directed the Marx's brothers films as well as "King's Row" with Ronald Reagan.) From old records I learned that in the late forties he formed an organization called the Motion Picture Alliance for the Preservation of American Ideals and was its first president. The MPA worked hand in hand with the House of UnAmerican Activities Committee and Congressman Richard Nixon in an effort to purge Hollywood of its 'left-wing' elements.

Wood's wife couldn't have been too crazy about the house because as soon as he died, she sold a great portion of the property, keeping only the house on the three acres and her daughter wound up living there. I kept wondering how many people knew it as I did and how they had felt about it. Was Richard Nixon ever there, planning. preparing his moves? It would seem logical that he might have visited his collaborator to scheme his infamous campaigns against the Hollywood 'pinkos.' I wondered how Sam Grosvenor Wood could have felt seeing the dismal results of his 'patriotic' work – or whether he ever realized he helped plunge Hollywood into a decade of mediocrity from which it has never quite fully recovered.

What was on the minds of the people who had lived within these walls? I wandered through the gardens trying to decide how to landscape it and after I had made up my mind and planned it all out and the gardeners proceeded accordingly, I discovered I was actually restoring it to the way it used to be. Where I decided on gravel walks, when the wildly sprouting shrubbery was cut back, it revealed remnants of gravel exactly in the places I wanted it in. I used to fall asleep devising new ways of restoring and improving the property.

But the most upsetting aspect of this new existence was that I never could stay long enough to suit me.

I was getting sick and tired of New York, Miami Beach, and Las Vegas which were the places we appeared in most often. But there was nothing I could do about it. Los Angeles, culturally and entertainment-wise was a wasteland. Had there been a resident ballet company I would have joined it immediately. I cursed America's lack of support and interest in culture – the narrow-minded, provincial mediocrity, the kind of values and attitude that left little room for things Europeans wouldn't and couldn't do without.

Whenever we had to leave, I was devastated. Yet once I got into the routine of working, it went well, and I could enjoy it again.

However, out of that time, only a few events stand out in my mind, and the rest seems to blend into that monotonous labyrinth of sameness.

CHAPTER TWENTY-SEVEN

Just before the end of the Batista regime, we went back to Cuba for a short engagement, and Havana welcomed us with open hearts and undiminished devotion. It was then that we met Liberace and became fast friends. Since both Lee and us were prone to be mobbed in the streets, the Chief of Police of Havana took upon himself the task of 'protecting' us. He would go everywhere with us; for dinner after the show and later, he would try to provide for our entertainment. As far as I was concerned, my favorite entertainment was to sit around and listen to Lee's jokes. He knew hundreds of them and his delivery was first-class. I loved it. One night our chief of police decided to give us a real treat. I had no idea where we were going or what kind of entertainment could be found in the old part of Havana which was where he drove us. It was in the early morning hours and that part of town looked dead. He pulled up in front of an old, somber house and started banging at the door.

The place looked deserted. I felt like going home, but he kept banging until someone finally opened up. We all piled into a big foyer. There were several young women, one of them black, all stacked and kind of brassy looking. The place seemed in an uproar over our arrival and more women were drifting in. Lee seemed to be looking them over and finally pointed to two. One was the black woman. For some reason this seemed to upset one of the other women so that she began crying and Lee pointed to her as well. Then we were ushered into a big room furnished with old but comfortable armchairs and sofas, all facing a small stage covered with a thick, red rug which continued up the small, elevated podium and even the walls.

The three women appeared and began taking off their clothes. Then a guy came up on the stage – stark naked. He looked cock-eyed and mentally retarded. Anyway, he sported this big, moronic grin and a huge cock. Finally it was beginning to dawn on me I was about to see my first stag show courtesy of our chief of police. I was utterly mortified – not only because of what I was about to see but mainly because they all knew me and seemed such ardent fans of mine.

The black woman strapped a dildo around her waist and went after one of the women while the moronic fuck-artist went after the other. There was a certain attempt to do it artistically, they assumed what they must have thought were graceful, arty poses and all the while the women kept glancing at me as if expecting approval. I thought I'd die. Lee appeared amused by the whole thing and kept dropping little lines such as: "Imagine! All this without music..." and "On second thought, tomorrow morning I don't think I'll have cream in my coffee." His manager, Seymour Heller, a pasty-faced flabby guy who didn't seem to own one single solid muscle, looked slightly bored but his beady little eyes didn't miss a thing and he seemed entertained by my obvious embarrassment.

I began to feel a bit sick to my stomach so I got up and went looking for the bathroom. Someone in the foyer pointed to a door which led out into a long, narrow courtyard. On both sides were doors leading to a number of small rooms and many were wide open revealing their dimly lit interiors where naked women lay sprawled on low beds. As I walked by they would poke their heads out and chatter excitedly and I could hear my name over and over. Well, in Havana I was a big hit even with the whores. Actually, it was only then that I realized I was in a whorehouse – and I had to walk the whole length of that courtyard to get to the bathroom. The realization of where I was made me so nervous that when I reached the toilet I forgot why I came. My guts were churning and I was afraid to sit down for fear of contracting some unimaginable disease. I decided not to go back to the 'showroom' but wait in the foyer.

When it was all over, they came to get me. The black woman was still naked sitting cross-legged on the podium eyeing us all in consternation and then started on the chief of police: "How could you bring 'our' Chiquita here, eh? La povrecita, mira la! Don't you see she's just a child? La pobre nina... Stupid jerk!" she yelled completely oblivious to the man's rank or his best intentions. "Don't you have no consideration for anyone?!"

To find my purity being defended by a whore was a bit too much to take. I felt incredibly relieved when we finally got out of there.

It isn't easy to break off a friendship with someone after living through such an experience together. Whenever we would work in the same city with Lee, we'd always get together after the show. He would play the piano, tell jokes, reminisce about our adventures in Havana or give us a preview of his latest wardrobe. Somehow, in retrospect, it didn't seem all that bad and it even made me feel rather knowledgeable and worldly. Since he also lived in L.A., we'd get together often, either at his place or ours. I really liked Lee. Besides being a lot of fun, I found the seemingly artificial friendly facade was indeed genuine. Lee was one of the nicest people I have met in the world of show business. And when Kay began working with us and suffered from nervousness and all kinds of insecurities, Lee spent endless hours explaining to her how every artist feels a little nervous before going on, and trying to impart some of his inimitable show-manship. It helped a great deal but Kay was never terribly enthusiastic about being on stage and although she looked and did great, she eventually dropped out to study medicine and wound up a surgical nurse.

I was heartbroken about it because I loved having her with me. Also, I liked the way it turned out musically. We had all our arrangements reworked to feature the electronic organ and it sounded fantastic. And Kay, tall and lovely with her long, blonde hair and "Sophia Loren build," as the reviewers liked to call it, was indeed an excellent asset which she never could believe or accept. She felt she hadn't made it herself. She felt pushed into it – promoted – and it didn't give her a sense of personal achievement.

We both had our problems to grapple with and looking at our parents, it was easy to see why. With Kay out of the act, living at the house, it became increasingly more difficult to leave. Understandably, I was interested in any offers which would allow me to stay and work in L.A.

Once, when whiling away a hot Las Vegas day around the pool, Ken Murray sauntered over with what turned out to be a fascinating offer. His plan was to try and revive the old Ken Murray blackouts and make it into a fine, high-class revue. He was very eager to have us join him promising us anything we wanted. He would give us a completely free hand to put together our own production, ballet or whatever. Of course, I was instantly interested. He said he thought of hiring a retired dancer to do the choreography, but he was willing to hire anyone else we'd care to suggest instead. Since I would be setting it anyway, we didn't care who he got so we agreed.

By the time we went into rehearsals, I had it all planned out. We decided on an oriental production based on "Scheherazade." We had a big cast and fairly free funds for the setting and scenery. For my presentation, we had a six foot gong made-up which stood on a small podium in the center of the stage. At one point in the production, a dancer hit it – somewhat like the guy in the Arthur Ranke pictures where upon four other dancers picked it up, turned it face down and supported it on their shoulders. I was on the reverse side, twisting and dancing while they slowly walked around with it. It was very effective and I had a marvelous time putting it together.

The choreographer was a pleasant guy, obliging and eager to help, so we worked on it together. I liked him so I let him take full credit for putting it together. That production turned out to be the most successful thing in the show and gave the choreographer a good start. Unfortunately, by the time we opened we had only six weeks left before going into the Fontainebleau with Jack Benny which we were already committed to. I felt terrible, but there was no getting out of it since Jack had been counting on us and the contracts had been signed months earlier. The show was a tremendous success for the six weeks we were there. After we left, it fell apart and closed shortly after.

But the time it gave me to enjoy the house in Malibu was filled with discord and disaster. First of all, we had a 'friend' of Jonny's, a Hungarian artist down on his luck, stay at the house and it was agreed he would look after things whenever we were out of town. I didn't much care for the arrangement because Janos had a few habits I wasn't particularly crazy about. He was forever burying himself in plaster, making casts of himself, and concocting some liquid rubber mixture and casting rubber masks of apes. Or he would be messing around with great piles of smelly buffalo hair which he painstakingly worked into monkey suits. I think the ambition of his life was to be a monkey, or at least create the best imitation of one. No matter who came to the house, he'd quickly slip into his 'costume' and come creeping up upon the unsuspecting victim.

He would do this particularly with those visitors who were in a position to either hire his 'talents' or recommend him to someone who was, and there was nothing I could do or say to stop him. No matter how much I cajoled, pleaded or threatened, he was like an obstinate jackass, fanatically committed to his objective, and did it anyway. His favorite style was to get into the whole outfit and come swinging from a tree. But if there wasn't enough time he'd content himself with just the headgear and creep up on the unfortunate prey to his ambition. This way he scared half of my friends shitless.

I will never forget the amazement and terror in Jack Benny's face when Janos appeared wearing the enormous, hideous ape's head. We were all sitting at the bar looking out at the ocean when Janos crept up and tapped on his shoulder. Jack turned around, gave out a yelp and fled behind the bar. But Janos was fast on his heels, picking on him and emitting the strange, jabbering ape sounds which he took such pains to get down pat. Jack kept backing away saying in a shaky voice: "That's... that's terrific... really... I've seen it now... You can take it off." But Janos kept it up. Simple words were never enough.

Janos was determined to 'conquer' Hollywood, come hell or high water. When auditioning for a job somewhere – a casting office, studio, prospective agent, whatever, he would dash into the men's room, change into his suit, terrify the secretaries and barge in on whomever he decided to see and 'impress.' He'd jump all over the desk, swing from the chandelier, toss papers around and make a general nuisance of himself. The poor bastard he decided to pick on, didn't stand a chance. Finally, however, it paid off. Janos wound up as the bear upstaging Andy Williams every week.

That was then Jonny's friend. The only friends I had at the time were a Canadian couple who were as far removed from show business as I was from my final objective – total freedom. He, Jim, was an interior designer, she, Pete (nickname for her maiden name Peterson) a buyer for some company. I think she was the only female friend I had ever had. If I survived it all, it was largely thanks to them. Somehow, they added a semblance of normalcy and sanity to my whole existence. Whenever we would come back home, I knew they would be there, waiting, ready to listen, to be with me, cheer me, or whatever I happened to be in the need of at that moment. Pete could not understand why I couldn't go anywhere without Jonny and her simple, earth-bound reasoning seemed perfectly logical and sane and made me feel that perhaps my wanting, needing, at least the tiniest bit of freedom wasn't altogether crazy or unreasonable after all. She had this marvelously composed, sober and practical way of thinking that made Jonny's rules simply ridiculous.

When I told her he would have an absolute fit if I were to go anywhere at all without him, she just wouldn't believe anything like that was possible. We were having dinner with them one evening and she had to go to the market which was only a couple of blocks away and so she decided that was a good opportunity to see what would happen if I were to go along. I was afraid to do it, but her attitude gave me the necessary courage.

"I'm going with Pete to the market," I said casually. "It's just around the corner and we'll be right back," I added seeing Jonny's threatening glare.

"Don't worry," Pete added laughing.

Jonny said nothing but the air bristled with tension and unvented objections, but I went.

As we got to the market, the manager was waving at Pete already. "Mrs. Duthie! There's a call for you." It was Jonny checking whether we got there all right. Pete couldn't believe it.

Jim was one of those rare individuals who could maintain his cool no matter what happened and the easy, relaxed humor that was so much a part of his personality was always there. They were the most fantastic friends I ever had. Unfortunately, for some unfathomable reason, when I stepped out of the limelight – our friendship suddenly and inexplicably disintegrated. Up to this day I hate to speculate on why this happened. I cannot allow myself to believe they were my friends because of the position I was in. I prefer to think our friendship, as it often happens, had outlived its usefulness and that was that.

It was while we were in Ken Murray's blackouts that the biggest disaster hit us.

It had been a dry winter, and a few fires were breaking out. Till then I had no idea I chose to live in a city that is continually threatened. There is always something. Not enough rain – you worry about fires. Too much rain – you worry about mudslides, and practically the whole state worries about the earthquakes.

This was 1958 – the year of the big fire. I got up in the morning to see a black cloud of smoke far in the north beyond Malibu around Zuma. Since we were planning to go out and do some shopping, I called the fire department to check how things looked. They asked my address, then told me I had nothing to worry about. Thus reassured, we went off never giving it another thought.

Toward the later part of the afternoon, when approaching the coast returning home, I was alarmed to see a great wall of black, threatening smoke somewhere near our area. At Sunset Blvd, Pacific Coast Highway was already closed and the police were only letting residents pass. Approaching our hill, I saw it enveloped in thickening smoke and the air was filled with tiny bits of ashes floating and settling to the ground like snowflakes, I knew then we had to prepare for the worst.

My sister was already at the house with a very close friend of

ours, a Czech woman by the name of Mrs. Vacek whom we called
Brouk which means bug. The poor lady was a semi-invalid and I
knew we had better get her out of there. The fire police came up and
told us we had to evacuate. It was a panic. We first loaded up Brouk's
car and Kay went with the old lady to her apartment in Hollywood.
Then we proceeded to load up our two cars and the old jalopy Janos
drove. In all the confusion, I seemed to be packing all the wrong
things. My furs and jewels were almost forgotten.

Janos was surprisingly calm and resolute and convinced we
would be all right. By the time the two Cadillacs were packed it was
twilight and the place was being showered with gleaming particles of
burning ash. Both cars were convertibles and there was a danger their
roofs might catch fire so we moved them down onto the beach side of
the highway. Then we raced back up the hill.

Janos decided he would stay. The fire was now just beyond
the rim of the nearest hilltop and approaching rapidly. We had no
municipal water supply at the time and our only source of water was a
private well and a reservoir which, during the dry months, had to be
supplied with additional water from the city. Now the pressure was
equivalent to a boy pissing but Janos was doggedly watering the roofs
of the two guesthouses which were nearest to the approaching fire.
The big house was a solid stucco structure with a Spanish tile roof so
there was little danger from the rain of burning cinders. The fire had
leaped across the hillcrest and was racing rapidly down the sloping
land toward our hill. There was no doubt now we were in its path —
and there was no stopping it. Jonny decided to stay as well, and I was
sent down to the highway to look after the cars and call the theater to
tell them we wouldn't make the show.

I hurried along the road hoping for some miracle to stop the
fire knowing well it was futile. Our neighbor, John Brahm, was leading one of his horses to the beach. Considering he was in his mid-six-
ties and had lived on the hill for some twenty years, he seemed
surprisingly calm and cool as he went about what had to be done. I
knew well how attached he was to the place yet he didn't show the
slightest apprehension or concern. John was indeed amazing.
Although he was a Jew, he projected the stoic, Germanic pragmatism

– solid and unshakable no matter what the circumstances. He was completely bald except for a neatly trimmed fringe of gray hair. His face, always deeply tanned and surprisingly smooth for his age, never showed any emotion. Nor did his eyes, as clear and blue as porcelain, ever betray what was on his mind. Even now, he wore that curiously detached, enigmatic expression as he looked at me. The horse, a big stallion named Chief, was nervous but he held the reins steady, unconcerned as he examined me appraisingly.

"You are too upset," he said matter-of-factly, as always understating the obvious.

"My God! How can you be so calm?!" I retorted almost resenting his composed, dispassionate attitude.

"Andert es etwas wenn man sich Sorgen macht?" he retorted with a hint of a smile. We most often spoke German together. John was from Hamburg, but he left Germany in 1933 when Hitler's persecution was beginning to make itself apparent. Coming from a family prominent in the theater, his uncle Otto was reputed to have discovered Max Reinhardt, John followed the family tradition and started out his long career as an actor but soon turned to directing.

By 1933, he was one of the leading theatrical directors in Germany and Austria but he didn't hesitate to leave it all behind and start all over in England where he fled in his effort to get away from the increasing oppression. Eventually, he left England as well and came to the U.S. where he directed such classics as "The Lodger," "Hangover Square," "The Locket," and many others. His first job in Hollywood was to replace D. W. Griffith on the last movie the aging giant was ever to make. From then on, his career was booming. Perhaps this dispassionate stoicism and utter calm which he projected is essential to a director having to deal with huge casts such as he had when working in Italy on "The Thief of Venice."

Viewed from that perspective, the fire must have indeed seemed of little importance, particularly since he could do very little about it aside from seeing to it that his wife and children were taken to safety and looking after the horses. But at that time I didn't see it that way.

"I have to go and get Bonnie," he said when he deposited

Chief on the beach. "Will you be all right?"

I nodded and he departed as calmly as he came, off to get the other horse, never caring that the fire was getting very close now. It came with a threatening roar that mingled with the calm, steady sound of the surf breaking on the beach below as if nothing so terrible was happening.

Darkness was descending rapidly and only the angry flames whipping about like gigantic fiery tongues, illuminated the landscape with an infernal, nightmarish crimson. I asked the people in the beach house across the highway to let me use the phone. Ken Murray was profoundly shocked, expressing his dismay and sympathy but added: "I know it's terrible, sweetheart, but the show must go on..."

I couldn't believe I heard him correctly. "Are you crazy?!" I yelled. "My house is about to go up in flames and you expect me to do the show? Not on your life!" and I slammed the phone down.

Outside, a thick rain of cinders flickered in the darkness like mad fireflies. John Brahm still hadn't come back with Bonnie. Three fire trucks were parked on the highway and the firemen stood around debating what to do. A small, scattered crowd of people were watching the spectacle.

Suddenly, a huge wall of fire was seen coming down the small canyon directly across the street threatening to cut off the only road from the hill. The people began jabbering excitedly and some ran to their own houses as the firemen shouted orders to evacuate the beachside homes. Realizing Jonny and Janos had no way of knowing they were being cut off, I asked the firemen to go up and get whoever was still up there. They seemed surprised to hear some people still hadn't left but were reluctant to comply with my request.

"We're not supposed to go up dead-end drives."

"What about the three people still up there!" I screamed. "In a while there'll be no way for them to leave!"

When they saw I was resolved to go up there and get them myself, they finally took one of the cars and drove up. By that time the flames were leaping across the road and the whole hill was on fire. I didn't know what to do. I was so worried I couldn't think straight. The rain of cinders was getting so thick, and the particles so big I knew I should move the cars further up the highway. It was then that I discovered I had the keys to only one of the cars. Another disaster – and more reason to panic. What was I to do?! Drive up only one car and leave the other behind? How would I get back? What about Jonny and Janos? Why the hell hadn't they come already?

I looked around. Everyone seemed to have vanished into thin air. I began to weep with fright. John hadn't come back yet either and his house was enveloped in flames.

Then I saw a dark shape of a man ambling toward me. He looked tall and thin and in the red, flickering light of the fire his face looked strange and menacing. He came up to where I was leaning against the new Eldorado and smiled showing a wide gap where one of his front teeth was missing.

"Don't cry. It'll be all right..." he said in a soothing tone but there was a hint of hidden threat behind it.

I looked around. There wasn't a soul in sight. "I don't know... it looks pretty bad..." I said trying to wipe the tears from my voice.

"You'd better get the car out of here. I suppose you have all your valuables in there..."

I nodded realizing instantly I made a stupid mistake.

"Do you have the keys?" he asked gently glancing at my hand resting on the white hood in which the keys were clearly visible. "Let me take you to safety," he said as if talking to a small child. "Don't cry, little girl, I'll take good care of you... give me the keys."

"I don't know..." I said hesitantly looking feverishly for someone to appear.

"Come on... don't be afraid..."

By this time he was pushing me toward the car door and grabbing my hand with the keys. Suddenly I saw the beams of two headlights sweep out of the driveway of the first hill property. In the next instant it cut across the highway illuminating us. At that moment I pushed the man away and streaked across the highway toward the car. It looked like the car of the lady who owned that property. There was a man behind the wheel so I thought it was her son.

"Jack! JACK!!" I screamed as I ran. It wasn't Jack at all, but I didn't give a damn. I was sobbing with fright. "There's a man – he tried to take my car keys and..."

"Where?"

I looked back and saw only a shadow disappearing in the darkness. But I was so relieved I couldn't stop weeping. I was safe. The hill was an insane, howling inferno of flames as tall as many storied houses – but I was safe. But my feeling of relief was quickly replaced by terrible anguish. What was going on up there? Were they safe? I knew nothing could save my house. Although I couldn't see it from where I was, I knew it must be in flames. John's house, also stucco and tile, was a black silhouette against the flames surrounding it and I knew if his house went, ours certainly didn't stand a chance and I wept bitterly, cursing the lousy fate. I had lived there only a few short months – and now it was gone.

John, leading the mare, suddenly appeared from nowhere and behind him was Jonny. "I gave up," he said. "Janos and few of the firemen are still trying to do what they can. But it's pointless..." The three of us stood there huddled together watching the terrifying scene. "Don't cry," Jonny said reassuringly. "We'll build another house – even better and bigger than that one."

"I don't want another house, I liked that old one... I don't want another house – not ever again..."

I stared at the ocean mirroring the macabre scene thinking of the irony of it. There was all that water, capable of squelching all the flames with just one of the calmly rushing waves, but there was no way of getting it up there.

But the fire had swept quickly across the hill, leaving charred, smoldering ashes and countless hotspots which kept flaring up. I knew that everything – every tree, every shrub, every blade of grass was devoured by the insatiable, overwhelming power of one of nature's most vital, but also most destructive, elements.

We stood there stunned, wondering when we would be able to go and survey the extent of the disaster. Fire engines were driving by. A car stopped and a chief of the fire police came out to talk to us. We asked if we could go up, but he said it still looked too hot but that he'd go up and see.

It was eleven-thirty at night – December 31 – New Year of

1959. We had planned a New Years Eve party after the show. The turkey was all made and the refrigerator was stacked with champagne. I watched the man walk up the driveway until he disappeared.

It was dark now – the flames had raced away devouring everything in their path. The hill was dark too, except for the patches of glowing cinders or smoldering branches gleaming in the darkness. John was silent, waiting patiently, stoically as ever – as if the whole thing didn't even concern him.

After what seemed an eternity. I finally saw the fireman strutting down the driveway with sure, resolute steps. He crossed the highway and headed toward us. I held my breath. He smiled and said: "You can go up now. My boys and your housekeeper are up there celebrating New Years with your champagne and turkey. One of my boys fell into the pool but no greater catastrophe happened. I tell you one thing though, you'll be busy with replanting."

I couldn't believe it. The house was intact. All the houses were intact – even John's – he assured us.

We hurried up. Surprisingly, the dark shapes of the cypresses along the road looked unharmed, but the sloping hill, full of eucalyptus trees and century cactuses buttressed by a wall of sandstone that curved along the driveway was a field of smoldering ashes and here and there a black stump of a branch pointed an accusing finger to the starlit sky. It was a fine, clear night and the heat rising from the scorched, smoking ground dispelled the December chill.

Ahead of us we could see the dark shape of the house and every window ablaze with lights. I thought how lucky we were. In the outdoor spotlights I could see the pool surface – black with soot and ashes. Hardly anyone was seen outside. Evidently most of the action was in the kitchen. It was a strange feeling coming in and finding it crowded with sooty firemen busy gobbling food and washing it down with champagne. When they saw us, their tired, smudged-up faces lit up with broad grins and the champagne glasses went up.

"HAPPY NEW YEAR!! – Come and join the party!"

I hugged them all and cried with joy. We found Janos, the host on this occasion, beneath a yellow fireman's helmet explaining excitedly how he ran the whole show. Even though Janos was such a bug and I resented him most of the time, I could never forget all he did to help save the house. The place was an unbelievable mess, but it was unharmed. It was one of the happiest moments of my life.

But the daylight of the next day showed the grim extent of the damage to the gardens. There wasn't one green leaf to be seen anywhere. The hills looked desolate in the new sad colors of black and gray. There was nothing but ashes and blackened skeletons of shrubs and trees. Even the massive trunks of the old royal palm trees were burned and the fronds, scorched and brown hung limply from the crowns. I thought the lovely palm grove was ruined forever.

I got into my sweat suit and boots and wandered for hours through the hills. I had my wish. The house was spared. Even John Brahm's house which I saw in the midst of flames – with my own eyes – was totally intact. There is indeed nothing like solid stucco.

The houses were sandblasted and repainted, but it took many years before the gardens began to look as they used to. And even the palms eventually recovered.

Although this experience was shattering and traumatic, to say the least, it never occurred to me to want to move away. There were other places in the world I liked at least as well as Southern California – Hawaii, for instance – but as much as I loved it, I seemed wedded to Malibu.

CHAPTER TWENTY-EIGHT

Hawaii was something entirely different. We went there for the 50th State Fair headlining a show at the Waikiki Shell with Johnny Cash and the Kingston Trio and to do a few concerts with conductor Carmen Dragon.

Although I immediately fell in love with Hawaii – I never once considered living there. To me, Hawaii was a fairyland, an enchanted paradise that had to be taken in small doses. I loved to ride up into the hills, which looked down on Waikiki, shrouded in constant mist. The first time we went there looking for a famous orchid grower, an Austrian by the name of Oskar Kirsch, it seemed like a strange dream. The day was sunny but the higher up we drove, the more humid and drizzly it became. Yet it was a fine, pleasant and warm mist that could hardly be felt. Walking into the gardens was like entering another world – a safe, friendly world where time stood still – a secure, inviting womb of strange familiarity fragrant with the rich, pungent smell of soil, of fertility, and the intoxicating breath of hundreds of the most exotic of all flowers.

I wandered around in a daze feeling as if I'd come 'home' – feeling like I never ever wanted to leave the place again but knowing that it wasn't a place to stay. There were countless varieties of orchids ranging from the grape-like clusters of tiny green or deep purple orchids so fragrant one couldn't bear to smell them up close, to the huge showy blossoms of purple Cattleyas that have no scent at all.

I wandered beneath hundreds of long slender stems bending under the weight of countless snowy blossoms of the Phalaenopsis, the butterfly orchid that is so beautiful it doesn't even look real. I became so enchanted with orchids I bought several hundred dollars worth of rare specimen and within less than a year managed to kill every single plant.

The Waikiki Shell was a copy of the Hollywood Bowl except one felt closer to the audience there than at the Bowl. The orchestra was so big that extra parts had to be written of our music which Carmen Dragon wrote out himself. He was a perfectionist, extremely cooperative and inexhaustible. We rehearsed until it was as perfect as humanly possible. To be dancing to a full symphony orchestra was an indescribable experience. I felt I couldn't ever be happy with anything else, nor dance as well ever again. Carmen Dragon was so delighted with the result, he was anxious for us to work together again. But we were booked up months ahead and later, we somehow never got around to it because then things were beginning to break up.

I was getting tired. Tired of my whole existence. I couldn't understand how Jonny could be content with the sameness, the maddening monotony which we had blundered into. But he was. He was perfectly content to go on – the same way, with the same act – indefinitely. My insistence on changes – new routines, concepts, choreographies – was a bother to him. But it wasn't just him. I'd seen other performers, grinding out the same thing, year after year, decade after decade, playing the same dates, pumping out the same style, the jokes forever seeming the same, the arrangements of songs following the same pattern, the cute patter and delivery never changing – and they are still doing it today – the people who were veterans when I arrived all fresh and new – a starry-eyed teenager bent on conquering the world! Dance teams were passé, they told us then. You came a decade too late. But I didn't care. I knew we had something different, something unique. And we put dance teams back on the map. A few weeks after we arrived, every club, every theater in the country wanted to book us and we didn't know where to work first. All sorts of dance teams who had already resigned themselves to oblivion were revitalized – again in demand, and new ones were quickly being formed to supply the demand. But after years of riding on the wave of success – an unchanging, constant grind – I was sick and tired of it. I wanted new challenges, new mountains to climb.

Years earlier when I was in Athens, I had a dream. It was one of those incredibly real dreams that somehow seem prophetic and stay with you forever. I dreamt I was climbing a mountain. A terribly steep, almost vertical mountain. Way up high, at the top – which obviously was my destination – I could see a brilliant, blinding white light illuminating my path. On both sides and below me I saw other people climbing laboriously, hanging by their nails, clawing at the mountain, many dropping only to be replaced by others. On both sides, the mountain was flanked by dark, threatening clouds which were converging below me so that I couldn't see the bottom. The strain was terrible, but I finally made it to the top. The top of the mountain, paradoxically, was the moon. I walked in the whiteness of the light, almost floating across the soft, rubbery surface, feeling triumphant. I'd arrived! Instantly I headed to the soft, rubber post office to send a telegram to Earth to give everyone the good news.

Then suddenly I found myself making the same trip again but this time I sat in an airplane and flew effortlessly toward the summit of the mountain watching the steep wall crawling with people eager to get up there – still struggling and falling into the abyss. The black clouds were still there and the plane flew leisurely into the clear light of my destination. But after a while, even the fondest dream, the ultimate goal – once reached, once it is a fait accompli – even that pales and new goals must be sought. At least that was the way it had been for me. The constant, tormenting drive would not let up.

I kept thinking there had to be more to life than just traveling around and keeping my body in top shape for my work. I had everything anyone could possibly want – except such unrealistic abstractions as freedom – freedom of choice – freedom to throw it all to the winds if I so decided. I felt tied down – hopelessly, infuriatingly tied down. The pink sash had turned into the stultifying restrictions against which I felt as helpless as against that suffocating confinement of my infancy. But I did get my arms out then – and I would do it again! It was a struggle – a torment – but I was doing it, without even knowing it. Everything in me was protesting against it – so far only in silence beneath the surface – but there the resentment and frustration was reaching a boiling point.

Then one day, it all erupted – why, how, I no longer remember, nor is it important. It was, I am sure, one of those insignificant little things – the straw that broke the camel's back – that set it off. The main thing was that finally I found the courage to say how I felt. That I was tired of being kept on a leash – that I wanted to be myself free to shape my own destiny – no matter what it was to be – good or bad – it had to be mine and mine alone.

At first Jonny was flabbergasted. Then a terrible argument ensued full of senseless, groundless accusations, reproaches, put-downs, and each was chipping away at whatever good feelings I had toward Jonny. He felt slighted, injured by a 'disloyal ingrate' that he 'pulled out of nothing, that he created – made famous, rich, etc., etc., all for nothing!' But I had made the step and there was no turning back. I wanted a divorce, and I wanted to quit the act. A clean cut – a complete end, and nothing else would do. When Jonny saw I couldn't be bullied, maneuvered or challenged into retraction, he retaliated in the most effective way he knew of. He would give me a divorce, but all the real estate, acreage, etc., including the house and all, was his. The only way he would grant the divorce was if I renounced, gave up and signed away everything. After all, it was his act – he alone was responsible for its success and therefore only he was entitled its fruits.

I couldn't believe it. My proposition was – he should take all the land holdings, I would divide the Malibu property, give him the two level acres above the house, the fifty-foot beach frontage below, and I would keep the one acre with the house, which constituted bare-ly thirty per cent of our holdings against his receiving at least 70% of the total. I thought he couldn't possibly refuse such an advantageous proposition. I thought he would appreciate my willingness to give him more than his share of our investments. I thought he would be fair, or at least reasonable. I still couldn't believe he was serious – he couldn't have possibly meant it. But he did. There was no doubt about it. I had hurt his pride and he was resolved to strike where I would feel it the most.

No matter what Jonny had done, no matter how much I disliked his restrictive, stifling attitude – I had always believed he had integrity and a sense of fairness. I would have been willing to stake my life on the assumption that he would never take advantage of my inexperience but see to it that I would always be protected.

Now my faith was disintegrating, my trust fading, like foolish delusions, and I couldn't stand it.

I screamed at him some terrible things and he slapped my face. I stared at him incredulously, then the sudden anger exploded into a terrible rage and resentment and I picked up the half-filled suitcase I was packing and threw it at him with all the newfound strength of my anger and raced out of the house. I had no idea what I was going to do. My life was disintegrating, my illusions were shattered – there seemed little sense to going on. I kept running and then there was the edge of the cliff – the balustrade – a bare second's worth of hesitation – a glance at the steep, jagged cliff, almost vertical drop some hundred feet to the highway – then I leapt. The beach, the cliff studded with cactuses and sumac, the ribbon of highway, rocked in a dizzying pattern as my body swung out – then suddenly, in midair, I felt my wrist being grabbed and I crashed against the cliff. My wrist felt like it was being torn from its socket as Jonny yanked me back trying to pull me up and over the balustrade. I fought and bit and scratched but he wouldn't let go until he got me back all the while cursing and screaming at me.

I became completely hysterical and spent the next two days in bed – exhausted and aching – sedated most of the time.

But it was all over. Jonny agreed to the divorce, but was still adamant on the issue of the property settlement. There was nothing to be divided. Everything was his, and he would rather fight it out in the courts, no matter what the cost, but he would not let me keep the house. He knew where to strike – and he was out to draw blood. I offered another alternative – to reverse the whole thing. He would take the acre with the house – I would take the rest. He only laughed saying he wasn't crazy. I realized he knew he had the better deal – but he also knew I didn't care as long as I got the house. I knew then, if I wanted to prevent a long, drawn-out fight – which would result in a complete disintegration of everything – I would have to play it cool and reason it out.

Everybody was urging me to let it be decided in court – that I would be awarded everything. But I didn't want that. I wanted Jonny to have more than his share because he was so much older – while I had my whole life still ahead of me. I would have so many other chances. All my friends, my family thought I was insane, or stupid at best. Several lawyers refused to take my case because of the inequity of the proposed property division, and because of their reputation.

Finally, I found one who, after fruitless arguing, gave up and took the case. But I insisted it would be up to me to settle it – to get Jonny to accept my terms. I didn't want to end it with a huge quarrel. If Jonny was content to spend his life doing one and the same thing, that was fine – I wasn't. I wanted freedom – Jonny didn't have it in him to give it. Our differences were obviously irreconcilable but that didn't mean we had to destroy each other and part as mortal enemies. If he wanted to continue with the same kind of work – I'd help him continue. I promised to keep working until he found someone else and to help him set a new act.

It was a calculated risk, one I knew was likely to backfire but I felt it was the only thing to do. The alternative was to give in to my friends' encouragement and 'fight it out.' And who would have anything to gain by it except the lawyers and the press?

Perhaps it was the recollection of my traumatic childhood experience in court during my parents' divorce, perhaps it was the California divorce laws which I considered unjust. Whatever it was, I was resolved to do it my way. I didn't want to add yet another guilt complex to my already impressive collection by ripping-off someone who, after all, was responsible for an important part of my upbringing. Of course, I didn't know then that Jonny used to drop fortunes in the Las Vegas casinos while he kept insisting he was always winning.

Much later, one of Jonny's friends mentioned of knowing of one instance when Jonny dropped $16,000 in one night at the crap tables and that he often had losses in the thousands. I will never know how much of the money was mine, or how Jonny ever figured these things.

But at the time of the settlement I had no idea about these 'minor details.' Thus I was only concerned with 'doing the right thing.'

My mother, who had since moved with my stepfather to L.A., drove me crazy insisting my decision to continue working gave Jonny an opportunity to 'get rid of me' – that sooner or later he was bound to drop me so that he'd get to keep everything. (My mother was always a trusting soul.) I knew it was sheer nonsense but her constant harping unnerved me. And Jonny's cold, menacing looks during the performances kept reviving the senseless fear my mother tried to instill in me. We were back at the Moulin Rouge at the time.

But gradually, very gradually, Jonny was simmering down and my hopes that we would be able to resolve our relationship amicably didn't seem so crazy after all.

But Jonny, the conditions of our divorce, and my mother wasn't all I had to worry about. I had to get adjusted to a completely new kind of existence which was by no means easy. Strange, how the things we want most seem less than desirable once we have them. My newfound freedom didn't turn into the utopia I once thought it would be. I didn't go berserk overnight and start running all over the city screwing every guy I met. Quite the contrary. I was afraid. All the self-confidence and self-assuredness I usually projected was gone. Finding myself so suddenly alone – free – I didn't know what to do. Just to get up in the morning – to decide how to spend my day seemed an impossible task.

At first, even going out alone, shopping, driving to the store, even just crossing a street – was a monumental, traumatic event. I had never handled money before – hardly even knew what the bills and coins looked like – now I had to learn it all quickly. I had to learn not to forget to pay – not to forget the package, or both, which I was likely to do in all my confusion. The end result was I hated to go out. At first, the best solution (the most convenient and appealing one anyway) seemed to hole up at home and contemplate my future which suddenly seemed rather bleak.

When word about our separation leaked out, the columnists had a field day. I don't know why it's always the gossip columnists and show biz reviewers who have the worst style of writing and an unpleasant way of digging at the people without whom they wouldn't have a damn thing to write about. Walter Winchell, for instance, wrote: "...it's open season on Chiquita. They're getting divorced..."

I was furious. I thought it was the crudest thing I ever read. But he pegged it right. The wolves were only beginning to crawl out of the woodwork and test the ground. But now that I was really free to do as I pleased – I didn't. Suddenly, it all seemed meaningless and futile. I was free – but I was still walled in – by an invisible wall of my own making.

After the Moulin Rouge, we went to Miami Beach for a three month engagement at the Carillon Hotel. Not wanting to spend all that time living in a hotel room, I moved in with a couple of friends – Francois Piroska, a Hungarian cancan dancer who brought to mind Toulouse-Lautrec's paintings of the slim, wiry Moulin Rouge dancer, and his wife, Christine, a lovely French girl who progressed from a moody chanteuse to his partner.

In the state of mind I was in, it was the best thing I could have done. Piroska was a dancer who liked nothing better than to organize long practice sessions which kept me from brooding myself into catatonia, and Christine, a resolute and good-natured, if somewhat brusque Parisian, was a completely devoted and loyal friend who gladly took me under her protective, motherly wing and tried to teach me the 'facts of life.' She was also a damn good cook and my three months in Miami netted me good company, extraordinary meals and at least three marriage proposals.

Under Christine's guidance, I began dating, usually two guys at the same time – for safety. Why these silly, platonic and certainly superficial relationships, equivalent to casual, teenage dating of yesterdays, should have resulted in marriage proposals, is one of those insolvable mysteries.

Meanwhile, Jonny was busy screwing every available showgirl. Suddenly, the fact that he used to consider them worthless tramps for all those years was a thing of the past. I was glad. I was hoping this might lead him to finding someone he could dance with. But it seemed he never mixed the two.

Besides, as I was afraid, he made no attempts to find anyone, and I was racking my brain how to prod him along without aggravating the progress I was making toward the settlement. For at last, Jonny was beginning to see the advantages in the property settlement I proposed. I had my lawyer draw up the documents (Jonny didn't even have a lawyer – why should he?) and he signed them. This meant that I was responsible for the house, the payments, etc. and also that within a specified period, I was to subdivide the Malibu property giving him the beach and the two acres free and clear. The last provision finally did it. What it boiled down to, is that everything seems to be merely a matter of money – as always. Each of the two pieces of land was valued at the same amount we originally paid for the entire property – together twice as much. Within a year Jonny would sell them both – but that no longer concerned me. What was more important – I could sleep at night. I could live with myself knowing I hadn't ripped-off anyone. I had done what I considered the decent thing to do. The fact that most of my friends – mainly my mother – thought I was a fool, mattered very little.

While all this was going on, the Miami columnists were giving me a rough time. I hated to see constant references to our private lives which I felt was no one's business. The result was that all the people I knew began giving me 'practical' advice, offering their lawyers and so on. Eydie Gorme, an old friend with whom I used to share a dressing room, kept telling me I have to 'look out for myself.' I noticed that American upbringing techniques of the females tended to create a single-minded objective: Make those bastards pay! Eydie could have hardly escaped it.

Eydie was a funny girl. Her pre-show nervousness made itself apparent in a peculiar way – she had to run to the bathroom a lot and sometimes even just before her performance. To save time – she would use the sink in the dressing room. (But not before she asked my permission.) So there she would be, in a gorgeous gown sitting on the

sink with her skirts piled high, looking at me judiciously and philoso-
phizing about one thing or another while she waited for her capricious
bladder to decide – to pee or not to pee – that was the question!

Her husband Steve was more practical, and certainly clannish
if the male breed can be defined as a clan. We would sit at the bar and
he used to get all burned up over Eydie's advice.

"You should get it all, don't you see?" she'd insist. "You're
the whole act, kid. Without you..."

"Why don't you just leave her alone, hunh? Can't you just let
her do as she pleases, for God's sake?! If her conscience tells her to
be generous, who are you to butt in? There should be more broads
like that."

There they were, yelling at each other, their loyalties divided
along the border of the sexes and I felt responsible. But they were
very sweet indeed. Seeing me so lost, trying to adjust to a new, unac-
customed existence, they dragged me along wherever they could – to
whatever party they happened to attend. Eydie even tried to marry me
off to her manager, a pleasant but totally uninteresting, unexciting,
prematurely bald youngish man, she used to be crazy about before she
got married. Generous soul Eydie was.

CHAPTER TWENTY-NINE

One of my suitors was incredibly funny. A sharp, energetic comic rapidly approaching middle-age but – nobody knew it – or wouldn't have even believed it – or so he thought. He was vain, slightly pompous, but very entertaining in a brash, aggressive way. Evidently he had an age-old romance going with an actress-singer who was waiting (in suspended animation) for him to take the fatal step. Now, suddenly, after a few casual, insignificant dates during which he progressed as far as holding my hand and gazing at me with somewhat paternal concern, he fancied himself being in love with me.

"Say you'll marry me," he begged, "or I'll do something rash, something I'll regret for the rest of my life – like marry whatever her name is..."

All I did was laugh and shake my head which exasperated him no end. But he was so amusing – even in his despair, he couldn't help being funny. And he was persistent – but then, so was I. I was not about to get trapped again. My one, short attempt at what I then considered to be the most odious, the most unsavory of all legal institutions, was more than enough. One mention of it was usually enough to send me running.

Some time later I ran into the comic again. "Why'd you let me do it?" he wailed, gazing at me reproachfully. "I'm miserable!"

"Oh, come on Jack..." I chided him.

"I am!" he insisted. "You know damn well I am still in love with you."

"Bullshit!" (By that time I was loosening up.)

"I tell you, I don't love her!"

"If that's true, why don't you get a divorce?"

"I'd like to – there's just one problem."

I sighed. "What's that?"

"Well..." he hesitated prudently, "we just finished furnishing this unbelievably elegant, sumptuous apartment. It would be such a pity."

And I thought I was being immature, irrational and childish! I could have screamed with delight. I wasn't the only idiot – a hopeless lunatic running lose on the face of this earth after all! And I was entitled! I was only 21 then! At least I had some excuse, some justification for being childish and silly! But he – he was already an old man – an infantile, irrational old man!

I guess it was then that I consciously began to look at other people – observe their behavior, attitudes, life-styles. This accomplished two things: It kept me from worrying too much about myself and my own problems, which was good, and started me worrying about other people's problems, which eventually led to political, sociological, mental and eventually to environmental and even cosmic problems – which was bad. In fact, it was worse. Gradually I realized there was really something to worry about. I didn't know then that in the years to come these problems would mushroom until the possibility to eliminate, or even control, them would appear beyond human capacity. Like a malignant, cancerous growth, they would spread until they would threaten to engulf – to destroy all rich and poor, the free and the oppressed, the villains as well as the just.

Often, when watching all the insanity proceed in the most orderly, dedicated fashion, I would wonder – has man grown so mighty, so deluded with self-importance, self-righteousness and delusions of omnipotence that he cannot see how helpless and ineffectual and self-defeating he really is? Has he grown so blind, so narrow-minded that he can't realize that the same power – the same cosmic law – that elusive something that succeeded in creating as complex a mechanism as the human being, is also perfectly capable of smashing it all down again – obliterating the whole misbegotten experiment?

Or is there, I would wonder, some deeper, complex law beyond the capacity of human understanding governing all that we do? The good, as well as the evil – the positive – as well as the negative?

These contemplations led me from worry to fear, from fear to hopelessness, and I wondered what it was that I really wanted or needed? Wasn't I as lost as everyone else? What was left but, as Bertrand Russell had said: "Unyielding despair" while watching the mad rush toward self-destruction...

At the time I was breaking with the only kind of existence I knew. I had to face the fact that I had already dedicated 16 years of my life to making myself into a successful, unique entity and at 21, I felt my life was a pointless, useless mess – my goals futile, empty concepts and my future a bleak space – an empty void.

What did I really want out of life? I knew what I did not want. The constant running after a new success – a bigger conquest. But what would I replace it with? The last question was purely academic since I hadn't quite extricated myself from the web of my obligations.

And so it went on, as if nothing so monumental had happened – as if I weren't about to pull my life apart, turn everything upside down without having the foggiest notion just what I would do instead. I continued playing my role like an old pro – the ham actor who knows his part a little too well because he played it a little too often.

After Miami Beach we went back to Mexico City – the city of our first triumph on the American continent. Although I was rather indifferent as to what we did or where we went, I had never anticipated nor wanted to leave the country.

However, a couple of months earlier, Christine, who inherited a rare talent from her grandmother – the ability to read cards – prophesied this unlikely event. I didn't believe her, but it was diverting going through the whole charade and allowed me to forget my plight for a while.

She'd sit there as inscrutable as a Buddhist monk, as serious as an executioner, and slap those cards face down, then turn them face up studying each intently while screwing her face into various expressions of doom, gloom, disaster. As it was, she never had anything good to tell me. It was nothing but bad luck all the way through. She would read the cards every week and it was always the same story: Disaster after disaster.

"I see your mother in a hospital," she would declare stoutly and throw me a significant look from those bright, slanted cat eyes. "...An accident..." She hesitated. "...No.... the accident comes after the hospital."

"Oh, for Chrissake! Whoever heard such nonsense?!"

She made an impatient gesture and pouted her lips like a school teacher. "Qu'est-ce que tu vent, alors? I don't understand it either. But there it is again."

"Listen, Christine, if you've got nothing better to tell me, let's forget it." But she was staring with undivided attention at the next batch of cards.

"Be quiet! I want to know what's coming up."

After a few minutes filled with breathless rumination, she would start all over again. "Aha! You will go to a foreign country!"

"Not again!..." I moaned.

"It's still here because you haven't gone yet," she declared with judicious finality. "Wait a minute, there's something else now..."

I remained quiet. No use asking her. She'd tell me anyway.

"Your sister will call you there..."

"Where?"

"How do I know?! Wherever you'll wind up going!"

"OK, OK. So she'll call me there. Terrific! And she'll say, hello, how are you..."

"No, she'll tell you she's got a big problem. A big sickness..."

(When reading cards, Christine talked a funny English, or I should say, French.)

"I want to know one thing. How come only I get the shitty

predictions? While Claudia gets all the good stuff?!"

"Merde alors!" she'd say disgustedly. "I can tell you only what I see. But don't believe it," she added in a voice soft with tolerance. "Claudia doesn't believe it either, and perhaps she's right. It's all sheer nonsense. Don't take it seriously – please."

Claudine, the French production singer, was a blonde, blue-eyed character with a touch of nymphomania and a drop of quicksilver up her ass. Anyway, that's the impression she gave. There was a rich guy from Nevada she was all set to marry and was only waiting for him to say the word. Meanwhile, however, she wasn't wasting any time. There were always plenty of guys she could and did amuse herself with.

Anyway, Christine finally found some calamity in her cards as well. There was to be a crisis and she warned her to be very careful, something was to happen that might 'jeopardize' her grandiose plans with the rich guy and it was all involved in some triangle. She might just as well have said octagon for Claudine wasn't stingy with her favors. Just at the time there was a French guy staying at her apartment (all perfectly innocent – 'he was like a brother to her,' after all), when her moneybag had the bad grace to suddenly appear. Panicsville! But Claudine wasn't one to lose her head. She was never particularly crazy about me, but now suddenly I came in handy. I was to pretend that old French guy was mine, and she was lending me her apartment for the duration of his stay. Since it didn't matter to me one way or another, I went along with it.

Claudine spent the night with her 'fiancé' at his hotel and I, bright and early in the morning, had to race to her apartment and when they arrived, there was good ole Pierre in his pajamas – making me an authentic French omelet while I watched the procedure with dispassionate curiosity. Up till then I was under the impression that the longer you cook eggs, the softer they get which gives a fair-indication about my culinary talents. The deception came off par excellence. Fortunately, Pierre had the good sense of departing the same day so I didn't have to carry it too far for the benefit of Claudine's flame who didn't wind up marrying her anyway.

After this little episode, however, Christine's card reading got

me thinking. But I found a quick rationalization. With Claudine's car-
ryings on, something like that could have been easily predicted even
without cards.

CHAPTER THIRTY

Much later, when I had all but forgotten what Christine had told me, a sharp, sleek Mexican impresario came to see us about a return to Mexico. I didn't feel like going, but he made it sound extremely attractive and Jonny thought it would be most imprudent to refuse. The man was also an aide to the wife of the then current President (I think it was Cortinez) in charge of raising funds for charities via benefits, etc., had his own TV show and seemed in general a classy operator. Needless to say, Jonny decided we would go. It was only later that I remembered that Christine had prophesied that trip.

Arriving, we were greeted by a mob of fans and newsmen with TV cameras covering the 'big event.'

We were to appear at a theater and the Club Senorial where Nat Cole had just closed. From the airport we were taken to the Club where a big reception, or rather a surprise party, was waiting for us. When we arrived, the Club was dark but as soon as we entered, lights went on, music set in, and the gathering, comprised of old friends and acquaintances, came to life with cheers and lots of noise. It was all corny as hell but at the same time strangely moving. I was touched by the devotion that didn't seem to have diminished by the years of absence and by all the old, faithful friends who acted as if we had never left.

Our 'manager' had arranged everything with extreme care never leaving out a single detail. The accommodations he provided were two lovely suites of rooms at the then new Tecali Hotel, a modern hotel, exquisitely furnished in fine, stylized Aztec decor. Each suite had a huge, sumptuous bathroom all white and gray marble and a glass-enclosed steam cabinet.

Surprisingly enough, I found I was beginning to rather enjoy it and didn't mind much when the one month planned had stretched into six.

Meanwhile my mother and stepfather suggested I should lease the house to which I agreed to spare them having to look after it. They had their own house by then and some income property to worry about. Someone else would be living in the house on the hilltop – but it didn't seem to matter. Nothing mattered. I would do my work and try to evade the guys hanging around with dogged persistence – waiting... Some were hard to ignore.

I have since learned that the more you run away from something, the more it runs after you – and vice versa. Had I wanted to remarry, I bet I wouldn't have been able to find anyone even remotely interested in the proposition. But instead of looking at it that way, I found it rather irritating at the time.

Our manager's younger brother, a droll little man who could put away incredible amounts of booze and recite mournful poetry improvisations until he moved himself to tears became, much to my horror, my most ardent, and certainly most persistent, suitor. Although he claimed sole ownership to these effusions of his poetic fervor, I found them richly embroidered with lines borrowed from many a great poem. Although I hadn't given him so much as a second look after the initial introduction, let alone even the barest encouragement, for some obscure reason the man seemed to have decided I was destined to marry him and thus proceeded to follow me like a persistent shadow wherever I went.

Being Oxford educated, he liked to sport his immaculate English whenever he could. At thirty, his pale blonde hair was already thinning, revealing an odd, egg-shaped head that went rather well with the impression he wanted to project. Obviously, he identified with someone like Shelley or Byron for he liked to dress like an English dandy and affected the mournfully tragic, resigned expression he must have thought was characteristic of poets and philosophers.

He was a news reporter and a political analyst which in combination with his fiercely radical, aggressive spirit and the government's unquestionable super sensitivity in certain areas made for an explosive combination. This proved to be a constant embarrassment to his brother, for Luis never missed a chance to openly attack the government.

Consequently, he was thrown off the paper several times and his brother had to rush and pull the necessary strings to get him rehired. But he was terribly proud of his little brother. After all, it was he who struggled, schemed and slaved to put him through Oxford and now Luisito was doing his damnedest to drink himself to death. But first, he would hunt me down, break my resistance and fulfill his intoxicated dream.

Wherever I'd go, he was bound to show up in no time, like a persistent shadow ever-present as a bad conscience, and recite his endless odes, often winding up on his knees with tears as big as peas welling up from his pleading blue eyes and rolling down the wan cheeks and staining his immaculate, expensively attired, chest. Oh, God! Luisito sure was a terrible pain in the ass! And yet, I was sure he never cared for me in any way. He needed someone to 'act upon' – he wanted to feel miserable. He enjoyed playing the part of the heartsick, rejected suitor and wallowed in the exquisite torment and self-pity with the delight of a pig in mud.

Instead of paying attention to his political columns, he took to writing long, nonsensical essays full of obscure innuendoes and hidden pleas. Why they were ever printed only God knows. In short, he was utterly embarrassing and continued, in spite of my complaints to his brother, to interfere with my schedules.

My days were crowded with all sorts of interviews, TV appearances and picture interviews. Every day the press was heralding our presence and reporting faithfully all our activities. But all in all, it was rather a bore although I did manage to run into some interesting experiences here and there, as for instance, at the press reception for Cantinflas (or Mario Moreno) returning from his promo trip for "Pepe" where I was asked to head the welcoming committee and found myself again the only female amongst all those newsmen. I was still far from as confident as I used to be and these affairs made me feel rather uncomfortable. But it had its rewards. I was presented with a gift, a lovely ring with a huge topaz that looked more like a weapon than a ring and which Walter Winchell would later almost knock his teeth out with when trying to accomplish the old continental feat – kiss the hand and gaze deeply into the eyes at the same time. It was one of those terribly awkward, paralyzing moments when you see someone heading for disaster, unable to utter a sound.

But the most interesting aspect of it was that I got to study, close up, Mario's extensive face-lift. It wasn't exactly new to me because he had looked me up during his earlier visit to L.A. but I never dared to take a close look then. We had become quite friendly during our first visit to Mexico and I liked the soft-spoken, gentle and humble comic who happened to be the biggest moneymaker and unrivaled favorite of the Latin audiences. His face used to be open, relaxed and full of friendly wrinkles. He had just finished "Around The World in 80 Days" and made his 'mark in Hollywood' when he called to pay his respects. We had made a date to meet, but when I got there I didn't see him. There was only this odd, smooth-faced, gigolo-type but old Mario was nowhere in sight. I passed the man never giving him another look when I heard him call my name. I whirled around and stared. It was Mario – one look and I knew what he had done. I thought it was such a pity – and so unnecessary. But then, if it made him feel better, what the hell! I didn't want to embarrass him by staring so we spent the whole evening playing gin and I won every single game because my mind was elsewhere.

During the press reception however – I felt perfectly at ease and I watched him intently as he delivered his speech. Then it was my turn to say something short and witty and soon after that, the affair was over.

At the hotel, I found my rooms flooded with flowers accompanied by a card with the most extravagant message: "Para Chiquita: Lamujer mas enchantadora de todas las epochas." (To Chiquita: The most enchanting woman of all ages.) That was stretching it a bit too far, I thought.

Nevertheless, as much as I wanted to escape the empty, superficial world of entertainment, all the compliments and adulation, no matter how meaningless and transparent, it still had the capacity to entice me – the insatiable monkey on my back still lapped it up as greedily as ever and hungered for more. It was still a struggle between what I was conditioned to crave, to want and need – and between an unknown something I instinctively knew was worth a great deal more than all the fame and fortune in the world. But there were still times when I'd say to myself – you've got to be kidding! What could possibly be worth more than that?!

An important part of the struggle was to shed all the puritanical nonsense which kept me uptight, aloof and afraid to let go of myself. But my own apprehensions, the senseless fear of involvement and its consequences, but mainly that exaggerated sense of 'morality,' still held me back.

It's odd that morality in this society is associated mainly with sex. The word 'immoral' instantly brings to mind some sex deviate or at least a promiscuous or over-sexed personality. The immorality of lies, deception, killing, wars – brutality and inhumanity – we never are that concerned about. Then all kinds of rationalizations are conveniently invented and restated until they are regarded as the only acceptable norm. In the name of business, profit, progress, technology, national security, everything is permissible. No matter what is said or written about it, the brutal, idiotic and certainly self-destructive rape of this planet, which indeed must support us all, can never arouse as much consternation and vindictive fury as the rape of a woman.

I wasn't in any way different. We are nothing but a sum total of our upbringing and conditioning. Where the parents leave off, the society takes over. But whatever the odds against succeeding, I was resolved to make myself over – to recondition the conditioning, to break with it all. I knew it would be a long and hard battle. But I was ready to fight everything and everyone – even myself.

During all those months in Mexico, I managed to go out with two men. These were, as was to be expected, two of the least aggressive, or 'safest,' I came across. One was an older, father-type of a man, the composer of several internationally famous songs, who was very gentle, unassuming, and undemanding. He looked somewhat like an aging Yves Montand. He was a good listener and since I was an avid talker, we got along famously.

The other was a young man, rather American looking, suave, well-educated, extremely cordial and proper and I could never figure out what he was all about. There was a certain aura of mystery about him which I couldn't penetrate even had I wanted to. I enjoyed his company because he wasn't aggressive or pushy, that is to say, he didn't try to fuck me, which was nice. I kept thinking, and was out to prove it, that men and women could simply be friends without winding up in a romantic entanglement. With Rolando, evidently, I didn't have to worry. One day, however, he surprised me by proposing marriage. I was shattered. Where did all that come from so suddenly? My strong aversion to marriage hadn't diminished any and I told him so. He said nothing but I had a feeling he didn't quite give up.

He said then he had been preparing a party at his parents' house for me and that most of the invitations were already sent out – and would I go to the party with him? I was reluctant to agree, but finally did.

When I was in Miami, a few months earlier, I had a peculiar dream. I dreamt I was in a house – a big, English mansion, a typical Tudor – all brick and beams – the kind I disliked. It stood in the midst of a huge garden – a square covering many blocks – surrounded by a tall, ivy-covered wall. I remember wondering what the four narrow structures built into each corner were all about. What was behind the neatly cut holes in the ivy? I had no idea why I was there, yet somehow I had a feeling it was home – the place I lived – owned. I thought – No! That can't be – I'd never live in such a place! I hated the neat symmetry of the typically English landscaping, the rose garden with pink roses bordered by a meticulous box hedge; the dull, somber look to everything. To the right of the wide, elaborate wrought-iron gate was a row of old cypresses facing a large rectangle pool – brick-inlaid deck – to the right of it the stables. Opposite was another gate, pretty much like the front gate, with the same lanterns adorning the columns flanking it. It all seemed terribly depressing and the most upsetting part about it was that I was a part of it – boxed in a situation I didn't care for. I woke up feeling disturbed and dissatisfied.

When I was driving with Rolando toward his parents' house, I had a feeling I shouldn't have come. What did I really know about him? He never spoke of his parents nor about his work nor plans. I only knew he seemed to have a lot of money – at least enough to frequent the most expensive restaurants and clubs. I kept wishing I could get out of it somehow – but it was too late.

We drove through a lovely suburban section of Mexico City when he said we were almost there. Soon he turned into the driveway of an old estate. A heavy iron gate began to open; I glanced left and right at the tall, green wall surrounding the property finding it strangely familiar. But it wasn't until we were driving past the English rose garden toward the old Tudor house that the similarity struck me. That's impossible, I thought. I glanced to the right. There were the cypress trees – the lanterns on each side just as I had remembered them. Yet I knew I'd never been there before.

"Is there a pool facing the cypress trees?" I asked.

Rolando smiled. "And a big one!"

"Rectangle?" He nodded. "And stables behind it?"

He nodded again looking puzzled. "You've been here before."

"Is there another gate in the back with the same lanterns?"

"Say, you know it pretty well! When have you been here?"

I was staring at the mass of pink roses so identical to those in my dream – the box hedge and all.

"Tell me," I said suddenly, "what's behind the holes cut into the ivy in each corner?"

He seemed to hesitate. "My father is a pretty important person..."

"So?"

"He has many enemies. – Those are guard towers with a

machine gun in each."

We were driving toward an area where several cars were parked already.

"Would you take me home, please?!"

He stared incredulously. "Is it because of the machine guns?"

I shook my head.

"Why then? What's the matter?"

"I can't explain it. I just want to go back."

And that was all I would tell him. I was petrified, and I could hardly wait to get out of that car. In my dream I was stuck there – I seemed to belong there. I would never live in a place like that. It was just too depressing. I wanted none of it – and that included Rolando.

At the hotel I slipped out of the car even before he cut the engine. "Wait! Can't you at least tell me what upset you?"

"No! There is nothing to say. And please don't call me any-more!"

He looked terribly hurt.

"I mean it," I said with finality. I felt very sorry for him, but there was nothing I could do. I never saw him again but the peculiar coincidence remained a disturbing memory.

CHAPTER THIRTY-ONE

There are many things which cannot be explained away with mere logic and as much as we may push them away – even negate them – they are there, defying all reason and logic. And Christine's predictions were a good example of it. Although I had dismissed them long ago they were only beginning to come true and I didn't even know it.

We were putting together a production at the theater in Mexico when I received the call from Kay. I was in the middle of the rehearsal and a cast of fifty was waiting. Kay was weeping and it took some time before I could make out what she was saying. She had quit work because they found she had tuberculosis which she evidently contracted during the two months she spent in training at a TB sanatorium. Now she was told she had to recuperate somewhere in the mountains. Mexico City with its altitude seemed an appropriate enough place so I told her to come immediately. I tried to sound cheerful but as soon as I hung up I fell apart. Although considerable progress had been made it that area, nevertheless, the ancient specter surrounding that disease obliterated everything else and I wept with fear and anger, blaming myself for letting her pursue that wretched profession.

The rehearsal had to be canceled, everyone sent home, and I went to the hotel to wallow in my misery.

This time I immediately thought of Christine's prophesies and cursed myself for listening to her. Wasn't it better not to know anything? Then suddenly I thought about mother. I immediately called back but learned she was fine. I breathed a bit easier. I tried to make myself believe it must have been merely a freaky coincidence but the uneasy apprehensive feeling was still there.

Kay arrived looking pale and terribly skinny. Her work in surgery didn't affect her too well. She couldn't even look at meat, much less eat it! I tried to talk her into giving up nursing but it was useless. She insisted she'd go back and give it another try. It took me quite a while to reconcile myself to it.

Meanwhile, I saw to it that she got the proper treatment, ate a lot, and rested up. Gradually, she began to look better and even gained some weight. Fortunately, it turned out to be a mild case of tuberculosis and in a couple of months, in spite of my protestations, she was heading back to L.A. to resume her work.

Shortly after that, mother went into surgery to have a kidney stone removed. It was a big one, and they had to go into the kidney. A week after she got out of the hospital, the deep incision barely healed, she had a car accident. Fortunately, she wasn't badly hurt but in her condition the experience was shattering. By that time I had gained a healthy respect for Christine's 'talents.' But my sense of logic wouldn't let me fully accept it. How could there be something to looking at those stupid cards? Whenever I had asked Christine about it, she'd say it wasn't just the cards. She claimed to get certain impressions, specific thoughts which would pop into her mind. Somewhat like strong intuitions and the cards actually had little to do with it. As anyone else, I looked at it with much skepticism and even after all these things had happened, I still couldn't believe it. I even began to doubt my own memory. Had she really predicted all that?

Evidently, I'd spent a long enough time in the U.S. to be affected by the pragmatic, American way of thinking – the realism-trip, the need for scientific rationale, a tangible proof, which left little room for things outside the realm of our physical existence.

In a way I was sorry I had let her read those cards. What if she had predicted a fatal accident in the future? Who wants to know about such things?

Yet years later there I was like a bloody fool letting her read those damn cards again. That time she predicted 'death in the family' and inheritance for me as a result which would cause me much grief. Sounds like the usual drivel? Right! Yet a few months later my aunt Mimi died in Vienna leaving me her parents' apartment house – the ancient building with the winged angel above the entrance I remembered so well from my early childhood, and which turned out to be nothing but a big headache.

As our stay in Mexico was extending, I found that once again, my life had settled into the dreaded monotony – everything seemed at a total standstill as if nothing had happened. Jonny apparently took for granted I would continue indefinitely in the act while I was getting more and more impatient to leave it. After Mexico we went for a month to Caracas where we had our own TV program. This necessitated setting up a new routine every day – twenty shows in total. At least that was a challenge I liked. Jonny hated it. Every rehearsal became a torment. Jonny was like a wet rag, sullen, uncooperative, resentful.

Just to follow directions went drastically against his grain. I was selecting the music, setting the routines, choosing the costumes. The show called for one dance number together and a couple of solo dances. Since time was always so short, I wound up doing what I liked the most – improvisations. These turned out to be the most enjoyable part of it all because they were unprepared and totally spontaneous. Once, while appearing with Jack Benny in Miami, George Burns said something which I considered the finest compliment I'd ever received.

"The act's so great," he said, "that it seems completely spontaneous – as if improvised. Yet at the same time you know what a tremendous amount of training and just plain hard work had to go into it to make even the most difficult parts appear effortless. But that's what makes it so great."

Frequently, I'd run into people – so-called pros – who'd give me well-meaning advice I didn't need.

"Chiquita, honey, you shouldn't make it look so easy – let the audience see how difficult it is."

I've never enjoyed seeing a performer strain and sweat and slave up there. It always made me feel like saying: Don't kill yourself for me – it's not worth it – quit already and rest up... And so I didn't want to perpetrate the same feeling upon my audience. I wanted it to look like a game – carefree, enjoyable play. I liked when people would come up to me and ask, "Do you really enjoy it as much as you seem to?"

"Of course! If I didn't, I wouldn't do it!" I'd retort instantly.

That last month in Caracas showed me it was high time to find a way of ending it and that it would really be up to me to do it. I decided I would start looking for a substitute as soon as we returned to L.A. The house was still rented and the tenant, Burl Ives, had another month before he would vacate it so I would have to stay at mother's during that time. We had a couple of months before going into a three month engagement at the Statler Hilton which would give me five months in L.A. During that time I would have to find some-one and set a new act. Mother had a large, comfortable three bedroom house and although she was very happy to have us both there, for me it was a torment. She wouldn't stop talking about 'the terrible mis-take' I'd made. I could hardly wait to get back into the house in Malibu.

Once, right after I arrived, I went up there to see the Ives' on some matter. It was the first time I was to see the house since the set-tlement had been agreed upon. It was a strange experience full of con-flicting impressions. There was the feeling of triumph, of tremendous satisfaction on the one hand, for the question whether or not the house would be mine which had plagued me for such a long time was finally resolved, yet on the other hand there was this unsettling feeling that I was only a visitor, a stranger in my own house – a stranger to the strangers who were calling it their home for longer than I'd lived there at any one time.

I drove along the long, familiar curve of the driveway beneath the grove of whispering eucalyptuses watching the house grow in the distance wondering what shape I would find it. The house stood there stoic, waiting, like an ancient patient giant. I walked timidly into the front yard. The pool was clean, the rattan deck furniture had disappeared to make room for the sturdy redwood furniture, bigger and more robust to withstand Burl Ives' 325 pound bulk. I hated it immediately. There was nothing graceful about it.

Mrs. Ives, a small, blonde woman who managed to convey an aura of shrewd, unbending will in spite of the plump softness of her immense, better than 200 pound form, came out of the kitchen to greet me. In spite of the tremendous weight, she was quick and agile, and although she acted friendly, there was no mistaking the fact that she was a sharp, efficient buffer between her husband and the outside world.

"Come in, my husband would like to meet you!" she announced as if she was handing me a rare gift. I glanced around noticing new colors in landscaping and Mrs. Ives quickly explained she wanted more flowers around so she had the gardener plant some.

Entering the living room, my eyes were instantly drawn to the incredibly huge, massive man sitting in the largest and strongest armchair in the house and filling every inch of it. I have never seen such a large, obese man at such close range. It was rather a formidable sight and I am afraid I stared. The huge, elephantine thighs, the massive trunks of the arms – the white, bulging flesh – it just didn't look real. I felt like a mere wisp of a child – while he sat there like some mythical giant defying all logic and imagination. But the pale-blue eyes, almost buried in the pale, pudgy mess of flesh, had a kind, good-natured look to them and I realized with a shock that beneath all the hugeness was a very gentle, sweet man.

He was looking at me with a frank, open curiosity, pretty much the way I was inspecting him.

"So you are the great Chiquita," he said with a tone of curiosity satisfied, expectations fulfilled.

"Yes, and you are the great Burl Ives," I said never betraying that I never saw one single film he was in nor heard a single song he sang.

"You have a nice house here, I'll hate to leave it. I hear you aren't interested in selling. Any chance of reconsidering?"

I shook my head. "Sorry."

"Pity," he said, then his eyes crinkled with a knowing smile. "Isn't it a bit too large for you alone?"

He must have heard. I shook my head again.

They weren't bad tenants. The place was neat, but Mrs. Ives, dealing with my mother and stepfather – a couple of foreigners hardly speaking the language – bought whatever she wanted from thumbtacks to those horrors of garden furniture and deducted it all from the rent. She also bought two huge sets of china I didn't need but at least Kay, realizing our tastes were hopelessly clashing, went with her selecting what she knew I'd like.

CHAPTER THIRTY-TWO

As soon as the Ives' left, I moved in. With all the traces of the previous occupants removed and everything restored to the way it had been – minus Jonny and Janos – minus everyone – the house was as silent and awesome as a ghost. I gave no parties, encouraged no visitors, as if I reveled in the feeling of abandonment the self-imposed isolation evoked in me. I tried to get Kay to stay with me, but she wouldn't. She was working at a hospital in Santa Monica and mother's house in West Los Angeles was closer and besides – I couldn't measure up to mother's cooking. Kay was looking for having it easy, and living in Malibu didn't fit into it. Not that I could blame her.

So I remained alone. All my busy plans seemed to have evaporated and I did little besides wander about – letting everything come together in my mind. It was probably the most crucial time in my life. I tried to understand what I was doing and why. Why did I have this need to tear it all apart? What was there to replace it with? Wasn't that the most important thing? Wasn't that drive and ambition I was so eager to shed regarded as the most desirable asset in one's personality? Desirable for what? To drive yourself insane with the unsatiable greed – the want to achieve more and more? But what did I really want to do? Wasn't my attachment to the house just as intense and sick as the ambition I was so desperately trying to pull out by its roots? The ambition that millions of parents were eagerly cultivating in their offspring. Was everyone else crazy, or was I? What did I want with this big, empty house? What did I need four bathrooms for or the five bedrooms I'd wander through like a lost, restless soul?!

Being completely alone in the house, on a solitary green hill, an oasis on the edge of miles of wilderness and mountains stretching undeveloped all the way to the Valley, was a strange experience. During the day all was well. I felt lonely and bewildered by the thoughts that were crowding in my mind, but I'd play the stereo and the hill would echo with music. I had a whole day's program all set up and the daily repertoire would never change. I was wallowing in the exquisite torment of my loneliness and indecision. I wept often, not knowing why, and stared at the endless span of the Pacific spreading beneath – forever changing, forever the same – eternal in its awesome immensity. I might sunbathe or swim in the womb-warmth of the well-heated pool and watch the day fade away. In my self-imposed imprisonment, I was by no means uncomfortable.

My diet consisted of frozen TV dinners and sandwiches and milk. Food was altogether an unimportant part of my life except to provide the necessary nourishment to sustain the physical part of me.

At night, however, I was afraid. As soon as it got dark, the house seemed to assume a different personality. It creaked and moaned and sighed. The rustle of the trees mingled with the ominous sound of distant footsteps, the creaking sound of a door, a tremble of a window pane. I slept with a .22 rifle, as taut as a spring, ready to jump up and go tearing after the elusive sound with my rifle pointed, ready to shoot at the ghosts of yesterday – as if I didn't know the old wood, settling, creaking, was playing games with my fantasy – too colorful for comfort.

Mother tried to talk me into leasing the house again, but I wouldn't hear of it. At first anyway. But gradually I began to see I couldn't go on living there all alone. With extremely mixed emotions I gave the listing to a real estate agent and waited.

The first (and last) appointment the agent made was a disaster.

The interested party was to show up at six in the evening. By seven-thirty, when it was already dark, and no one showed up, I assumed they wouldn't come anymore. I shut off all the lights and went upstairs to read. Barely ten minutes later I heard a car drive up. I went down, putting on a few lights as I went. Someone was already knocking at the door.

The couple who came in immediately appeared very favorably impressed and seemed all set to take it. The man began inquiring about who would pay the gardener and such. Now, on a windy night, the house had the strange habit of emitting a fearful, bloodcurdling sound, somewhat like a tortured lunatic's scream which we were never able to determine where it came from. Sometimes it would be a low wail or shoot right up to the loudest possible pitch. When heard for the first time, it was well capable of scaring the shit out of anyone and I saw strong, fearless men pale at the sound of it.

Now, at this precise moment, the capricious devil decided to make itself heard. The living room was lit dimly since I had had time to switch on only a few lights and so the effect was one of the best. Both, the man and his wife, paled noticeably and exchanged alarmed glances.

"What the hell was that?" the man whispered through a constricted throat.

"Oh, that? That's nothing. Just the wind blowing through the vents or something. Whenever it's windy, it goes crazy," I said lightly adding challengingly, "You aren't afraid, are you?"

"No, of course not," he assured me quickly but after a forced, short discussion during which he said he'd be in touch with the agent, they departed – rather hastily, I thought.

The next day, the agent was most curious to learn exactly what had happened because they told him they could never live there as the house seemed haunted.

That, however, made up my mind for me. The house didn't want to be rented. Why else would it have given the finest demonstration of its uncanny talent just at the crucial moment? It was altogether silly to let myself be talked into renting it again. What was there to be afraid of, I told myself in the light of a sunny day. The dark and a few easily explained creaks? There were far more real things to be afraid of – such as some people and their sick minds.

There were the fellow motorists I passed on my lonely, nocturnal treks back to the beach from the many benefits we were inclined to do when in L.A. There were countless charitable organizations or societies which would put on big shows and get stars to either donate their talents or work for a token salary to satisfy the unions and the proceeds would go to the various institutions in need of support.

We've appeared at benefits from the City of Hope to Friends of Barry Goldwater raising funds for campaigns. In those days, Barry Goldwater was just one of the many senators I'd met at the White House, and what political views he did or did not hold mattered precious little. I was faithfully following Jonny's ideology.

The masters of ceremonies on these occasions were people such as Ronald Reagan and George Murphy, actors who didn't do too well in films anymore so they got busy in civic affairs. However, most didn't do any better as MC's than as actors. I thought Ronald Reagan was a little too self-conscious and too uptight to do a decent job of announcing the performers. Like most actors, he was lost without a script and we had long conferences about what he should say about the act. No matter how often he had announced it, he still wanted to know exactly what he was to say.

Most performers didn't mind doing these dates because they could deduct from their income tax the salary they didn't get as a donation to charity. But it still was a hassle to pull these shows together. Subsequently, the coordination of the talent for these shows was left to well-known film producers because they had the necessary pull and connections. It was their job to cajole and flatter whoever they felt would draw the most attendance into participation. Most often these attempts were obvious, sugarcoated ploys to get you to do it. I'd have much preferred a straightforward approach, devoid of all the bullshit.

Once I received a call from one of the 'greats,' obviously soliciting.

"How is my favorite dancer?" he cooed. The jovial tone

couldn't have been more intimate had we been bosom buddies for the past decade. Yet I hardly knew the man. Hearing him lay it on so thick I instantly knew what it was all about.

"What can I do for you?"

Ignoring my matter-of-fact tone, he continued undaunted. "Darling, you know how I feel about you. Everybody knows you are the greatest dancer in the business – not to mention the most charming and beautiful..."

"What's on your mind?" I managed to interject.

"Darling, there is this absolutely fantastic benefit next Saturday which I am putting together and you'll be the icing on the cake. There'll be only the most important and influential people in the business – that's why I can't do without you. We must have only the very best. I know you wouldn't want to miss it."

I tried to interrupt him a few times but there was no way I could stop the enthusiastic sales pitch cascading like a bubbling, torrential river.

"I'm sorry," I managed to get in at last. "I'll be on a plane in the morning heading for Canada. We're opening Friday at the Petroleum Club in Calgary."

"Oh, I see..." The voice dropped from L.A. August to Alaska December. "Well, goodbye then."

And the phone went dead with a sudden click.

That was Hollywood at its finest. Phony flatteries, empty promises, plastic, opportunistic people blatantly obvious in their intentions. I was ashamed for him but not really surprised. The moment they can't use you – you're a zero, a nonentity until the next time.

But I really didn't mind doing benefits. At least some of the proceeds were bound to get where they were needed.

However, the trip home from these dates was something else again. After all the excitement and turmoil, having to face the long, lonely ride home and the empty dark house was a terrible letdown. But nothing really mattered that much. I was still facing the most crucial part of the problem – the division of the property – and there were still so many decisions and changes facing me all of which I found so overwhelming and confusing that I hated the very idea of having to cope with them. Life seemed altogether an intolerable state but not intolerable enough to end it. Instead, I began taking stupid chances and caring very little about things in general. I drove like a maniac and accumulated speeding tickets at an alarming rate in spite of being lucky enough to talk my way out of a great many of them. Most cops readily fell for the little-girl-lost-or-fatigued-or-distressed-over-some-unimaginable-calamity routine but of course not everyone was obliging enough to swallow it.

My conscious reason for racing was that I hated to drive alone late at night. At that time the city seemed to be swarming with weird characters cruising around and looking for whatever their idea of excitement happened to be.

Most often I was dead tired, hardly able to keep my eyes open, and certainly not in the mood for anyone's silly jokes.

Once, when racing again as fast as I could toward the attractive prospect of grabbing my rifle and sinking into the cool softness of my bed and a deep, restless sleep, I suddenly noticed a small sports car hot on my heels. I stepped on the accelerator but the car stayed with me. I was on Sunset Blvd. – just leaving Beverly Hills where all the crazy curves begin. The screeching of the tires was terrible, but seeing my pursuer determined to scratch at my heels, I kept it up. I had no idea what the lunatic was up to and I wasn't sticking around to find out. I was resolved to lose the bastard as quickly as possible. But I just couldn't make it. Finally, somewhere in Brentwood a red light put a stop to the mad race. Seeing it loom up ahead, I came to a screeching halt. There wasn't another car on the road, but I wasn't about to chance smashing into crossing traffic.

The other driver pulled up alongside and was yelling something. He didn't look anywhere near as menacing as his wild pursuit led me to believe, so I pushed the button and the window came down.

"Hey, that was a bit of good driving!" he yelled appreciatively.

I thought I'd faint. He scared me shitless and now he was complimenting me on my driving.

"What kind of a lunatic are you?" I yelled back but he just

grinned.

"You should try racing. You'd do well! I should know! I'm a race car driver!"

"I'd have never guessed!" I snapped, stepping on the accelerator and tearing off with the changing yellow light.

But my racing days were all but over. I received a warning that unless I reformed, I'd lose my license. I tried but it wasn't easy. When driving alone I found myself lost in thoughts in no time at all, never knowing where or how fast I drove. Often I didn't even remember passing through certain sections of town. It was as if I had blacked out for long periods of time – probably some form of partial catatonia.

I kept thinking, one more ticket and there'll be one more problem to cope with. I was resolved to prevent that no matter what. But, as often is the case, even the best intentions disintegrate under the barrage of thoughts and impressions assaulting us every moment of our waking hours.

And so on a fine, clear night, I was racing again – never aware of it – lost in contemplation of the labyrinth that was my life. I was only vaguely conscious of being on Pacific Coast Highway – the road was clear and straight – no other cars in sight. The speedometer was something totally incomprehensible, something outside the realm of myself. I was lost in the world of speeding thoughts, lost in a world where past and future blended and lost their meaning, where present was an empty concept – where even the red lights flashing in the distance – even, hypnotizing – became an integral part – an unconscious unit blending into the whole pattern of thoughts. It wasn't until the siren set in that I pulled myself back into reality and realized with a sinking feeling that I had done it again.

I pulled dutifully to the side and waited. Two young cops emerged looking rather grave.

"What did I do officer?" I asked with helpless innocence.

"Only about a hundred in a 35 mile zone," he retorted drily. "We've been trying to catch up with you for the past three miles."

"Heavens! I can't believe it!"

"You can believe it. We timed it."

I sighed deeply rubbing my forehead. "I hardly noticed... I'm so tired."

"You should be. It's one-thirty. Aren't you too young to be out so late?"

I gave him a well-practiced dazed look. "I shouldn't have done that benefit..."

"What benefit? What do you do?"

"Ballet. I just did a benefit for the crippled children." That usually did it.

"Really?" he said with interest then glanced at his partner who wore an indifferent look on his sullen face.

"Look, you aren't going to give me a ticket are you?"

The sullen face hadn't changed expression. I knew I was sunk. Those two didn't look as if they'd pull together. After a long hassle, I finally managed to get them to at least mark it down to 75 instead of the 100 miles they claimed I did. I knew it wouldn't make too much difference, but it was better than nothing.

I went to the auto club to find out what I was up against. In view of my previous record, the fine was estimated at $200 and there would go my license. My only chance was to contest it. I decided I had nothing to lose at that point.

With my day in court set, I began racking my brain for a likely excuse. I knew I'd have to come up with a damn good one but I couldn't think of anything that would sound reasonable enough. At last I had a brilliant inspiration. My capacity to retain trivia came in handy. I remembered Alexander King's "Mine Enemy Grows Older" and the marvelous excuse he came up with when faced with a similar dilemma, and I decided I'd use it. If it worked for good ole Alex, why shouldn't it work for me?

On the day I was to appear in court, I rose early and prepared myself meticulously for the task. No make-up, hair combed straight, tied neatly with a ribbon, flat shoes, a demure little dress and an expression to go with it.

But when I drove out of the driveway and the protectiveness of my secluded domain, I was full of doubts and even debated whether I should go through with it. But when I put on the radio, there was my favorite song (I think it was "The Theme from a Summerplace" at the time), and I knew everything would be all right. Learning that my judge would be Leo Freund, I was fairly certain nothing could go wrong. Freund means friend in German. How could a man with such a name do anything rotten to me? Thus resolved, I faced the courtroom bravely – only to recoil. At ten in the morning it looked like a bad scene from a B-movie. The drunks, derelicts and sex-offenders, looking like a remnant of a long lost, beaten battalion of the French Foreign Legion, were lined up on one side, we, the traffic violators, on the other. Everyone in my row looked with distaste at the sick, haggard faces stubby with a few day's growth, and dirty with puke and blood, undoubtedly wondering, as I was, what the hell we were doing there.

Leo Freund was like his name. A small, sympathetic face that tried to settle into stern lines but never quite made it. I trusted him immediately. The only problem was that there were so many people. Should I tell my story which in the sober light of the courtroom began to appear silly?

But when my turn came I fortified myself somehow and decided, for better or worse, I would go with it. The judge reiterated the details of my 'crime' ending with the inevitable: "Do you plead guilty to the charges?"

I could hardly deny the facts so I admitted quietly: "I do, your Honor, but can I explain?"

He nodded resignedly and the look on his face told me he was wondering what kind of crap he'd get to hear this time.

"I was doing a benefit for the crippled children that night."

He blinked. "What do you do?"

"I'm a performer, your Honor."

His eyes went over me quickly. I knew I didn't present the expected image but that was just fine.

"I see," he said judiciously.

"I really shouldn't have consented to do it... because I'm under doctor's care and that day I got a dehydrating shot."

Fortunately that was true – partially anyway. I was getting shots but they were B-12s and similar junk because I was anemic.

"What kind a shot?"

"A dehydrating shot," I repeated slowly watching that bit of obscure information turning around in his brain. "And under the circumstances, the only thing I could do was to try to reach a gas station in time..."

I let that sink in again, looking at him with an apologetic little smile colored lightly with a plea for understanding. He nodded his head slowly.

"I see..." he said again then gave it some more thought.

"It was a clear night – no traffic at all," I added helping him make up his mind.

"Very well. I can see the justification for your haste," he said trying to suppress the merest hint of a grin. "Let's make it then a small fine – six dollars and it won't go against your driving record."

I could have screamed with joy. Good ole Judge Freund! I love him to this day.

CHAPTER THIRTY-THREE

The driving ticket was just one problem I managed to avert. There were others. The most important one had to be resolved very soon. The day when I had to subdivide the property and provide Jonny with the deeds to the two parcels was approaching rapidly. I spoke to the Marlowes hoping they'd agree to the subdivision and to my assuming the responsibility for the remainder of the mortgage which wasn't all that much anyway. However, much to my surprise, they seemed reluctant to trust me as the party solely responsible for the payments, especially under such conditions.

They were well aware that the checks were coming from me for quite some time but that didn't seem to matter. I suppose, had it been the other way around, they'd have agreed. It was the first time I realized that women in this country didn't rate as highly as men. This was substantiated further when I tried to refinance the property to get the Marlowes out of the picture.

Then an old agent I knew suggested I should meet a friend of his, a banker who was the head of a chain of banks – one of the largest in L.A. – assuring me he would accommodate me.

When I went to see the man, whom I shall call Hal Garth for

reasons which will become obvious, I was amazed at the drastic difference in treatment. Had I been about to drop a multimillion dollar deal into his lap, I couldn't have hoped for anything better. It was red carpet treatment all the way. I'd sit in the president's sumptuous office, showered with attention, served with refreshments, or whatever I wanted, while he chatted as if it was a social occasion and all the while top officials and high ranking executives were hustling in and out – taking care of every detail with the utmost speed and efficiency.

Garth was a smallish, balding man somewhere in his late fifties or early sixties – I assumed – with blue eyes fading with age and a weak, tremulous chin. His lips seemed forever wet either because he kept licking them or because he was drooling.

I assumed the reason for all the cordiality was the close relations between him and the agent who sent me there. However, I had this vague, uneasy feeling mainly because of the way he kept looking at me and licking his lips – somewhat like a cat that was about to pounce at the unsuspecting mouse – and inquiring ever so often if I wanted a drink, or something to eat and patting my hand or putting an arm around my shoulders whenever he could. The whole transaction took a few days and he kept asking me to join him for lunch which I never did. I always found something 'urgent' to do. When the whole business was over (I got exactly the kind of deal and conditions I wanted), he insisted I should stop by whenever I was in Beverly Hills and have lunch with him, and if I ever wanted or needed anything else, he was at my service. I thanked him, but never stopped in to see him.

Several weeks later, he called asking why I never came to Beverly Hills, carried on some idle chitchat for a while then made me promise I'd stop by at the earliest opportunity. Again I didn't. About a week later he called again. This time, he simply said he wanted to see me on some matter and could I meet him that afternoon. It sounded like business so I agreed. The place he chose to meet was a swanky cocktail lounge in the middle of Beverly Hills.

I appeared at the appointed time wondering what was the matter, hoping it had nothing to do with the deal we made. Garth was already there dressed with the contrived casual elegance of a Hillcrest

Country Club golf-buff. He ordered a couple of cocktails and some hors d'euvers and as soon as the waiter disappeared, delved into a serious dialogue.

"I had to see you on a matter of great importance."

"Anything in connection with the house?"

"No, of course not," he assured me quickly. "It's something entirely different."

For a while he was quiet. The cocktails arrived and some time was spent with that. After the first few sips, he resumed.

"I don't want to waste your time so I'll come right to the point."

"Good," I said for lack of anything better to say. I was eager to get home. The place depressed me, and I didn't like the look in those staring, faded eyes.

"You know that you have the most beautiful eyes I've ever seen?" he said suddenly quite irrelevantly. I failed to see where that had to do with anything we were likely to discuss, but I smiled my thanks. No use contradicting him. I was used to all sorts of compliments and could let it wash right over me.

"I've just received my brand-new Maserati which was made up specially for me," he informed me matter-of-factly, and gave me a long look. "You can have it if you like..."

I stared at him flabbergasted. Then he delivered what must be the world's greatest cliché without seeming in the least ashamed for it. "I'm married, but my wife doesn't understand me. We stay together only because of the children..."

He gave me another long look as if he expected me to applaud him for divulging that gem of intimate information. I remained quiet waiting for him to finally say what he wanted. He seemed puzzled by my silence but went on.

"I could forget about the entire mortgage if you'd like... I would do, invest, buy anything you want – but I want to live with you."

I felt as if someone had poured a bucket of scalding water over me. Somehow it reminded me of the time we were in Montreal at the sumptuous Queen Elizabeth Hotel with its own subterranean railway station, elegant suites and clientele and lots of hookers, some from the ranks of local housewives eager to supplement their allowances who were reputed to get fifty bucks a lay. The show was over and I had just arrived in my suite and threw myself into a deep, comfortable chair when the phone rang. I picked it up, but all I heard at first was a lot of heavy, raspy breathing then a hoarse, male voice blurted out: "Chiquita, I'm willing to spend a hundred dollars to fuck you."

For a moment I was mute with shock, then I took a deep breath and came back with: "Go and fuck yourself, you filthy son-of-a-bitch!" and slammed the receiver down, trembling with rage. (I'm afraid I said fack and fucked the whole effect.) Then I called the operator and tried to have it traced. Evidently it was a call from within the building, but of course, no one would tell what room it came from. I wanted to annihilate the bastard.

But only a couple of days later another similar communication took place. I was just passing the hallway when I happened to glance at the door and saw what looked like a visit card emerge from beneath it. For a while I stared at it fascinated then picked it up. It read: "Have prick, will travel." Room No. Three hundred or something... Who can say TV doesn't influence people!

I thought I'd go mad. Was the goddamn hotel full of sex-fiends?! In throes of moral indignation, I called the house detectives, gave them the card and demanded they do their duty. They looked rather sheepish about the whole thing, undoubtedly they thought I was being terribly uptight about it all, but they had no choice but to do something about it.

They banged on the door of the room in question, but no one answered. They tried to unlock it, but it was bolted from the inside which left them no alternative but to break it down. The search of the room produced two lanky kids in their late teens staring with cold defiance at their captors, who looked rather uncomfortable as they led them away. What punishment, if any, they were subjected to, I have no idea. But I felt I had at least made an effort to right the existing state of affairs at that hotel.

Jonny surprised me by laughing the whole thing off and saying: "Who are you to raise the prices?" perhaps he began to realize his puritan upbringing had created an unbending monster.

Anyway, although I was trying to break out of the confining restrictive grip of puritanism, that kind of a deal was a bit much. As far as I was concerned, Garth's proposition amounted to more or less the same thing, and the drastic jump in value didn't change the basic aspect of it in the least. He was making a deal to buy me. I didn't consider myself a commodity for sale. The whole damn proposition was so insulting to me I could have smashed my fist into his face.

"Do you have a boy friend, perhaps?" Garth inquired politely, but before I could as much as open my mouth to answer, he quickly cut in. "No, don't tell me. That's none of my business. You can do as you please."

What the hell was he telling me? I could fuck anyone I wanted? Perhaps he was a voyeur and all he wanted was to watch. What was I to do? Follow my impulse and slap his face and storm out of there? But this wasn't Victorian England nor was his proposal presented as crudely as those in Montreal.

Finally, I gathered my resources and began as matter-of-factly as he had.

"Look, Mr. Garth, I appreciate your frankness and not to waste any time, I'll be equally candid. The answer is no."

He looked as if he couldn't believe I had said that. But his surprise soon vanished. He was not about to give up. He was used to tough dealings.

"I want you to take into consideration that I travel a great deal which means I'd spend perhaps three days a week at your house. Neither does it mean you have to sleep with me, you see? I simply like to have a beautiful young lady to take out and show off, so to speak..."

Now, what did that mean? Was he telling me he was impotent? In spite of my relative naiveté I sensed many hidden messages behind these words which I couldn't quite grasp. What kind of a freak was he anyway? I flashed suddenly the picture of the scene I witnessed in the comic's dressing room and I shuddered.

"The answer is still no," I said coldly.

"Is it perhaps you don't like older men? – Some women do, you know."

"I don't."

"Nevertheless, I would suggest that you think it over. I think it's an excellent proposition... It might be wise not to make a rash decision at this point. I'd do anything you'd want – refurbish, remodel your house... anything. The Maserati is yours to take right now."

"Mr. Garth, please don't. It's completely useless. I won't change my mind."

"My dear," he said gently, "you don't realize what you're doing."

"And you don't seem to realize, Mr. Garth, I don't need any money. And the answer will remain no and if you insist anymore, I'll be very angry."

"I wouldn't want that," he said quickly. "I want us to remain good friends. However, should you change your mind – anytime – just call me."

I shook my head and got out of there as fast as I could. My head was spinning. Today I realize how lonely and desperate a man Garth must have been, even though he may not have been fully aware of it. Negotiating like the banker he was, for a piece of ass. He too had everything he wanted, success, money, position, power – but it still wasn't enough. The things that ought to come free – he had to buy. How hardened must a man be not to react to such a refusal, such a put-down, any more than he'd react to losing a banking deal.

Some time later I saw Garth again at Bart Lytton's house where he was one of the one hundred and fifty bankers invited to a party Lytton threw in honor of Edmond von Rothschild – the European financial wizard.

Lytton had spent some $35,000 on that party which was the most extravagant affair and the most flagrant waste of money I've ever witnessed. The entertainment provided featured us, Stan Kenton and his orchestra and a small group of jazz dancers.

In the afternoon, during the rehearsals, Lytton was running around the patio swarming with workmen, caterers, gardeners, all busy converting it into an exquisite outdoor cabaret. Every available spot was filled with every kind of orchid, the showy blossoms sparkling fresh and fragrant, amidst the richly set tables gleaming with silver and crystal. Lytton, the great patron of the arts, had a smart, basically simple stage set up to emphasize a piece of gigantic abstract sculpture standing in the background – the work of his protégée. He seemed resolved to personally conduct the entire affair – with the virtuosity of a master puppeteer. One moment he was fussing around with the orchids, the next he was on the stage insisting Stan should work toward the sculpture instead of the band. I was hoping Stan would say he wasn't conducting a sculpture but an orchestra, but he only smiled and said nothing.

When I started rehearsing with the orchestra, Lytton streaked up on the stage again telling me the same thing. "The audience is not important – it's the sculpture. You are admiring it, dancing for it." I was wondering why he had spent all the money on the party if the audience didn't matter. I looked at him patiently. "Mr. Lytton, why don't you let me do my job the best way I know how, OK?"

He looked perturbed. "Well, as long as you know what I want." Stan grinned at me and winked.

In the evening, I danced without once looking at the monstrosity behind me, and gave all my attention to the dance and the audience. I could see Hal Garth sitting there salivating and licking his chops, and I had to laugh. I wondered if he was still waiting for me to come to the conclusion he had offered me a 'great deal.'

Baron von Rothschild looked about as aristocratic as Archie Bunker. Small and stocky, tight, neatly combed curls, bland, blue eyes behind thick, gold-rimmed glasses – he seemed more like a polite, unassuming bank teller than the man who controlled the Rothschild fortune. But it was nice. I thought it was a welcome change from the overbearing men of finance imbued with their own self-importance.

Lytton insisted I should dance with the Baron and teach him how to do the twist and he obligingly complied, awkwardly following every move I made, chatting easily, casually, until we finished. When he then suggested that Lytton should try it himself, the banker flatly refused and when a few people pressured him, he really became indignant. I saw Rothschild observing him with an amused, speculative smile. Then he turned to me asking if I could put up with another try at it.

With all the money Lytton sunk into the party – it took over three weeks before we were able to collect our money.

CHAPTER THIRTY-FOUR

The engagement at the Statler Hilton turned out to be a lot of work for me, but in some ways it was also an unusual and mainly illuminating experience.

We were headlining a revue which had several rather good productions in which I starred en solo. Actually, that was the only way they could afford to pay us the salary we were used to getting. Los Angeles – is a real live town.

It came out very well and altogether ran four months which was some kind of a record for the Statler Hilton. We had rooms at the hotel but the only time I stayed over was when it was so foggy it was just impossible to drive home. So I used the room mainly to warm-up and prepare myself for the show. I had many costume changes, some very fast ones, and those I did in the showgirl's dressing room. Finally, I was in the midst of the element Jonny had kept me away from for all those years. And I wouldn't have missed the experience for anything. At first I listened in silence, amazed at the language I was so suddenly exposed to. I had never heard such language since my Latin Quarter days. I couldn't believe it! Those girls could out swear Julius La Rosa or any of the stars behind that thin wall. I was shocked but also fascinated by it. It seemed such a completely open and natural way of speaking I wished I could do it too. If one felt like saying shit, why not say it? The problem was that I didn't understand most of the words they used, and the ones I did know, I wasn't sure how to pronounce. And I was ashamed to ask. I didn't want them to know I was such a ninny.

One girl in particular was a riot. She must have used the word fuck at least three times in every sentence. She was pretty and viva-cious, part Cherokee, as she proudly informed me, but besides the wide cheekbones and black hair, there was nothing to suggest her background. She was blue-eyed and snub-nosed but the latter feature looked like some plastic surgeon's idea of what a nose should look like. She sounded older, wiser and worldlier in her fast, earthy assess-ment of her own as well as everyone else's problems which inevitably centered around men – their existing, or anticipated relations with them and mainly the failure for something 'concrete' or 'permanent' to materialize.

They all appeared eager to get married – to hold on to whom-ever they had or hoped to get. It seemed silly to me. One girl, a bright, blue-eyed redhead with the whitest complexion I'd ever seen was liv-ing with some guy for years supporting him through some lofty ven-ture and waiting breathlessly for him to marry her. The question, just when and if, seemed to be the sole object of her preoccupation. But not quite. She also kept on saying how horny she was. At that time, I hadn't the vaguest notion what that meant.

"I'm so horny I could just die," she'd say at least a dozen times a night. I felt terribly stupid and intimidated by their smart jar-gon and kept wishing I would learn to talk that way too.

Once, when searching for an elusive part of my costume or something and feeling rather brave, I ventured a casual comment: "Where the fack is it?"

The part-Cherokee stopped brushing her eyelashes and stared at me in astonishment. "What?"

I felt destroyed – humiliated! Where did I go wrong? They said it all the time. "I said where the fack is it?" I repeated as confi-dently as I could.

"Oh," she said nodding.

I sighed with relief. But she got up walked over to me and put her hand on my shoulder in a half-maternal, half-comradely fashion.

"It's not fack, honey. It's FUCK – FUCK!"

"Fack?..."

"...No, no. Fuck like... like duck, see?"

"Fuck like duck," I repeated carefully, "Duck, fuck – fuck..."

"That's right. Now you've got it!"

"Gee, thanks, thanks ever so much," I said pumping her hand enthusiastically. I later overheard her saying to the redhead:

"The poor kid's off her rocker. Stiff as a prick. And such a good dancer too. Pity."

"Uptight cunt," the redhead commented drily.

That was another word they kept using all the time. What the hell could it mean? It sounded vaguely like the cigarettes I was beginning to smoke to look more sophisticated. (I gave it up soon, though, because I hated the taste and could never learn how to inhale the smoke.) But I knew instinctively it was another goodie. I was determined to find out just what it was. For some reason I felt less self-conscious around the boy I did a bit of dancing with during one of the productions so I decided I would ask him. Ron wasn't a terribly good dancer but what he lacked in talent, he made up in looks and enthusiasm. He was ecstatic about dancing with me even if it was just for a few minutes because it gave him a certain distinction and a boost to his career.

I found Ron backstage, eyeing the musicians. He was forever on the make. "Ron," I asked without preliminaries, "what's a kent or cant?"

"Cunt?" he whispered furtively.

"Yes, that's it! Cunt!"

"Shhh..." he said quickly glancing around. "You shouldn't use such a word."

"Why? The girl's use it all the time."

"They would, those cunts!" he hissed disapprovingly.

"But what does it mean?" I was getting impatient with him.

"It's nasty," he declared piously.

"How nasty?"

"Well," he said glancing around again then pulled me aside. "It's the... the female thing... you know?" He seemed all flustered about it and even blushed. The poor bastard. He was as bad as I was.

"How do you pronounce it?"

"C-U-N-T, cunt!"

"Oh, cunt – like hunt?..."

He sighed. "Christ, why do you want to learn such things. What do you need it for?"

"What's an uptight cunt?" I asked paying no attention to his moral indignation.

"Who said that?"

"Never mind, just tell me what it means."

He had a tough time explaining it adequately but I finally got the gist of it. Needless to say, I was sore as hell and determined to do something about it.

When I came down again for my first costume change that night and couldn't find my comb right away, I looked around the dressing room saying sharply: "OK, which one of you cunts borrowed my comb again?"

The silence that followed was so profound one would have heard a pin drop. I felt their startled eyes examining me quizzically to determine my mood. I gave each a tough look then grinned. As if on command, they all started shrieking with laughter.

"We're corrupting her!" the redhead declared passing me my comb.

"Balls!" exclaimed part-Cherokee, "We're just improving her vocabulary, that's all."

"I knew it must have been the horny cunt again," I said as casually as I could and began combing my hair. They roared again. Our relationship was definitely improving. The lines, drawn by class differences – status – star vs. chorus girl – were disappearing to be replaced by a new status – teachers vs. pupil. Jonny would have been positively horrified. Seeing my interest in acquiring new 'knowledge,' they eagerly took to teaching me every filthy expression they could think of.

Everything that happened presented an opportunity to learn something new. A few days after this major breakthrough, I started out a perfectly marvelous Malibu morning by slipping and crashing down the stairs. They were carpeted, but as I fell backwards I came down hard on my ass and bounced off each step all the way down. It was one hell of a way to start such a glorious day and for a dancer, totally inexcusable. By the evening I was terribly sore and it hurt even just to walk.

"What's the matter?" part-Cherokee inquired solicitously seeing me limp in after my first dance.

"Just pain, terrible pain," I said gingerly touching my abdomen.

"Oh," she nodded knowingly, "been balling all night, eh?"

I stared at her uncertainly. "No," I said finally. "I tried it once but didn't like it. My fingers kept getting stuck."

Part-Cherokee's face was blank with utter bewilderment. "Stuck?" she repeated uncertainly.

"Yeah! In the ball."

"Oh... I didn't say bowling! I said balling!"

Now I looked at her uncertainly. Here was definitely a gap in communication if ever there was one.

"Balling isn't like bowling?" I asked.

"No, not exactly," she said grinning. "You're pronouncing both the same way. That's wrong. Bowling starts like bowl – bowl like owl and balling starts like ball... balling... like fucking."

"Like fucking? Really?"

She sighed in exasperation. "Man, where have you been all your life?"

I was devastated. Why did I always have to come off as such an ignoramus? When would I stop being so stupid?

"Well, did you?" she inquired tartly.

"Did I what?"

"Ball, for Chrissake!"

"No, I fell down the stairs. Came down hard on my ass."

She made a face. "Try balling. It might go away," she said smugly, trying for the air of a doctor making a snap diagnosis and went back to slapping make-up on her face.

They talked like tough, hard-boiled broads but underneath all that brass they were simply girls. Some nicer, some cuntier, but all pretty much vulnerable. There wasn't one among them who hadn't come in, at one time or another, with reddened eyes, weeping over some calamity having to do with a boyfriend. Even the one I thought looked so sweet and unspoiled came in one night weeping bitterly. It appeared she was pregnant and had no idea what to do about it because she wasn't sure just whom to hold responsible. Ron told me later she was the 'hottest fuck' of them all and that she had balled all the musicians (and he hated her guts for it) and even made a pass at him! he informed me with a horrified look.

Poor Ron, as delighted as he was with his new status, it evidently wasn't meant to last. He was strong and tall and although all he had to do at the end of the production was to pick me up (all of my 102 pounds) into a very simple lift, but even that turned out to be too much for him. One night he lifted me, and after the curtain and I came down, he sort of sunk to the floor with a dramatic heave and stayed there. I thought he was kidding but even if I hadn't, there was no time to find out. I had a very fast costume change coming up and so did the girls and since everyone is well aware of the phrase some idiot phrased ages ago for some obscure and idiotic reason that "the show must go on" – everyone was running and hopping over him while he lay there moaning. It wasn't until the finale that we learned Ron was taken to the hospital in an ambulance with a wrenched back.

But all in all, the Statler Hilton was fun. Our bandleader choked to death on a piece of meat, a musician's wife drove over their kid while rushing to the hospital with the other, and I learned every dirty word in existence thus preparing myself adequately for the life of a 'liberated' female.

CHAPTER THIRTY-FIVE

I didn't know it then, but that was the last 'long' engagement of my career. Had I known, I might have been able to enjoy it more. As it was, my constant preoccupation with when I would get out of the whole mess at last, kept me miserable. But in a way, I still loved the dancing – the doing of it. However, that didn't keep me from looking for someone to take my place. But no matter whom I suggested, Jonny wasn't happy with the choice and made no effort to really give it a go. I tried out several girls, but it just never worked out. I bitterly resented Jonny's attitude. At that rate, I'd never be able to quit. The need to resolve it, to have it all behind me at last was like a thorn jabbing at my brain – never letting up, never giving me peace.

My life at the house wasn't improving either. I still hadn't adjusted to living there alone as I had hoped I would. So as great as it was to be alone, it was also miserable.

It was the time of year when L.A. is swept by banks of heavy fog which blankets the beaches in the early morning, then drifts inland or the other way around. Sometimes late at night when I was leaving the Statler Hotel, the city looked like a mirage, a phantom town of soft contours blending in and out of the fog, yet the closer I would get to the beach, the clearer it became. But it had to be really bad before I would spend the night in the hotel room.

I don't suppose anyone who hasn't lived through it can really understand what it means to spend years in different hotel rooms – the cold, impersonal atmosphere which settles like an icy blanket of loneliness around your gut and makes you feel as if you hadn't one single friend in the whole wide world nor a spot to call your own. To reach the comfortable familiarity of my own home – no matter how dubious the safety of it – I'd have traveled a lot further and through a lot worse weather. But that didn't make me like the long, nocturnal treks any better. There were good reasons for it too. There wasn't just the abstract fear of the menacing darkness I drove through and the mysterious creaks of the old house waiting for me. I had several unpleasant experiences, one of which ended with me shooting above the heads of a couple of persistent pursuers, who followed me all the way up to the house, and scaring them into a hasty flight. Because of such incidents, I had a tacit agreement with the Malibu sheriff station that a car would patrol the area and drive up ever so often. I must say, the Malibu cops were fantastic. They truly fulfilled the role they were intended for – and more. Aware of the situation, they waited for me almost every night at the bottom of the hill then preceded me up and even searched the house just so I'd be certain there was no one hiding behind any corner. Sometimes they'd stay for a cup of coffee and since I knew only how to make instant coffee, they showed me how to brew it. Whenever I panicked out over something – real or imagined – all I had to do was call and they were there in no time. I am afraid that most of the time, I called them needlessly. But once it was very real – and it wasn't even at night. In fact it was in the middle of a lovely, sunny day.

I had been swimming and then strolled around the deserted gardens. I was in the front yard which borders on the wide sweeping driveway and the grove of ancient eucalyptus trees, where a big volarium full of finches and canaries, surrounded by philodendrons, stood facing the big picture window of the living room. I was gazing at the waterfall cascading with a gentle murmur across the rocks covered with bird shit and ended in a scalloped pond where a finch was busily splashing around when I heard a voice coming from where it had no business coming from – the oceanside. In that direction, there was nothing but the pool, the lawn, a narrow terrace spanning the entire width of the property and then nothing but the steep face of the cliff dropping down to the highway.

"Oh, there you are!" exclaimed the voice ringing with the familiarity of old friendship yet I instantly knew I had never heard it before. When I turned around to inspect its owner, I saw a total stranger. In fact the strangest stranger I'd ever seen. At first glance he didn't seem extraordinary in any way. Short, stocky build, dark, fuzzy crewcut, pudgy, pasty face – an ordinary man of an ordinary appearance. Yet there was this strange feel about him – a certain vague something I couldn't quite grasp. Perhaps it was the strange gleam in his weasel eyes – the peculiar grin revealing yellow, wide spaced teeth or the half-silly – half-shrewd look he wore.

I assumed the protective homeowner's air.

"Where did you come from?" I inquired sternly but not too much so.

"From back there..." he said pointing to the cliff.

"But there's only the steep mountain."

"I know," he said grinning conspiratorially. "But I climbed it."

"That's impossible! Where?"

I let him proceed toward the pool area. He walked by the pool, crossed the lawn and headed toward the ancient, half-overgrown steps that no one used any more which led down to my neighbor's house. Evidently, he must have seen John's house and climbed the less steep hill there and probably finding no one home, roamed around until he discovered the old steps.

"There," he said pointing down the steps.

"You shouldn't have done that. Do you realize you are trespassing?"

He nodded dutifully. "But I've got to make a phone call. I ran out of gas down there," he said pointing to the beach side, "and I want to call my buddy to come and get me."

"Couldn't you get a ride to the nearest gas station?"

He grinned again showing those horrible teeth. "I ran out of cash."

I couldn't see a single vehicle on the other side of the highway. "I don't see any car."

"It's back there, past those beach houses," he explained obligingly.

I didn't like the sound of that at all. "Why didn't you try to call from down there then?"

"You'd be surprised how few people will let you use their phones," he confided, his face twisting into that strange grin again.

"What made you think someone up here would?"

"Cause I climbed all the way up." His little weasel eyes gleamed unpleasantly and a deliberate grin crinkled the massive face. His logic, somehow pathetic and like the rest of him strangely, disturbingly off-key, made me uneasy and irresolute. What was I to do? I flashed the rifle in the bedroom upstairs and wondered how I could possibly get it if I should need it. For the moment, I felt there was only one thing to do.

"OK, you can use the phone," I said heading toward the kitchen door. I could hear him hurrying after me. "No!" I said sharply. "You stay out here. I'll bring the phone out."

He did as he was told. For a moment I considered the possibility of slamming the door shut, but quickly gave up the idea. Some five other doors were wide open and I knew there wouldn't be time to shut them all if he really wanted to get in. So I decided the best approach was to act perfectly natural and unafraid, as if his appearance and request weren't at all unusual. But I was terribly disturbed and my heart felt as if it were beating in my throat. What was it about the man that frightened me so? My reason told me I was being paranoid, but my intuition rang all the alarms in my system. I unplugged the the telephone and walked outside again, unhurriedly, deliberately, plugged it in and handed it to him.

"Isn't Granite a toll call from here?"

I nodded.

He looked worried. "What could it cost?"

"A quarter perhaps. It doesn't matter."

"Naw – I wanna pay for it," he insisted fishing around in his pockets. "I gotta have a quarter somewhere..."

"Never mind. Just make your call."

My tone was resolute and he quickly obeyed. The call he made was most peculiar. His language was that of a simple, uneducated man and his dialogue consisted of 25% garbled account of his misfortune accompanied by a good 75% of moronic laughter that ranged from low, horsey laughs to maniacal shrieks. I was getting more and more uneasy. I didn't know what to do so I just stood there watching him – waiting. At last he hung up.

"Sorry I took so long. That sure must've been more'n a quarter."

There was nothing wrong with what he said except for the way he said it. Again it rang flat and somehow unreal – as if he were playing a role and playing it badly. "It doesn't matter. You made your call, now you had better go."

He was looking at me guardedly – appraisingly. "Which way?"

"The same way you came," I said pointing to the stairs.

He nodded and started shuffling in the direction of the steps. A few times he hesitated glancing back at me. The strangely appraising, inquisitive quality of his look was unnerving. It seemed to suggest he was trying to decide what to do about me. But I remained calm and followed him as if to make sure he really left. After descending a couple of steps he stopped and looked back at me.

"Did you lose a black hose?" he asked abruptly.

"No." I had no idea what hose he was talking about and I didn't care.

"I saw it down there. Looks like a good hose too. They sure cost a lotta money. I could bring it up..."

"I don't want it. I just want you to leave. And don't come back."

He stood there for a while longer as if deciding whether to go or not. I stared back at him steadily and at last he began descending. I listened for his steps, making sure he was really leaving. – He'll come back – the thought flashed through my mind with such certainty, I raced into the house, up the stairs, grabbed the rifle and raced down again. As I suspected, he was coming back. I heard his steps ringing on the cement stairs. When he emerged, he found me standing there pointing the rifle at his gut.

"What do you want? I told you not to come back." My voice was harsh with the effort to keep it from trembling.

He was carrying a short piece of black garden hose that must have laid there forgotten for years. Seeing the rifle pointed at him, he stopped for a moment. I watched with morbid fascination the corners of his fat lips twist into a slow, ugly grin.

"I thought you might need it." Somehow, the voice was different. It turned slow and dull and it gave me the creeps. Suddenly he began advancing – slowly, methodically, the hose swinging in his grip. I began retreating.

"You had better not come any closer," I warned him but he seemed oblivious of the rifle now. I released the safety catch. The sound of it made him stop for an instant, but he soon resumed his slow, steady approach, his eyes never leaving mine. I didn't know what to do. I couldn't just go ahead and start shooting at him.

On a sudden inspiration, I turned abruptly and walked quickly, but evenly, toward the telephone. My back felt prickly with a sick apprehension. I half expected him to lurch for me at any moment. Reaching the ledge where the telephone stood, I whirled around picking up the receiver and pointed the rifle at him again. It was a neat trick to hold the receiver with my chin, the rifle with one hand, dial the operator with the other and look menacing at the same time. But once that was behind me, I felt reasonably sure again. Or as sure as anyone could be under such circumstances. But I managed it all in a matter of seconds, keeping an icy, unshaken resolve.

"This is an emergency. Get me the police." I said it coolly, but the operator must have sensed the urgency because I had the sheriff on the line almost immediately. The man was gazing at me irresolutely, his face working in concentration over the options available to him which I tried not to think about. But I had the distinct feeling he was wavering between taking flight and jumping me with that hose. I gripped the rifle tighter and pointed it at his head wondering whether I could really pull the trigger if it came right down to it.

"I want a squad car up here immediately."

The officer began asking something. I interrupted him instantly. "I am holding a prowler at rifle point. You'd better hurry. This is Chiquita." Then I dropped the receiver, letting it dangle there.

The man was ambling hesitantly toward the steps. I followed him at what I considered a safe distance. By the time we reached the steps the faint sound of a siren approaching rapidly drifted up from the highway. I thought it must have been a lucky coincidence. It couldn't have been more than a couple of minutes since I called. But the man listened tensely for a moment, then dropped the hose and began running down the steps. The sound of the siren grew and soon I could hear it coming up the driveway. As if in answer, another one started wailing in the distance. I still stood there looking down the steps where I saw the man disappear. Then I heard a squad car come to a screeching halt in front of the house. It was only then that I raced up front. Two officers were rushing toward me.

"He ran down the steps." My voice sounded strange to me and seeing the officers' glances I became conscious of how I must look brandishing a rifle in a wet bikini.

"Get into the house and lock all the doors," the officer snapped. I was only too happy to comply. A second squad car was pulling up. In minutes, the policemen were gone – the search for my strange caller had begun. Occasionally I could hear them yell from somewhere around John's house below. It seemed to take forever before they came up with the man between them, handcuffed and screaming incoherently.

"Is this the man?"

I nodded. Seeing me he began screaming something about the phone call, and fighting them off. It was a horrible spectacle. Just as they were taking him away in one of the cars, a friend came driving up. Until then I managed to stay calm – holding myself together. But the moment I saw a familiar face, I fell apart. The tremendous will I had summoned from some unknown source dissolved and all the pent-up terror broke loose in great, engulfing waves. But it wasn't over yet. The officers were patient and gentle but I had to tell them exactly what happened so that they could make out their report.

Although they never said it, I felt they thought I had panicked, or overreacted at best. Still, they promised to let me know the result of their investigation.

It took many hours before they called. But the tolerant, slightly condescending tone was gone.

"You had a close call, young lady," the officer said cheerfully. "The guy is a psychopath. We finally traced him to the state mental hospital at Camarillo, and we're taking him back there."

"Just how sick is he?"

"All I can say right now is that he's classified as potentially dangerous."

"What does that mean?"

"That he is liable to do just about anything."

Once the initial shock wore off, I began to feel sorry for the man. People don't become mentally ill all by themselves. Someone, something – helps it along. We live in a baffling world where man and his needs seem the last thing the society is concerned about; where material value has superseded human value; where technology, meant to enhance our existence, has been left to proliferate until it seems beyond anyone's power to slow it down long enough to reevaluate and redirect it to fulfill its original purpose. And man, overwhelmed, overridden by the unchallenged assumption that machines are more efficient, more reliable than he himself, is blundering around in the maddening labyrinth – the sordid mess of his own making, unable to find a way out of the circle of errors crowding him more and more and making his escape impossible. Is it really surprising that he tends to throw it all aside and escape into a very private realm where the harsh realities of his existence dissolve like a nightmare with the light of day leaving only the misty phantoms that inhabit his dream world? Isn't it indeed, this absurd, irrational world we've created for ourselves which is making us neurotic and then offers no more than a few mental hospitals available that are ill-equipped and totally inadequate to deal with the alarming increase of mental disorders the world over? The best the society can do is call the reaction to it all a crime wave and stiffen penalties. But whoever stops to consider that mental diseases are as dangerous as cancer. And who is doing anything about it?

I've often thought about the man and wondered what finally became of him. He had frightened me, but he also showed me a side of the human personality I hadn't given much thought to before. He showed me something that dwells in every one of us – the capacity to flip out – to tune out of it all when we are driven to the limits of our endurance. Can we then still call it criminal or is the term more applicable to the society that allows it to happen – that doesn't stop to examine and reshape itself in order to put a stop to it?

What comes to mind here is part of the narrative from the film, "Man Isn't Dying Of Thirst," by a man and filmmaker whom I greatly admire:

Where actually is the border between reality and fantasy?
Where does the human capacity to create values end and where begins the feverish need to escape – to find more and better ways to dull the senses?
What is causing civilized nations, in their search for solutions, to turn to escapism in the form of alcohol, cigarettes, sedatives, and modern-day rituals?
Every day over a thousand people commit suicide and another eight thousand attempt to. We all bear witness to a mass crippling of the psyche in the name of progress and civilization.
We all are the accusers and we all stand accused.
Cultural and emotional poverty is as devastating to man as hunger.
To achieve mental balance we don't need robots or tranquilizers.
We cannot give meaning to life by escaping reality. There is no turning back...

There is indeed no turning back. I began to realize I couldn't live in a vacuum – concerned, as Jonny wanted, only with myself, my work and the things that immediately affected me. But there were many things which 'immediately affected me.' I was curious. There were things I wanted to know. Things such as why people had to be so goddamn greedy and dishonest – willing to do anything – rip-off anyone for a few dollars.

CHAPTER THIRTY-SIX

It must have started long ago because in Africa, Jonny gave me a primitive ivory carving of the three monkeys and told to always keep it and remember its lesson: don't hear, don't speak, don't see. But I couldn't do it! I still have the little statuette but its message doesn't strike me as wise – it seems more convenient and cowardly and smacks of the self-serving but also self-defeating ostrich-philosophy so widely practiced today. But it solves nothing and never will.

In a way I was guilty of the same thing. I was procrastinating even though I knew I had to face all that bothered me and change it. I felt I had to shed that terrible ambition that drove me on and on and turn at last to things I considered more important – whatever those would turn out to be.

As it was, I felt stifled – but I just blundered around – searching for something that kept eluding me. But there was one thing I knew for sure. If I was to continue dancing it would have to be in a different form and in a different environment, and until I found it, there was no use going on. I had no idea if and when or how I would find it. I only knew I had to try. I loved dancing too much to let it shrivel and dry up in monotony until there was no passion left in me for it. I was ready to give it up rather than let that happen.

Dancing should be a joy – something vibrantly alive – full of changes, dynamic new ideas and styles, as varied as music itself. Because dance is the physical interpretation of music and both are important parts of the human existence. As the language is a tool to interpret our thoughts, so the dance is a tool to express what that music conveys to us. And I felt I wasn't accomplishing that anymore and all the success we continued having couldn't convince me otherwise or make up for the lack of that elusive something that I felt was missing. But I knew it had something to do with change. And change doesn't come about without some upheaval and pain. Not to mention hard work. Perhaps that's why we are so afraid of changes. We are afraid of the new – of the unknown. And we prefer to stick to the old – the outdated, outlived, no matter how rotten only because it's comfortable and convenient. But as painful as any change may be, it is also healthy and indeed vital. Because without changes, we don't live – we only stagnate.

I knew all this instinctively, as we all do, but I too was afraid. Yet I knew, as I watched with sadness the joy evaporate from my work, that there was no changing it within the confines of where I was at. The longer I continued – the more I saw it. Yet the realization that I would have to face what might turn out to be a long, perhaps futile search to find – I knew not exactly what – filled me with fear and despair.

I vacillated between all sorts of conflicting emotions, and it left me feeling lost and useless. I couldn't bear to continue dancing yet I couldn't envision a life without it. I was tossing about in what might be termed as an existential crisis and I saw no way out of it. How different was I really from the unfortunate man who blundered upon my hill? We both had problems we couldn't extricate ourselves from. But I wasn't ready to tune out of it – I had no dream world I could lose myself in and not give a damn about anything.

And so I went on. From engagement to engagement, from one flight to another, never caring if the plane should crash, laughing with delight when something went wrong, watching hopefully for black, threatening clouds in the skies.

But I knew it couldn't go on like that. I had to pull myself together and initiate the break. I had to get someone to take my place so I could quit with a clear conscience.

I called an audition and went to work. The girl I finally chose was a disaster but she looked good, was light, supple and I thought I could teach her. But I forgot one cannot overcome a lack of will. The girl lacked the one thing I was so desperately trying to lose – ambition. The only reason she wanted to be 'somebody' was because her mother pushed her every inch of the way. The girl just didn't care – not inside – where it mattered. She was like a wet rag. Wherever I put her, she stayed, whatever I told her went right through her like through a sieve. She'd look at me – no expression on her face – nod, but nothing I ever said really penetrated.

Her mother, eager to see her daughter in the limelight already, was 'working' on me and Jonny to presumably 'cement' the partnership. It looked as if she hadn't the confidence her daughter would pull it off without her assistance. She was right, of course. She knew, instinctively, unconsciously, that her daughter couldn't and wouldn't do it. But she kept hammering away at it. She would wine and dine us whenever possible, trying to develop a relationship which would make it impossible to reject the girl. Actually, if it hadn't been for her parents, I'd have given up long before. But I felt sorry for them. Sorry for the foolish dreams they spun, the hopes that would remain unfulfilled. They too couldn't just let go and leave their child to find her own goals, to carve out her own future – as she saw fit. They just couldn't do it. And I couldn't do the thing I should have done long ago – tell them the truth.

The weeks turned into months and I was getting nowhere. In spite of all the time invested, the results remained dismal. Jonny, seeing how determined I was to quit, actually did his best to help. But no matter how hard we tried, it didn't work. I even began to doubt my capacity as a teacher. I had to keep reminding myself of the results I was able to achieve in the past. It wasn't that the girl was stupid – her body and mind were simply out of tune. That was her defense against the parents' pressure. She knew what I wanted, her body simply refused to do it.

Finally, I had to accept the fact that it was hopeless. You can't grow a birch out of an acorn. Some things just can't be done. However, there was an engagement to fulfill which Jonny had booked way ahead of time, assuming that by the date of the opening, the 'new' act would be long set, polished and ready to roll. But in the beginning we never figured that it would actually be an impossibility.

So once again I had to fall back into my old role.

I was lamenting the time and effort wasted, but even that experience taught me something. Every minus can be turned into a plus. The seed of the positive lies within every negative. This last experience taught me I couldn't initiate things for someone else. Everyone has to do it for himself. I realized then I had to give up. Just give up and I knew I'd soon have the strength to do it.

CHAPTER THIRTY-SEVEN

It happened after the next engagement – a four week run in San Juan, Puerto Rico. We were at the Americana Hotel, Harry Belafonte was at the San Juan Hotel next door. The last time we worked together was at the Plaza Hotel in New York and it felt ages ago. And we were both still doing the same thing. The same style, the same everything.

There had to be a way out, for Christ's sake!! I couldn't bear it a moment longer! All the things that were my entire life were falling apart – everything was dissolving in me – nothing mattered anymore.

And so, after the engagement ended, I did it. When Jonny was going to accept an engagement in Miami Beach, I said I wasn't going.

"Just like that?" he asked bitterly.

"Just like that! I can't. It's been two years since I said I wanted to quit. I'm 23 and I want to be free at last."

Of course he didn't understand. How could he? He only saw that I was casting away a 'fabulous career,' a successful act that could go on and on and on...

"That's what I'm afraid of... That it's just going to continue on and on..."

"But you promised. I won't be able to find anyone."

But it didn't work anymore. I was shedding the guilt syndrome. I was past all that bullshit.

"You will have to," I said quietly. "And when you do – then I'll help you."

It wasn't easy to leave him sitting in Miami Beach. He thought if he refused to leave Miami I'd stay. But I didn't. I boarded the plane and that was that. He stood there looking suddenly very helpless and lost, but I knew I'd never go back again. I had to start moving forward – no matter what he thought of me for doing it.

Sometimes the kindest gesture is the most brutal one – a move without pity – but it has to be done swiftly and without hesitation.

As I expected, Jonny did find a girl soon after that and I did help him put a new routine together and he was ready to start all over again. Soon he was on his way, working as I knew he always would. That was his thing – it worked for him, I saw it, accepted it and gave up trying to make him see something he couldn't. The only thing I got him to understand was that his way wasn't mine and so we just had to end it.

And finally, finally I was free – free of guilt – free from my obligation – free to let myself experience anything I wanted. And so the search, the decade long search began. At last I made it – I could anticipate and savor the joy, the excitement of 'doing' again. The sheer joy of exploring new, uncharted regions – fantastically new, exciting realms. But this time I wasn't searching for fame and recognition. I was searching for – myself and although I wasn't quite aware of it – the search had already begun.

FINIS